Ubiquitous and Pervasive Computing - New Trends and Opportunities

Edited by Rodrigo da Rosa Righi

Published in London, United Kingdom

Ubiquitous and Pervasive Computing - New Trends and Opportunities
http://dx.doi.org/10.5772/intechopen.100785
Edited by Rodrigo da Rosa Righi

Contributors
Sara Cannizzaro, Rob Procter, André Luiz Tinassi D'Amato, Wellington Oliveira de Andrade, Peter Stubberud, Boaz Lerner, Oded Zinman, Gabriel Kabanda, Rodrigo da Rosa Righi, Bárbara Canali Locatelli Bellini, Fernanda Fritsch, Vinicius Facco Rodrigues, Madhusudan Singh, Marcelo Pasin

First published in London, United Kingdom, 2023 by IntechOpen
IntechOpen is the global imprint of INTECHOPEN LIMITED, registered in England and Wales, registration number: 11086078, 5 Princes Gate Court, London, SW7 2QJ, United Kingdom

British Library Cataloguing-in-Publication Data
A catalogue record for this book is available from the British Library

Additional hard and PDF copies can be obtained from orders@intechopen.com

Ubiquitous and Pervasive Computing - New Trends and Opportunities
Edited by Rodrigo da Rosa Righi
p. cm.
Print ISBN 978-1-80356-389-3
Online ISBN 978-1-80356-390-9
eBook (PDF) ISBN 978-1-80356-391-6

Meet the editor

Rodrigo da Rosa Righi is a professor in the Graduate Program in Applied Computing at Unisinos University, Brazil. He is a researcher and advisor for undergraduate, graduate, master's, and doctoral students. His postdoctoral degree was obtained at KAIST, South Korea. Rodrigo works on the following topics: performance evaluation, load balancing and adaptation in the cluster, grid, fog and cloud, healthcare computing, and the internet of things. He is a senior member of both the IEEE and the ACM, He has also had experience in coordinating international projects with companies such as Siemens, HT Micron Semiconductors, and Dell.

Contents

Preface

Today, 5G communication, cloud computing, the internet of things (IoT), robotics, and the feasibility of artificial intelligence (AI) computing algorithms are contributing to redefining ubiquitous and pervasive computing. We live in an age of digital transformation where connectivity is more and more visible to end users. We are also experiencing new business models, transformations in industry, and the adoption of new applications and computing frameworks, with both hardware and software in a process of continuous redefinition.

The aim of *Ubiquitous and Pervasive Computing – New Trends and Opportunities* is to outline the novel and interdisciplinary concepts in this research area that we can expect to see during the next ten years, with their associated challenges. The chapters focus on data science, the internet of things, big data, Industry 4.0, high-performance computing, cybersecurity, intelligent applications, and cloud computing environments. A collection of old and new topics relevant to ubiquitous and pervasive computing are discussed throughout the book. Sometimes, old issues are revisited with a new vision. For example, the internet is being redefined with 5G mobile communication and IoT protocols. We are confident that we are passing through a revolution that is in its infancy. In the next ten years, the internet, connectivity, and AI services will be increasingly present in our daily lives in a totally transparent way. It is essential to tackle the security, and specifically privacy, concerns that follow from this revolution. In this context, the move towards implementation of GDPR (General Data Protection Regulation) rules is a very positive one.

The book is divided into two sections: "New Algorithms and Frameworks" and "Smart Environments". The first section opens with a discussion of resource allocation in a distributed system, and explores novel topics such as quality of experience, quality of context and user satisfaction, and their relevance to the success of scheduling algorithms. The aim should be a satisfactory trade-off between (i) optimization, risk minimization and enhancement of income, and (ii) user satisfaction, quality of experience and quality of the offered context. Chapter 2 introduces a novel hybrid genetic optimization algorithm to analyze differential evolution in populations. Chapter 3 considers the increasing use by companies of big-data frameworks for decision-making, detailing the use of artificial intelligence and machine learning algorithms that employ the Hadoop MapReduce computing style for niche applications.

The second section presents three chapters that explore intelligent cities and the smart transformation of living environments. Chapter 4 connects Industry 4.0, the internet of things, and cybersecurity through a study of the use of IoT in a smart home, detailing aspects such as stakeholders in security solutions and privacy concerns. Chapter 5 introduces an edge–fog–cloud architecture for health services. The proposed architecture captures vital signs relevant to long Covid across the entire population and brings this data to the edge. Health services are executed in the fog, detecting health problems in individuals or groups through the use of serverless computing and federated learning. Chapter 6 addresses the mapping of social functions in an intelligent city. From a computational social science perspective, land-use details can be obtained through mobile phone data. Classification engines are used by machine-learning algorithms use to gain insights into the field of urban computing.

I would like to thank Author Service Manager Nika Karamatic for her hard work and excellent support. Also, I thank all the authors for their contributions, which will be useful for ubiquitous computing lectures and research purposes.

Rodrigo da Rosa Righi, Ph.D.
Applied Computing Graduate Program,
Universidade do Vale do Rio dos Sinos – Unisinos,
São Leopoldo, RS, Brazil

Section 1

New Algorithms and Frameworks

Chapter 1

A Resource Allocation Model Driven through QoC for Distributed Systems

André Luiz Tinassi D'Amato
and Wellington Oliveira de Andrade

Abstract

The trend of fog computing has generated challenges to establish resource allocation provided by this type of environment, since, in fog environments, the computing resource setting occurs on demand and at the edge of the network. Thus, ensuring both environment performance and providing user satisfaction imposes a severe technical problem. Since distributed systems are context-aware systems, the quality of context design can be applied to manage customer service, which aims to improve QoS, and provides system performance, for a given context. So, in this chapter, we propose a model to obtain runtime improvement for individual users and improve the global system performance using the quality of context in fog computing environment. The contribution of this proposal is to provide a resource allocation model, and metrics, based on QoC to deal with different distributed computing scenarios, in order to coordinate and enhance the environmental performance and user satisfaction. Experimental results show that our model improves system performance and users' satisfaction. For measuring workloads, estimates of users' satisfaction were performed. The proposed model obtained average results between 80 and 100% of users' satisfaction acceptance, and a standard deviation adherent to a flat surface for workloads with a large number of tasks.

Keywords: distributed system, fog computing, resource allocation, quality of experience, throughput, quality of context, users satisfaction

1. Introduction

The fog computing approach is an alternative to the cloud computing solution, once this paradigm reduces the amount of transmitted data on the network and the computational complexity required in the cloud. However, some approaches in the computing field try to take advantage of both approaches simultaneously. The degree of freedom presented by this new branch focuses mainly on the internet of things landscape, which needs an infrastructure that encompasses all its requirements, a situation in which fog computing fits, which allows the main focus on decision-making and data management locally [1, 2].

In fog computing, part of the data processing, which would be sent to a cloud, can take place between nearby personal devices situated at the edge network. Thus the latency problem can be mitigated, as part of the processing takes place close to the users' devices. In the fog computing model, edge devices could be set as small local data centers supporting multi-tenancy and [3] elasticity. Therefore, we can say that fog computing allows reducing the amount of data sent to the cloud, and consequently reducing the communication latency and the amount of data processed by it. Although fog computing is a good solution for dealing with the problems arising from cloud computing, this paradigm presents several challenges.

Fog computing is a solution designed to deal mainly with Internet of Things applications (IoT) [3], and this type of application tends to deal with the processing of information collected from one or more sources in real-time. From there, it is necessary to make decisions to satisfy the users' needs [3] while maintaining QoS and consequently QoE. However, relying exclusively on edge resources is not always possible, as some computing and data storage requirements may exceed the capacity of those of edge devices. In addition, a user resource configuration may not have enough capacity to meet user's request due to availability or even memory and processing limitations.

In addition, the technological diversity of edge computing devices, and the growth in user demand, generate difficulties to establish resource allocation in order to favor the environment and the applications individual. Edge devices impose a very high level of heterogeneity, making it difficult to allocate resources and establish technologies capable of dealing with different types of different devices. When performing an allocation of resources in any data center, it is important to meet the demands of the user; however, it is of fundamental importance to perform this task maintaining as much load balancing as possible so that the resources can be shared by other users. Therefore, resource scheduling in a fog environment must deal with the best fit between QoE and load balancing.

The related works considered in this article aim to establish techniques, to deal with computational resources management in distributed systems, focusing on system performance or user satisfaction. Due to the difficulty in establishing the trade-off between performance/satisfaction, the related works tried to focus on one of these parameters. Among the related works, knowledge models based on artificial intelligence and ontology are applied. Our proposal presents an approach to address this gap, considering the performance/satisfaction trade-off by developing and applying parameters of context and quality of experience. In this sense, this chapter is proposed a Quality of Context (QoC) based approach aiming at the user's QoE considered from jobs attendance time (makespan).

1.1 Paper organization

The remainder of this paper is organized as follows: Section 2 addresses the basics concepts used by the proposed model in Section 3, and 4; Section 5 discusses the experiment conducted and presents results; Section 6 addresses related works, while final considerations are presented in Section 7.

2. The relationship between quality of context and quality of experience

Considering computational or network resources, the performance perspective between humans and service providers is technically distinct. Service providers consider QoS parameters while, for users, the quality of experience determines the perceived performance [4]. The QoS metrics, for example, are determined from technical parameters: throughput; delay; network performance; loss packets rate, etc.

To evaluate the user QoE of a particular service provided by the network, opinion tests are applied in controlled environments. This type of test is known by the community as a *mean opinion score*. This technique is generally applied for evaluating multimedia systems [5]. However, due to the large number and diversity of applications, opinion tests are not the best alternative. In addition, opinion tests are criticized by some authors [6] and their criticisms are related to scoring scales used in opinion tests. The scale of opinion tests is considered by some authors such as [7] inaccurate and not representative. This occurs because scales used in MOS tests do not consider cultural differences in interpretation. According to [8], the MOS test scores determine absolute values obtained in controlled environments, which do not accurately represent real environments by not considering the influence of context variables.

According to [9], QoC describes context metrics, which can be applied to enhance application or service performance. Thus the QoC is used to establish the reliability of provided services. QoC modeling based on context parameters makes it possible to quantify, or predict, the quality of a service provided.

3. Proposed model

This Section discusses the proposed model addressing all proposed model components. First will address basic concepts of the model. Section 3.1 addresses the QoC metric and Section 4 addresses the QoE metric used in this work. In our work, it is proposed that the QoE is considered a utility function determined from QoC correctness parameter.

The model proposed in this work approaches QoE based on the concepts of resource utility when an application is submitted to a distributed system. The concepts of QoE applied, and the relationship between QoE and utility, are explained in Section 4. Is important to mention that application classes have a strong relationship with the concept of utility since each class has different needs regarding which resources they use on a larger scale. In this sense, the main information that a user describes refers to the application class. The classes referring to the application features are presented as follows: serial applications; parallel applications; network-oriented applications; CPU-oriented applications; I/O and storage-oriented applications.

3.1 QoC parameters

3.1.1 Correctness

In our work, the QoC is used to verify how much a given context is in accordance with what is being demanded by the application. As mentioned earlier in the introductory section of this chapter, the model proposed in this thesis meets different classes (or categories) of applications, each class is characterized by a different need for resources. Therefore, the parameter *correctness*, or correctness, provides a quantitative reference to determine if the current context of a particular resource is suitable to serve an application taking into account its category.

To obtain the value of QoC, an approach based on Bayesian probability theory is proposed. This approach is inspired and adapted from the solution proposed by [10]. The Bayesian probability combines information in a way that relates observed events to hypotheses. In other words, Bayes' theorem is used to calculate the probability conditional that a given event occurs given an observation. For example, calculation of the probability of overhead in allocating an amount cp_i of processes in a given node of a computational grid, in which an amount cp_j of processes available in that node was observed.

Proposed approach, aims to calculate the QoC using conditional probability from the contextual information specified in each submission of *job*, and from the status system update. A *job* is understood as a set of specifications for the execution of a certain task, these specifications being conditional on each other. For example, if context information reveals that the system has processes available in order to provide a processing rate x to execute a *job1*, it is also necessary to know the exact number of processes available to meet the application's execution flow. In other words, if the context manager determines the availability of a certain CPU rate for processing, it is also necessary to know if there are processes available to fulfill the request of *job1*.

In addition to the application demand, the approach proposed in this work aims to manage the workload exerted on the system. Therefore, one of the main functions delegated to the context manager is to collaborate for context-driven load balancing. Eq. (1) determines the probability that a given demand for a resource will be met without generating overload. Eq. (1) expresses the probability that a given demand cp_i for a resource i will overload a capacity node cp_j. Thus, the probability of the resource executing properly is determined by the completeness of Eq. (1). Therefore, the QoC for the resource i considering the available capacity cp_j is given by Eq. (2). The QoC defined in Eq. (2) is actually the partial correctness, considering only an amount of resource of type i on a single node j, named as $QoC_{i|j}$ just to facilitate understanding. For partial correctness, calculation $QoC_{i|j}$ is not considered the application class; therefore, the context for all resources described in *job* are calculated in the same way.

$$P\left(cp_i|cp_j\right) = \frac{P\left(cp_j|cp_i\right) * P(cp_i)}{P\left(cp_j\right)} \tag{1}$$

$$QoC_{(i|j)} = 1 - P\left(cp_i|cp_j\right) \tag{2}$$

3.1.2 Probability for each required resource

The probability for each required resource CP_i is given in Eq. (3), where $ENV_{resource}$ is the total capacity of the environment to provide the required resource. The $ENV_{resource}$ is given by Eq. (4), where n is the number of provider nodes in distributed resource facilities.

$$P(cp_i) = \frac{cp_i}{ENV_{resource}} \tag{3}$$

$$ENV_{resource} = \sum_{j=0}^{n} CP_j \tag{4}$$

The probability for each resource CP_j is given in Eq. (5), where $AVR_{resource}$ is the average of total capacity of the environment to provides the required resource. The $AVR_{resource}$ is given by Eq. (6), where n is the number of provider nodes in distributed resource facilities.

$$P\left(cp_j\right) = \frac{cp_j}{AVR_{resource}} \tag{5}$$

$$AVR_{resource} = \frac{\sum_{j=0}^{n} CP_j}{n} \tag{6}$$

3.1.3 Conditional probability

The conditional probability that associates the required and the available amount of resource is defined in Eq. (7). The probability of a required resource cp_i given an amount cp_j is defined by the magnitude correlation between what was requested and what is available.

$$P\left(cp_j|cp_i\right) = \frac{cp_i}{cp_j} \tag{7}$$

3.1.4 Conditional context parameter

Eq. (1) determines context evaluation from Dependent Context Parameters (DCP) set. Thus, is possible to achieve Eq. (8), where n is the applications context parameters (cp_i). The set CCP Conditional Context Parameters resulting from the Eq. (8).

$$CCP(cp_i) = \left\{P\left(cp_i|cp_j\right); j = 1..n \cap cp_j \varepsilon PDC_i\right\} \tag{8}$$

The correctness is calculated correlating CP_j, CP_i, and n for all context parameters that characterize cp_i. The $QoC(cp_i)_k$ is context association that characterizes cp_i for k-th CP. The Eq. (1) relates the application requirements with resources available resulting in Eq. (9) resulting in Eq. (15).

$$QoC_{(i|j)} = 1 - \frac{P\left(cp_j|cp_i\right) * P(cp_i)}{P\left(cp_j\right)} \tag{9}$$

The resulting correctines, Eq. (10), is obtained from resulting QoC.

$$Correctiness = QoC_{(X|Y)} \tag{10}$$

$$QoC_{(X|Y)} = 1 - \frac{P(X|Y) * P(X)}{P(Y)} \tag{11}$$

$$QoC_{(X|Y)} = 1 - \frac{\frac{X}{Y} * \frac{X}{Z}}{P(Y)} \tag{12}$$

$$QoC_{(X|Y)} = 1 - \frac{\frac{X^2}{Y^* Z}}{\frac{Y}{\frac{Z}{N}}} \tag{13}$$

$$QoC_{(X|Y)} = 1 - \frac{X^{2}}{Y^{2}}^{*}\frac{1}{N} \qquad (14)$$

Thus, the correctiness parameter for X amount of computation requested is defined by Eq. (15).

$$Correctiness = 1 - \left(\frac{1}{N}\right) * \left(\frac{X}{Y}\right)^{2} \qquad (15)$$

The resulting QoC is given by Eq. (16), for all CP_j potential associated with CP_i, and from the number of all n possible CPs, where m is the number of parameters considered QoC resource CP_i. The expression $QoC(cp_i)_k$ is the k-th conditional element that characterizes the *job* J_i.

$$QoC(J_i) = \frac{1}{m}\left(\sum_{k=1}^{m} QoC(J_i)_k\right) \qquad (16)$$

From the QoC, obtained in our model, it is possible to quantitatively predict the user's experience. The relationship between QoE and QoC proposed in our work is presented in the following section.

4. Predicting the quality of experience: a quantitative approach

In our model, QoE quantitatively expresses the prediction of user's satisfaction from QoC-utility function not depending on subjective feelings. The reason is that quantitative metrics are not only more meaningful, but also provide an improved magnitude reference of the measured parameters. From this magnitude reference is possible to benefit the user, and the resource provider environment. In our work, the correctness and runtime are proposed as quantitative metrics for prediction.

In a fog environment, or any distributed system is acceptable that computing resources are provided on demand. The matching between available resources and application requirements is expressed by utility function. The utility function is expressed by the Eq. (17). Utility $U(p)_r$ assigned to a particular resource r, represents a metric proportion of resources adequacy for application, also given by p (*probability of correctness*). Correctness is the main metric applied to measuring the QoC to meet applications demands. The utility is given by Eq. (17).

$$U_r = correctiness_r \qquad (17)$$

The QoE directly depends on application runtime rt, and the response time t. Response time is given t by sum both execution time and waiting time. So, QoE is expressed in Eq. (18).

$$QoE = \frac{rt}{t}\sum_{r=0}^{R} U_r^{\alpha} \qquad (18)$$

The α value quantifies the resource importance, r, to application, and his value ranging between 0 and 1. The α parameter is related with application category, thus, is determinant for utility function. The α parameter is expressed by Eq. (19).

$$\alpha = 1 - U(p) \tag{19}$$

In this section, the metric used to predict users QoE was discussed. Next section covers the obtained results from experiments conducted.

5. Experiment and results

In order to test the efficiency of proposed model, experiments were conducted using the *SimGrid* [11] simulator. This simulator was chosen due their scientific community importance. The mentioned simulator are widely used in academic works in the area of distributed systems for determining a flexible test platform, which can provide hundreds of resources to be used in several experiments. The experiments were carried out aiming to verify the proposed model behaviour considering different workloads, numbers of users and context parameters.

The experimental evaluations, section 5.2, were conducted aiming at performance and QoE. The experiment, aims to insert an exhaustive workload in the tasks submission, and discusses the QoE and the performance of the environment. The QoC was obtained in experiments from the equations proposed in the 3.1 section, using as values for variables, the computational capacity for processing and network, number of processes, workload, and communication latency. The value of Eq. (1), CP_i corresponds to the value of the resource i requested by each workload, and the value to CP_j corresponds to the capacity of the requested resource available on a given node j.

The mentioned values were extracted from the simulation in the SimGrid environment. Programming codes were inserted into the simulation in order to collect data to simulate the *Context-provider*. The QoE for each workload was calculated according to the metric discussed in the 4 section. The QoE was obtained through the resulting QoC considering the parameter *Correctness*, and from the execution and waiting times.

The objective of this experiment according is to analyze the performance of proposed model and perform QoE estimates, when the model is subjected to thousands of *jobs* of different characteristics considering a well-defined interconnection grid, in the SimGrid environment. The SimGrid simulator provides a complete simulation environment to simulate point-to-point interconnection between computers in a grid. The SimGrid simulator has better support for managing *links* when compared to others simulators. In SimGrid it is possible to manage the allocation parameters addressed (Cpu speed, number of processes, transmission rate, latency) peer-to-peer. In general, SimGrid has support for simulating data transmission over the network. In this experiment, files in mrc format were used as input to specify the set of tasks to be simulated, and as output were generated *trace* files in mrc format containing execution data and QoE and QoC estimates. In this experiment, the execution times of the *jobs* and the QoE estimates obtained by user were analyzed. In addition, the central tendency and dispersion of the data were analyzed, as well as the *outliners* generated by the proposed model.

5.1 Infrastructure and workloads

The environment that configures the simulated infrastructure determines a heterogeneous test platform, aiming to measure the performance of our model. For this, 10 grid resources were configured, each feature is determined by a computational grid with the following specifications in **Table 1**:

Resource	Machines available	Mips per process
0	200	50
1	200	50
Baud Rate 1000000: Network between resources 0 and 1		
2	200	150
3	200	150
4	100	150
Baud Rate 500000:Network between resources 2, 3, and 4		
5	100	300
6	100	300
7	100	300
Baud Rate 200000: Network between resources 5, 6, and 7		
8	50	800
9	50	800
Baud Rate 100000: Network between resources 8 and 9		

Table 1.
Simulated resources description.

The environment configuration used aims to represent a heterogeneous set of resources. This type of environment is similar to those found in fog computing environments. The jobs used in this experiment aim to establish a diversified workload, in order to explore the features of the model proposed in this work. Therefore, a number of 20 different types of jobs were used, which are described in **Table 2**.

The environment used as a platform for carrying out the tests was the platform. xml file available along with the simulator. SimGrid is an ideal testing platform for resource allocation policies involving networks, as it has simulation classes that implement point-to-point communication mechanisms. The connection between the various nodes of a computational grid can be specified in SimGrid. The proposed *trace* file records the times obtained with the execution of *jobs*, together with the estimated QoC and QoE. The context-broker receives the file *mrc* as input, which must contain the description of tasks by users, which are:

- Category: Category of the application, cpu or network oriented, sequential or parallel;
- Process_amount_req: Number of processes required by the user;

Type of task	Process required	MIPS required	Type
1	200	200000	CPU/Network bound
2	200	200000	CPU/Network bound
3	200	1000	Network bound
4	200	100	Network bound
5	100	500	Network bound
6	100	500	Network bound
7	100	500	Network bound
8	100	100000	CPU bound
9	50	800	CPU/Network bound
10	50	100000	CPU bound
11	50	100000	CPU bound
12	50	50000	CPU bound
13	20	50000	CPU bound
14	20	100	Network bound
15	20	500	Network bound
16	10	50000	CPU bound
17	10	50000	CPU bound
18	10	50000	CPU bound
19	5	5	Network bound
20	5	200	CPU/Network bound

Table 2.
Workloads description.

- Computation_amount_req: Amount of computation in FLOPS estimated by the user;
- Communication_amount_req: Amount of communication in bits estimated by the user;
- Execution_time: Estimated execution time by the user.

The workloads were synthesized by generating random values for the mentioned parameters above, in order to simulate the unpredictable behavior of a real distributed system. A workload was generated with 3000 tasks randomly distributed among 20 fictitious users represented by numbers (IDs) from 1 to 20. The tasks (or *jobs*) were synthesized using the random function of the GCC library. The system clock time was used to calculate and generate the random numbers.

5.2 Results

The absolute values obtained by running the workloads using the algorithm *Round-Robin* and proposed model context-based strategy are shown in **Tables 3** and **4**, respectively.

The smaller standard deviation represents a smaller dispersion in the resulting runtimes. The users' QoEs are shown in the graphs in **Figures 1** and 2. The graphs present the average QoE values for each user's identifier represented in the ID_users axis. The number of users for the graphs in **Figures 1–4**, is fixed and equal to 20, with the QoE and standard deviation resulting from each user as the workload on the system increases.

The surface generated by the data referring to the average QoE of users when using the model proposed in this work. **Figure 1**, shows a global trend of QoE values around 90% of user satisfaction. This behavior is reinforced by the graph in **Figure 3**. It is

Number of tasks	Average	Standard deviation
100	31028.43	63988.94
200	35732.46	68043.18
300	35076.89	68064.07
400	36377.30	68674.47
500	37436.61	71239.62
600	38791.38	72928.67
700	38329.13	71744.08
800	38329.13	70564.11
900	37032.33	70093.15
1000	36626.69	69546.43
1500	37604.74	70032.94
2000	36255.30	69071.16
2500	36158.03	68628.92
3000	35713.19	67863.07

Table 3.
Average runtime of Round-Robin.

Number of tasks	Average	Standard deviation
100	31979.29	27697.15
200	32031.66	27756.22
300	30226.01	27179.46
400	29601.41	27145.35
500	30676.16	27611.36
600	30342.75	27571.99
700	30068.66	27620.44
800	30065.64	27616.27
900	30136.01	27558.11
1000	29872.54	27565.27
1500	30086.24	27400.14
2000	30270.34	27406.40

Number of tasks	Average	Standard deviation
2500	30507.55	27418.29
3000	30400.25	27429.05

Table 4.
Average proposed model runtime.

important to note that the values are shown in the range between 0 and 1 to represent a QoE from 0 to 100%.

The graph in **Figure 2** shows several QoE spikes revealing an imbalance in terms of user satisfaction with the Round-Robin and Dijkstra policy. Another situation observed in **Figure 2** is the instability of the Round-Robin and Dijkstra policy for QoE. According to the graph in **Figure 2**, users tend to be more dissatisfied when the task set increases. According to **Figure 2**, for a workload with a size of more than 1500 tasks, the users' QoE starts to decrease more sharply.

The graph in **Figure 3**, represents the estimated QoE standard deviation. The graph shows that as the number of tasks submitted to the system increases, the standard deviation becomes more linear. The graph in **Figure 3** reveals a more uniform surface for workloads with a quantity above 1000 tasks. This is because users' QoE tend to decrease with variability in resource states (totally free, fully occupied), especially when there are few tasks. For large numbers of tasks, resource variability occurs more "smoothly" and distributed over time.

The fairness generated by adequate load balancing, which respects the users' needs, is a determining factor in the overall QoE experience. This situation is shown in the graphs of **Figure 1**. The graph presents the average QoE values for each user's identifier represented on the Users_ID axis. The number of user's for the graphs in **Figures 1** and **3** is fixed and equal to 20, with the QoE and the resulting standard deviation of each user being shown as the workload on the system increases. The surface generated by the data referring to the average user's QoE, **Figure 1**, shows a

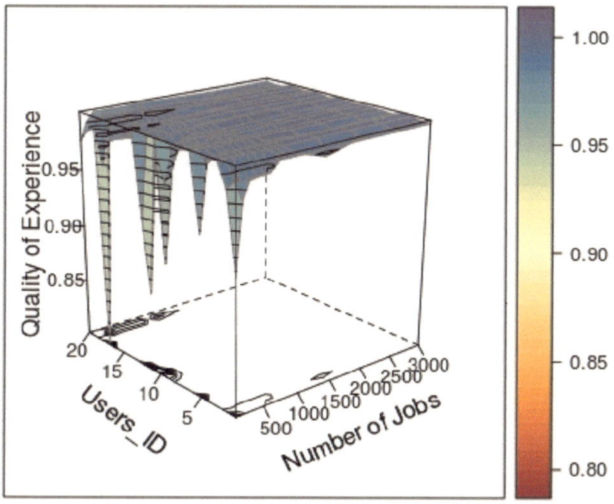

Figure 1.
QoE per user from proposed model.

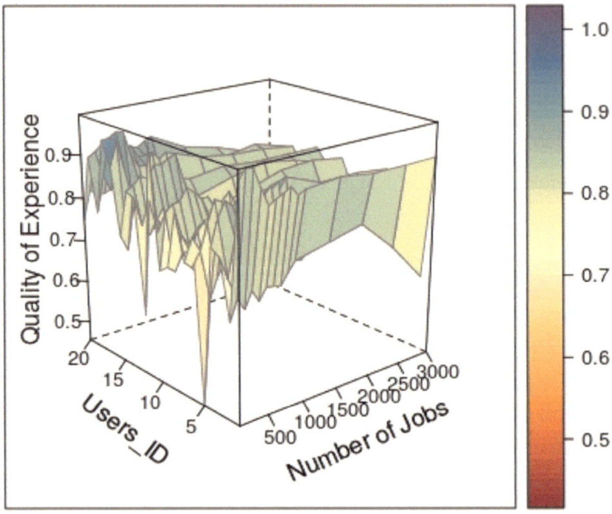

Figure 2.
QoE per user Round Robin and Dijkstra.

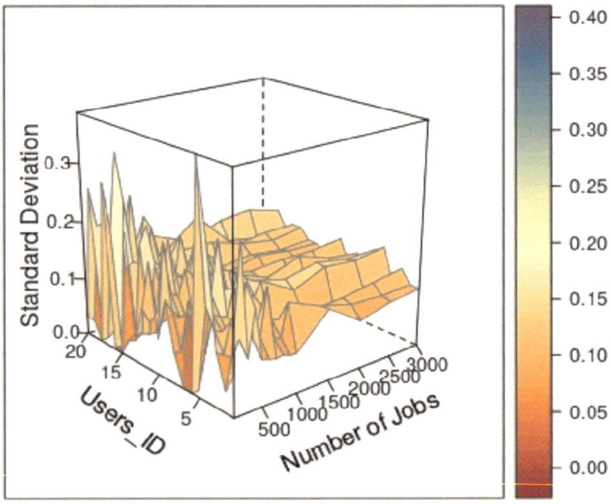

Figure 3.
Standard deviation for QoE per user from proposed model.

global trend of QoE values around 90% of user satisfaction. This behavior is reinforced in the graph of **Figure 3**. It is important to note that the values are shown between 0 and 1 to represent a QoE between 0 and 100%.

The graph in **Figure 4** displays the standard deviation of the estimated QoE using Round-Robin policy with Dijkstra. The graph reveals a greater variation in users' QoE when compared to our proposal. The standard deviation surface of the graph in **Figure 4**, presents irregular characteristics for the QoE of all users. For task sets of sizes 100, 200, and 300, the standard deviations are low, however, the values for QoE for these task sets have lower QoE for all users.

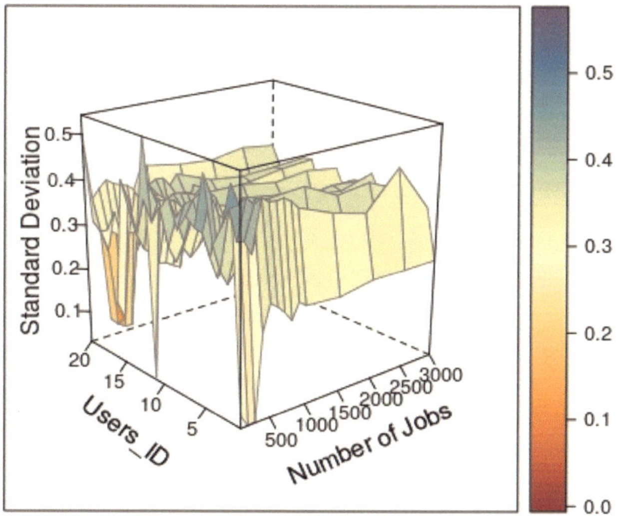

Figure 4.
Standard deviation for QoE per user from Round Robin and Dijkstra.

The proposed model presented better results and stability for QoE and standard deviation when compared to the Round-Robin and Dijkstra based strategy, which does not consider the context to provide resource allocation.

Figure 5 shows the number of tasks that were submitted by each user. The graphs in **Figures 6** and 7 shows the data dispersion in relation to the proposed model QoE. The graphs of **Figures 6** and 7, reveal that although the model is efficient in a global perspective, it is subject to undesirable *outliners* generated by unsatisfactory QoE. The box plot in **Figure 6** confirms the trend of user satisfaction between 80 and 100%, but reveals the cases in which these values did not occur. The same happens for the graph of **Figure** 7. The graph of **Figure** 7 shows the values of the QoEs obtained by each user. According to the graph, it is possible to observe that values close to 100% and close to 0% are not concentrated in specific users, but distributed among all users. Thus, it is possible to carry out a qualitative analysis, concluding that the model established (*fairness*) to resource allocation.

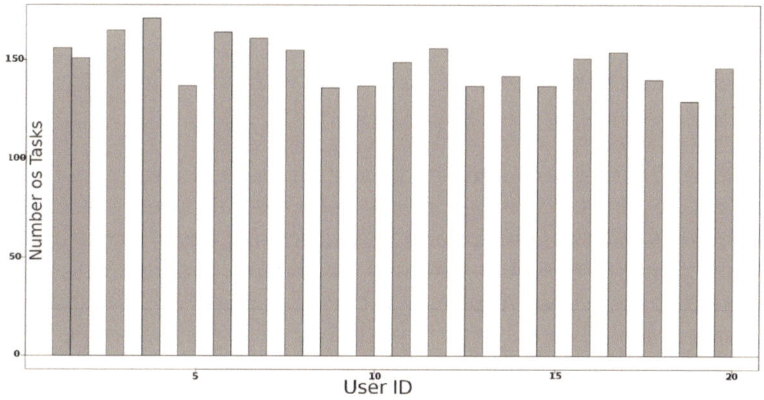

Figure 5.
Number of tasks submitted per user.

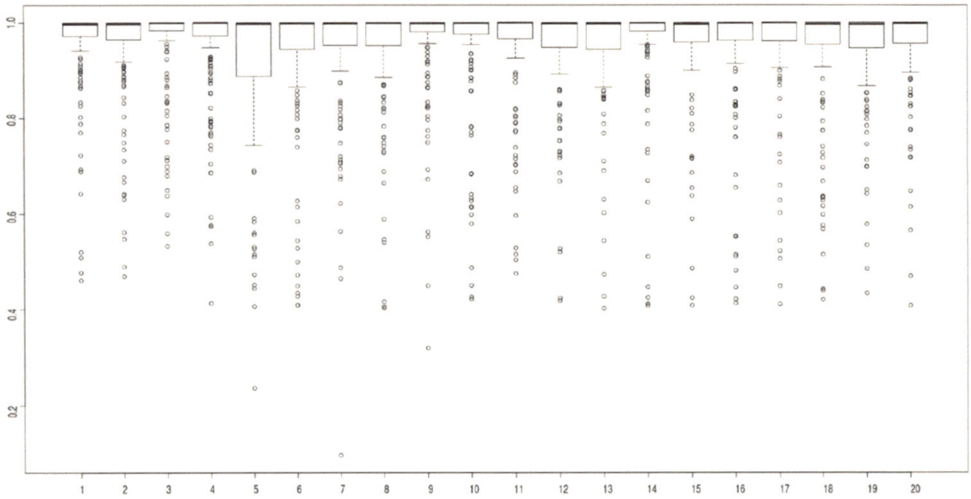

Figure 6.
Box Chart for Users QoE.

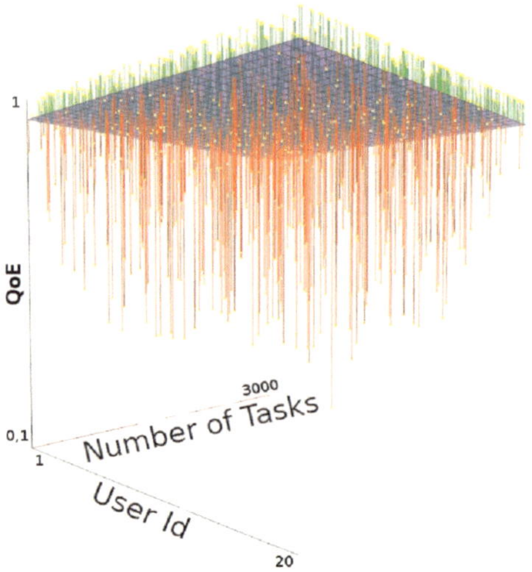

Figure 7.
Scatterplot for (QoE x amount of tasks) per user.

The objective of this experiment was to analyze the relationship between performance and QoE established by proposed model, when the model is submitted to thousands of *jobs* of different characteristics considering a well-defined interconnection grid, in the SimGrid environment. From the results obtained with experiment, it was concluded that the model proposed in this paper has better performance when compared to the *Round-Robin* algorithm with the routing based on the Dijikstra algorithm. For the workloads submitted to execution, QoE estimates were performed. The proposed model obtained average results between 80 and 100% of satisfaction for each user, and a standard deviation adherent to a flat surface for workloads with a large amount of tasks. In this way, the proposed model showed stability in terms of the QoE obtained. The results obtained also show that the proposed model established fair behavior, *fairness*, in resource allocation.

6. Related works

Messina [12] proposes an agent-based model to provide System Level Agreement negotiation. The authors use an ontology to establish the resources needed for each submission. Ontologies are used to provide knowledge to the environment. Therefore, it is possible to establish a more adjusted allocation of resources according to the application's input parameters. Ontologies generate knowledge about the semantic rules to perform the correspondence between the requested resource and the available resource. The work proposed in [12] uses an ontology to provide knowledge, however this approach does not handle situations not foreseen by the ontology well. The context-based strategy of the model proposed in this article provides the best configuration for running applications based on the updated state of the system. The approach proposed in this article performs the allocation of resources considering, in addition to the performance of the application, the performance of the system, which does not happen in the work proposed by [12].

Das uses a resource scheduling policy based on [13] artificial intelligence. However, Das uses the Teaching-Learning Based Optimization learning algorithm as a basis for his proposal. The justification given by the authors for the adoption of the learning algorithm in the context of resource allocation in computational grids is that Teaching-Learning Based Optimization is considered a light and efficient algorithm to find the global solution to optimization problems. Another work based on artificial intelligence is presented in [14]. The authors use an approach centered on estimating values for various data transmission parameters, such as latency and use of *links*. The approach used in [14] is applied only to provide service guarantees, based on QoS prediction through fuzzy logic. Parameters, or formulations, for controlling overall performance are not specified.

In [15] a dynamic resource allocation method, is proposed for load balancing in fog environments. For this, the method has a scheduler capable of performing dynamic migration of services to achieve load balancing for computing systems in fog. Negative aspects related to migration, QoS degradation, and QoE, are not considered in the [19] work. In the works [16, 17] scheduling strategies with real-time constraints are discussed. In [16], aspects of QoE and QoS are addressed but not in depth in order to propose directives to measure and improve these attributes. In [17], the authors develop a work in order to investigate how utility is affected by performance parameters in environments focused on fog aimed at healthcare applications. To evaluate the use of a fog data center, the resources of the iFogSim tool were used. In the work [18], a new resource allocation algorithm based on stable correspondence is proposed, in order to benefit users and providers in the fog environment. However, the authors do not clearly show how the aspects involving user satisfaction and the performance of the environment are treated. **Table 5** shows that our proposal establishes a model that meets QoE and makespan together. This tradeoff is not achieved in the works analyzed so far being our main contribution.

In [19] is proposed a pricing policy based on the QoE. This QoE is expressed from result of the allocation and try to optimize resource allocation from statistical information of the computational requests. This mentioned strategy is implementable in real-time brokers according to the authors. optimal dynamic allocation rule based on

Reference	Addresses a QoE model	Makespan	How implements resource allocation policy
[12]	Yes. SLA model	No	Knowledge model from Ontologies
[13]	No	Yes	Teaching-Learning Based Optimization
[14]	No. QoS only	No	Fuzzy logic to provide QoS
[15]	No	Yes	Dynamic Load Balancing
[16]	Yes. Aimed to Real-Time tasks	No	Neural Networks and Fuzzy Logic
[17]	No	Yes. Based on utility	Algorithm based on stable correspondence
[18]	In a non-detailed indirect way	Yes	Cost Load-Balancing Strategy
[19]	Yes	No	Statistical and real-time approach
[20]	No	Yes	Energy-Aware Load-Balancing Strategy
Our Model	Yes	Yes	QoE/QoC Tradeoff Model

Table 5.
Comparison between proposals.

the The developed solution is statistically optimal, dynamic, and implementable in real-time. The proposal in [20] is based on an energy and collaborative model in load balancing. The proposal in [19] is based on a statistical and dynamic model aiming users QoE. In [20] is proposed an algorithm to both: meeting the application latency requirements and providing energy efficiency in the heterogeneous edge tier. To the algorithm proposed in [20] implements a collaboration strategy at the edge of the network aiming at heterogeneous environment characteristics. According [20] is possible to reduces the waiting time for meeting requests. The proposal in [20] is based on an energy and collaborative model in load balancing. **Table 5** summarizes related work and shows a comparison with our proposal in terms of QoE, environment performance (makespan), and technical approaches to implementation.

7. Conclusions

The scheduling techniques to resource allocation in distributed systems do not generally meets jointly the user satisfactin and throughput. The QoE emerges as a differentiated paradigm to fill this gap. The QoE approach is particularly important for resource allocation, since the resource allocation adjusted to users needs must to consider contextual parameters. The use of QoC to make the resource allocation allows an efficient management, resulting in a performance gain achieved by a strategic load distribution, improving the level of users QoE. Aiming to act in this mentioned scenario was proposed, and evaluated through experiments, QoC-based approach to provide resource allocation in fog computing. The proposed model performs management decisions based on a QoC policy. The QoC is used also to predict the user's QoE. Our model quantifies resource feasibility considering an application demand. An experiment was conducted to analyze the performance of the proposed model. From the results obtained it was concluded, that our model shows a lower standard deviation, when compared to well-known strategies. From the use of the proposed QoC-based policy, was obtained average QoE scores between 80 and 100% considering each user. The resulting QoE values adhere to a flat surface for workloads with large amounts of tasks. Thus, our model shows a stable behavior considering obtained QoEs. Results show that the proposed model established fair behavior (fairness) in resource allocation. Our QoC-based policy stands out, especially when there are excessive workloads and a lack of resources. Among the works mentioned in related works, there are approaches to allocate resources considering the performance of the environment and user satisfaction. Although the related proposals aim to meet user demands, the authors do not provide metrics for effective measurement of user satisfaction. In addition to all that has been mentioned, the works found in the literature on resource allocation are generally applied to specific environments, which do not consider orchestrating different paradigms of distributed systems. Therefore, the main contributions of this work are a solution to the existing gap between user satisfaction and environmental performance (makespan) for distributed systems. Although this work aims to meet the needs of the system and the users, it does not guarantee the QoE individually for the users, it only proposes to improve the average satisfaction. Another limitation of the work is that although the model has been tried in specialized simulators, this model has not been implemented in a physically robust fog environment.

Abbreviations

GB	Gigabytes
GBps	Gigabytes per second
QoS	Quality of Service
QoC	Quality of Context
QoE	Quality of Experience
IoT	Internet of Things
MoS	Mean Opinion Score
DCP	Dependent Context Parameters
CCP	Conditional Context Parameters
AVR	Average
ENV	Environment
MIPS	Million Instructions Per Second
HPC	High Performance Computing

Author details

André Luiz Tinassi D'Amato*† and Wellington Oliveira de Andrade†
Universidade Tecnologica Federal do Paraná, Apucarana, Brasil

*Address all correspondence to: andredamato@utfpr.edu.br

† These authors contributed equally.

References

[1] Cheol-Ho H, Blesson V. Resource management in Fog/Edge computing: A survey on architectures, infrastructure, and algorithms. ACM Computing Surveys. 2019;**52**:1-37

[2] Jouret G et al. Cisco Delivers Vision of Fog Computing to Accelerate Value from Billions of Connected Devices. 2014. Available from: wsroom.cisco.com [Accessed: July 1, 2022]

[3] Shekhar S, Chhokra A, Sun H, Gokhale A, Dubey A, Koutsoukos X, et al. URMILA: Dynamically trading-off fog and edge resources for performance and mobility aware IoT services. Journal of Systems Architecture. 2020;**10**: 101-710

[4] Junaid S, Markus F, Denis C. Quality of Experience from user and network. Annals of Telecommunications. 2010;**65**: 47-57

[5] Fiedler M, Hossfeld T, Tran-Gia P. A generic quantitative relationship between quality of experience and quality of service. Network IEEE. 2010; **24**:36-41

[6] Katrien DM, Istvan K, Wout J, Tom D, Lieven DM, Luc M, et al. Proposed framework for evaluating quality of experience in a mobile, testbed-oriented living lab setting. Mobile Networks and Applications. 2010;**15**:378-391

[7] De Koning TCM, Veldhoven P, Knoche H, Kooij RE. Of MOS and men: Bridging the gap between objective and subjective quality measurements in mobile TV. 2007

[8] Marc S, James P, Philip K. Practical issues in subjective video quality evaluation: Human factors vs. psychophysical image quality evaluation. In: Proceedings of the 1st International Conference on Designing Interactive User Experiences for TV and Video. 2008

[9] Michael K, Iris H. Challenges in modelling and using quality of context (Qoc). In: Proceedings of the Second International Conference on Mobility Aware Technologies and Applications. Springer-Verlag; 2005

[10] Brgulja N, Kusber R, David K, Baumgarten M. Measuring the probability of correctness of contextual information in context aware systems. In: Dependable, Autonomic and Secure Computing, 2009. DASC '09. Eighth IEEE International Conference

[11] Quinson M. SimGrid: A generic framework for large-scale distributed experiments. In: IEEE Ninth International Conference on Peer-to-Peer Computing. 2009

[12] Messina F, Pappalardo G, Santoro C, Rosaci D, Sarne GML. An agent based negotiation protocol for cloud service level agreements. In: WETICE Conference. 2014. pp. 161-166

[13] Das D, Pradhan R, Tripathy CR. Optimization of resource allocation in computational grids. Journal of Grid Computing and Applications. 2015;**6**:1-18

[14] Kolomvatsos K, Anagnostopoulos C, Marnerides AK, Ni Q, Hadjiefthymiades S, Pezaros DP. Uncertainty-driven ensemble forecasting of QoS in software defined networks. In: 2017 IEEE Symposium on Computers and Communication. 2017. pp. 908-913

[15] Xu X, Shucun F, Cai Q, Tian W, Liu W, Dou W-C, et al. Dynamic

resource allocation for load balancing in Fog environment. In: Wireless Communications and Mobile Computing. 2018

[16] Talaat FM, Ali SH, Saleh AI, Ali HA. Effective Load Balancing Strategy (ELBS) for Real-Time Fog computing environment using fuzzy and probabilistic neural networks. Journal of Network and Systems Management. 2019;**1**:1-47

[17] Khattak HA, Arshad H, Islam S, Ahmed G, Jabbar S, Sharif AM, et al. Utilization and load balancing in fog servers for health applications. EURASIP Journal on Wireless Communications and Networking. 2019;**91**:1-12

[18] Battula SK, Garg SK, Naha RK, Thulasiraman P, Thulasiram RK. A micro-level compensation-based cost model for resource allocation in a fog environment. Sensors MDPI. 2019;**19** (13):1-21

[19] Farooq MJ, Zhu Q. QoE Based Revenue Maximizing Dynamic Resource Allocation and Pricing for Fog-Enabled Mission-Critical IoT Applications. IEEE Transactions on mobile computing. 2021;**20**:3395-3408

[20] Xavier Tiago CS, Delicato FC, Pires Paulo F, Amorim Claudio L, Wei L, Albert Z. Managing heterogeneous and time-sensitive IoT applications through collaborative and energy-Aware resource allocation. ACM Transactions on Internet of Things. 2022;**3**:1-28

Chapter 2

A Hybrid Genetic, Differential Evolution Optimization Algorithm

Peter Stubberud

Abstract

This chapter presents a heuristic evolutionary optimization algorithm that is loosely based on the principles of evolution and natural genetics. In particular, this chapter describes an evolutionary algorithm that is a hybrid of a genetic algorithm and a differential evolution algorithm. This algorithm uses an elitist, ranking, random selection method, several mutation methods and both two level and three level Taguchi crossover. This algorithm is applied to 13 commonly used global numerical optimization test functions, including a spherical, three hyper-ellipsoid, the sum of different powers, Rastrigin's, Schwefel's, Griewank's, Rosenbrock's valley, Styblinski-Tang, Ackley's Path, Price-Rosenbrock, and Eggholder's functions. This algorithm is applied 1000 times to each of the 13 test functions, and the results shows that this algorithm always converges to each of the 13 test function's global minimum.

Keywords: optimization algorithm, differential evolution, genetic algorithm, hybrid, Taguchi crossover

1. Introduction

Optimization algorithms are systems that determine an optimal set of parameters that minimize or maximize a cost, or objective, function subject to constraints. Optimization applications are common in engineering and other scientific and mathematical fields. For a typical engineering optimization application, a cost, or objective, function mathematically describes a metric of the error between a desired performance and actual performance over a constrained solution space. For such applications, optimization algorithms would determine an optimal set of parameters that minimize the cost function subject to physical constraints, such as the optimal parameters result in a stable system. As computing power has increased, many multimodal optimization problems have been solved using heuristic evolutionary optimization algorithms. An evolutionary algorithm is an optimization search algorithm that is loosely based on the principles of evolution and natural genetics and uses operators such as reproduction, selection, recombination and mutation [1]. Popular evolutionary algorithms include genetic algorithms [2], differential evolution [3], particle swarm optimization [4], simulated annealing [5] and colony optimization [6, 7]. Although no algorithm can solve all types of optimization problems [8, 9], genetic algorithms and differential evolution algorithms have become popular in engineering optimization applications because these method are simple, effective and flexible.

Because no algorithm can solve all types of optimization problems [8, 9], hybrid algorithms that combine the elements of an evolutionary algorithm with one or more evolutionary algorithms or search algorithms have been developed and have been shown to be effective search algorithms [10]. Because genetic algorithms and differential evolution algorithms have become popular in engineering optimization applications, this chapter presents a hybrid genetic, differential evolution algorithm. The algorithm uses an elitist, ranking, random selection method. Elitist selection methods assure the survival of the fittest individual, which is the candidate solution with the best optimization criterion cost, during the selection process. The fittest individual is also assured selection in all recombination and mutation operations. Except for the fittest individual which is guaranteed selection, the candidate solutions that survive the selection process are randomly selected for a differential evolution operator to improve convergence, a differential evolution mutation operator to improve diversity and a recombination operator that improves both convergence and diversity. The selection probabilities for the mutation and recombination operators are dynamic and change each generation, or algorithm iteration, to maintain a constant population size. After generating new candidate solutions using these operators, the new candidate solutions are added to the set of candidate solutions that survived the selection process. Except for the fittest individual (which is guaranteed selection), candidate solutions are randomly selected for Taguchi crossover [11] which is an effective recombination operator that creates near optimal new candidate solutions from two or more parent candidate solutions. Section 2 of this chapter describes the basic elements of genetic and differential evolution algorithms. Section 3 describes this chapter's algorithm in detail. In Section 4, this algorithm is applied to 13 commonly used global numerical optimization test functions, including a spherical, three hyper-ellipsoid, the sum of different powers, Rastrigin's, Schwefel's, Griewank's, Rosenbrock's valley, Styblinski-Tang, Ackley's Path, Price-Rosenbrock, and Eggholder's functions.

2. Elements of genetic and differential evolution algorithms

Genetic algorithms and differential evolution algorithms are evolutionary algorithms that typically define objective functions so that the set of parameters being optimized are represented in a vector [3]. Parameter constraints are implemented by restricting the available solution spaces for each parameter in the vector. The basic design strategy for such genetic and differential evolution algorithms is to determine evolutionary operators that balance the algorithm's ability to both effectively search the solution space and converge to an optimal solution.

Genetic algorithms and differential evolution algorithms typically begin by randomly selecting $K(0)$ vectors, called candidate solutions or individuals, in the solution space. This initial set of candidate solutions is called the initial population. A subset of $M(1)$ of these initial candidate solutions, or individuals, are selected as a function of their fitness, or cost, when evaluated with respect to the optimization criterion. Although many selection operators exist [12, 13], selection operators are typically designed to select a subset of $M(1)$ candidate solutions from the population in a manner that should improve the overall fitness of the population. The candidate solutions that survive the selection operator form the initial mating pool of $M(1)$

individuals where $1 \leq M(1) \leq K(0)$. Candidate solutions from the mating pool are then selected for recombination and mutation. Recombination operators create new candidate solutions by combining vector elements from two or more of the candidate solutions from the mating pool. Mutation operators in genetic algorithms create new candidate solutions by altering elements of candidate solution vectors. In differential evolution, mutation operators create new candidate solutions by using vector operations, such as addition and scaling, on two or more of the candidate solutions from the mating pool. Regardless of the algorithm, the new candidate solutions created by recombination and mutation are added to the mating pool to create a new population of $K(1)$ candidate solutions. This process of selection, recombination and mutation forms one generation, or iteration, of a genetic or differential evolution algorithm. This process iterates until a convergence criteria is met and an optimal solution is determined. A generic genetic algorithm or differential evolution algorithm can be summarized as follows:

Initialize population {$K(0)$ candidate solutions)}
$n \leftarrow 0$
repeat
$n \leftarrow n + 1$
Select $M(n)$ candidate solutions using a selection operator
Generate new candidate solutions using a mutation operator
Generate new candidate solutions using a recombination operator
Add the new $K(n) - M(n)$ candidate solutions to the mating pool
until convergence condition is met

where n is the algorithm's iteration number.

Genetic operators such as recombination and mutation generate a combination of new candidate solutions that can be either similar or diverse from the candidate solutions in the mating pool. Controlling the ratio of the diversity and similarity of new candidate solutions added to a population each generation is a fundamental design parameter of any search algorithm [14]. Creating diversity, or exploration, is the process of generating candidate solutions that lie in previously unevaluated regions of the search space. Creating similarity, or exploitation, on the other hand, is the process of generating candidate solutions within a neighborhood of previously visited points so as to converge to an optimal point in the neighborhood. Exploration and exploitation are typically conflicting processes of a search algorithm because a lack of diversity can result in a population converging to a local minima or maxima and a lack of similarity can impede convergence. Therefore, every search algorithm needs to design an effective ratio of exploration and exploitation of a search space. In general, an optimal ratio of diversity and similarity is not only dependent on the search algorithm but also the cost, or objective, function. For example, determining the optimal solution of a unimodal objective function typically requires less exploration than determining an optimal solution of a multi-modal objective function that typically requires more exploration. Also, different generations, or iterations, of a search algorithm typically have a different optimal ratios of exploration and exploitation. For example, a search algorithm's early generations require more exploration than exploitation until the neighborhood of the optimal solution is found. After the neighborhood of the optimal solution is found, a search algorithm's generations require more exploitation and less exploration. Therefore, the goal of any search algorithm is to design a ratio of adding diverse new candidate solutions and similar new candidate solutions to each generation so that the algorithm can effectively determine optimal solutions for different types of objective functions.

Genetic algorithms and differential evolution algorithms typically use three operators, selection, mutation and recombination, for controlling the ratio of adding diverse and similar new candidate solutions to their populations. Selection operators control the ratio of exploration and exploitation by varying the selection process. A selection operator that is designed to select the most fit candidate solutions, the candidate solutions with the best costs when evaluated with respect to the optimization criterion, biases the selection process away from exploration and towards exploitation. A selection operator that is designed to select the least fit candidate solutions biases the selection process away from exploitation and towards exploration.

Mutation operators for a typical genetic algorithm or differential evolution algorithm randomly modify individuals from the mating pool to increase the diversity of a population. As a result, a typical mutation operator increases the exploration of unevaluated regions of the search space. However, some mutation operators only slightly alter individuals from the mating pool. In such cases, these types of mutation operators can be classified as an exploitation operator because most of the mutated individual is preserved and the mutated individual still remains in the neighborhood of the parent candidate solution. A recombination operator for a typical genetic algorithm or differential evolution algorithm combines two or more parent individuals, or candidate solutions, from the mating pool to generate a new and possibly more fit candidate solution. As a result, a typical recombination operator generates new candidate solutions within a neighborhood of the parent candidate solutions. From this perspective, a recombination operator increases exploitation and improves the convergence of the algorithm. However, when recombination uses a mutated candidate solution, recombination can create a new candidate solution in a previously unevaluated region of the search space. In such cases, recombination operators can improve exploration of the search space. In most cases, mutation operators improve a population's diversity and recombination operators improve an algorithm's convergence rate; however, in practice, the combination of selection, mutation and recombination determines the ratio of exploration and exploitation in both genetic algorithms and differential evolution algorithms.

3. A hybrid genetic, differential evolution algorithm

This hybrid genetic, differential evolution algorithm determines a best solution with respect to an optimization criterion that has a solution space which is the subset of an N dimensional hyper-rectangular solution space although the algorithm can be adapted for other types of N dimensional spaces. The algorithm generates an initial population of $K(0)$ candidate solutions by randomly selecting $K(0)$ candidate solutions within the solution space. Each candidate solution in the initial population is evaluated by an optimization criterion and ranked. Except for the top ranked candidate solution that is assured selection, a subset of these candidate solutions are randomly selected as a function of their rank. The surviving $M(1)$ candidate solutions solutions from the initial mating pool, where $1 \leq M(1) \leq K(0)$, are randomly selected and employed in creating new candidate solutions using a differential evolution operator to improve convergence, a differential evolution operator to improve diversity and a crossover operator that improves both convergence and diversity. To ensure that the new candidate solutions lie in the solution space, one of two methods is used to move any unfeasible candidate solutions into the solution space. All the new candidate solutions are then added to the mating pool and candidate solutions from this set are randomly selected for Taguchi crossover, a type of recombination operator. After Taguchi crossover, the population should have an average of approximately $K(0)$ candidate solutions. After the Taguchi crossover operation, each candidate in the population is evaluated, ranked, and randomly selected for the next iteration. The algorithm can be summarized as follows:

Initialize population $\{K(0)$ candidate solutions$)\}$
$n \leftarrow 0$
repeat
$n \leftarrow n + 1$
Ranking and stochastic selection $\{M(n)$ candidate solutions$\}$
Differential evolution operator to improve convergence
Differential evolution mutation operator to improve diversity
Recombination operator to improve convergence and diversity
Ensure new solutions are in the solution space
Taguchi crossover $\{K(n)$ candidate solutions$\}$
until convergence condition is met

where n is the algorithm's iteration number.

3.1 Population initialization

To generate the initial population of $K(0)$ candidate solutions, candidate solutions are randomly selected so that the population is uniformly distributed over the solution space. For a hyper-rectangular solution space, an initial population of candidate solutions can be generated in Matlab using

$$\begin{aligned} G(0) = &\, kron(\mathbf{X}_c, ones(1, K(0))) \\ &+ diag(\mathbf{X}_s) * (rand(N, K(0)) - 0.5); \end{aligned} \tag{1}$$

where $G(0)$ is a matrix containing the $K(0)$ initial candidate solutions, $\mathbf{X}_c$ is a vector containing the solution space's center in rectangular coordinates, $\mathbf{X}_s$ is a vector containing the solution space's size for each dimension in rectangular coordinates, and N is the solution space's dimension. For example, for a two dimensional ($N = 2$) hyper-rectangular solution space of $[0 \quad -1]^T \leq \mathbf{x} \leq [6 \quad 1]^T$, $\mathbf{X}_c = [3 \quad 0]^T$ and $\mathbf{X}_s = [6 \quad 2]^T$.

This selection of initial candidate solutions can be adapted for other types of N dimensional spaces. For example, the initial population of $K(0)$ candidate solutions for a hyper-ellipsoid solution space can be generated in Matlab using

$$\begin{aligned} G(1:2:N,\ :) &= kron(\mathbf{X}_r, ones(1, K)).^{*}rand(ceil(N/2), K); \\ G(2:2:N,\ :) &= 2^{*}pi^{*}rand(floor(N/2), K); \end{aligned} \tag{2}$$

where $\mathbf{X}_r$ is a vector containing the the hyper-elliptical solution space's radii, the terms, $G(1:2:N,\ :)$, represent the magnitudes of each candidate solution and the terms, $G(2:2:N,\ :)$, represent their respective phases. If the solution space is not centered at the origin, then candidate solutions of the form $[r \quad \theta]^T$ and centered at $[0 \quad 0]^T$ can be moved to $[R \quad \Theta]^T$ and centered at $[r_0 \quad \gamma]^T$ using the transformations,

$$\begin{aligned} R &= \sqrt{r^2 + r_0^2 + 2rr_0 \cos(\theta - \gamma)} \\ \Theta &= \arctan\left(\frac{r \sin(\theta) + r_0 \sin(\gamma)}{r \cos(\theta) + r_0 \cos(\gamma)}\right). \end{aligned} \tag{3}$$

If appropriate, these initial candidate solutions could be converted to rectangular coordinates using

$$x_k = R\cos\Theta \quad \text{and} \quad x_{k+1} = R\sin\Theta. \tag{4}$$

3.2 Ranking and stochastic selection

This algorithm uses an elitist, linear ranking, random selection method. Because the selection operator is elitist, the fittest individual, or the candidate solution vector with the best optimization criterion cost, is guaranteed to survive the selection process. Elitist selection algorithms can increase an algorithm's exploitation and therefore increase the algorithm's ability to converge, especially when steady-state misadjustment is significant [15]. Linear ranking selection methods evaluate each candidate solution by the cost function and rank the candidate solutions according to their costs [16, 17]. Starting with the candidate solution with the best cost, each candidate solution is assigned a selection probability in linearly decreasing increments so that all candidate solutions have a nonzero probability of selection. This method of selection allows diverse candidate solutions that might contain useful vector elements but have a poor cost to survive the selection process. This can improve an algorithm's exploration and prevent the algorithm from converging in a local minima or maxima.

The selection operator is the first operation performed for each generation, or iteration of the algorithm. At the start of the algorithm's nth iteration, the selection operator evaluates the $K(n)$ candidate solutions, $\mathbf{x}_k(n)$, with respect to the cost function, J, and ranks the candidate solutions according to their cost. For a minimization problem, the ranked candidate solutions are sorted from highest cost to lowest cost and are assigned consecutive integers from 1 to $K(n)$ so that $\mathbf{x}_1(n)$ is candidate solution with the highest, or worst, cost and $\mathbf{x}_{K(n)}(n)$ is assigned to the candidate solution with the lowest, or best, cost. After ranking, each candidate solution is assigned a selection probability, $P(\mathbf{x}_k(n))$, so that

$$P(\mathbf{x}_k(n)) = \sum_{m=1}^{k} \Delta p_m \tag{5}$$

where

$$\Delta p_m = \frac{1}{K(n)}\left[\eta^- + (\eta^+ - \eta^-)\frac{m-1}{K(n)-1}\right], \tag{6}$$

η^+ is a constant, and η^- is a constant that is selected so $P(\mathbf{x}_1(n)) = \eta^-/K(n)$ which is the selection probability of the worst candidate solution [16, 17].

Because this algorithm uses an elitist selection method, the best candidate solution is assured survival during the selection process which implies that

$$P\big(\mathbf{x}_{K(n)}(n)\big) = 1. \tag{7}$$

Substituting Eq. (6) into Eq. (5), and the resulting equation into Eq. (7),

$$\sum_{m=1}^{K(n)} \frac{1}{K(n)}\left[\eta^- + (\eta^+ - \eta^-)\frac{m-1}{K(n)-1}\right] = 1. \tag{8}$$

Solving Eq. (8), an elitist selection method requires that

$$\eta^{+} = 2 - \eta^{-} \tag{9}$$

where $0 < \eta^{-} < \eta^{+}$.

The set of surviving candidate solutions are referred to as the mating pool. After this selection method, the mating pool's mean size is

$$E[M(n)] = \sum_{k=1}^{K(n)} P(x_k(n)) = \frac{2\eta^{-} + \eta^{+}}{6}(K(n) + 1) \tag{10}$$

where E is the expectation operator and $M(n)$ is the number candidate solutions in the mating pool after selection during the nth iteration. Because this algorithm uses an elitist selection method, Eq. (10) can be simplified by substituting Eq. (9) into Eq. (10) which results in

$$E[M(n)] = \frac{2 + \eta^{-}}{6}(K(n) + 1) \tag{11}$$

which is the expected number of candidate solutions that survive this elitist linear ranking selection process during the nth iteration. Ref. [17] shows that setting $\eta^{-} \approx 0.9$ often provides an adequate balance between selective pressure which allows for exploitation of the objective function and population diversity which allows for exploration of the objective function.

3.3 Differential evolution operator to improve convergence

Differential evolution algorithms generate new candidate solutions by adding a weighted difference between two randomly selected candidate solutions to a third randomly selected candidate solution. For this algorithm, the differential evolution operator to improve convergence generates a new candidate solution, $\mathbf{v}$, using

$$\mathbf{v} = \mathbf{x}_k(n) + R\left[\mathbf{x}_m(n) - \mathbf{x}_j(n)\right] \tag{12}$$

where $\mathbf{x}_k(n)$ is the candidate solution randomly selected for differential evolution, $\mathbf{x}_m(n)$ and $\mathbf{x}_j(n)$ are two randomly selected candidate solutions from the mating pool, and R is a uniformly distributed random number from the interval [0,1]. The two candidate solutions, $\mathbf{x}_m(n)$ and $\mathbf{x}_j(n)$, should be distinct and chosen so that $\mathbf{x}_m(n) \neq \mathbf{x}_j(n)$; however, this can become difficult when the algorithm is converging.

Because this algorithm is an elitist algorithm, the best candidate solution, $\mathbf{x}_{K(n)}(n)$, is always selected for this differential evolution operator. The other candidate solutions are selected randomly for differential evolution with a probability of $P_{DE1}(n)$. Because R in Eq. (12) is a uniformly distributed random number from the interval [0,1], the value R attenuates the difference between the two randomly selected candidate solutions. When this attenuated difference is added to the candidate solution selected for differential evolution, it creates a new candidate solution within a neighborhood of the candidate solution selected for differential evolution. As a result, this differential evolution operator improves the algorithm's ability converge to an

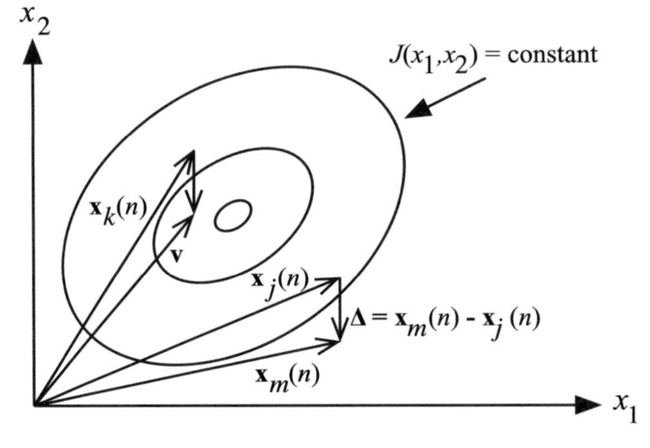

Figure 1.
A plot showing an example of the differential evolution operator that improves convergence for a two dimensional cost function, J. The plot shows the contour lines of the cost function and the candidate solution vectors involved in the differential evolution operation.

optimal point in the neighborhood. **Figure 1** shows a plot of the contours of a two dimensional cost function, J, and three candidate solutions selected for differential evolution. The figure illustrates how this differential evolution operator creates candidate solutions within a neighborhood of the candidate solution, $\mathbf{x}_k(n)$, selected for differential evolution.

On average, this operator creates

$$(M(n) - 1)P_{DE1}(n) + 1 \tag{13}$$

new candidate solutions.

3.4 Differential evolution mutation operator to improve diversity

Because differential evolution algorithms generate new candidate solutions by adding a weighted difference between two randomly selected candidate solutions to a third randomly selected candidate solution, the differential evolution operator creates new candidate solution vectors that contain elements that are different from the candidate solutions that formed the new solution vector. As a result, the differential evolution operator is often referred to as a mutation operator whether the operator creates similarity or diversity. In this chapter, the differential evolution operator that increases diversity is referred to as the differential evolution mutation operator.

For this algorithm, the differential evolution mutation operator generates a new candidate solution, $\mathbf{v}$, using

$$\mathbf{v} = \mathbf{x}_k(n) + \frac{1}{4}diag(\mathbf{R})diag(\mathbf{X}_s)\left[\mathbf{x}_m(n) - \mathbf{x}_j(n)\right] \tag{14}$$

where $\mathbf{x}_k(n)$ is the candidate solution randomly selected for differential evolution mutation, $\mathbf{x}_m(n)$ and $\mathbf{x}_j(n)$ are two randomly selected candidate solutions from the mating pool, $\mathbf{R}$ is a vector whose elements are uniformly distributed random number from the interval [0,1], and $\mathbf{X}_s$ is a vector containing the solution space's size for each dimension in rectangular coordinates or the diameters of an elliptic solution space.

Again, the randomly selected candidate solutions, $\mathbf{x}_m(n)$ and $\mathbf{x}_j(n)$, should be distinct and chosen so that $\mathbf{x}_m(n) \neq \mathbf{x}_j(n)$.

Because this algorithm is an elitist algorithm, the best candidate solution, $\mathbf{x}_{K(n)}(n)$, is always selected for this differential evolution mutation operator. The other candidate solutions are selected randomly for differential evolution with a probability of $P_{DE2}(n)$. Because the term, $\frac{1}{4}diag(\mathbf{R})diag(\mathbf{X}_s)$, in Eq. (14) is a diagonal matrix with uniformly distributed random numbers from the interval zero to $\frac{1}{4}$ the size of each dimension of the solution space, the term, $\frac{1}{4}diag(\mathbf{R})diag(\mathbf{X}_s)$, typically increases each dimension of the difference between the two randomly selected candidate solutions randomly. As the entire population begins to converge and the differences between any two randomly selected candidate solutions begins to decrease, the term, $\frac{1}{4}diag(\mathbf{R})diag(\mathbf{X}_s)$, increases these small differences and these increased differences are added to the candidate solutions selected for differential Evolution. Therefore, the new candidate solutions typically lie outside the neighborhood of the candidate solutions selected for differential evolution. As a result, this differential evolution operator improves the algorithm's diversity until the entire population begins to converge within very small differences.

The mean number of mutant solutions created by this process is

$$(M(n) - 1)P_{DE2}(n) + 1. \tag{15}$$

3.5 A recombination operator to improve convergence and diversity

Taguchi crossover can greatly increase convergence rates [11, 18]. As a result, when the differential evolution operators discussed earlier are combined with Taguchi crossover, this algorithm can converge too quickly. To prevent this algorithm from converging too quickly into a local minima or maxima, a recombination operator that creates a pair of new candidates is added to this algorithm. To improve convergence, this recombination operator generates a new candidate solution, $\mathbf{v}$, by averaging the selected candidate solution, $\mathbf{x}_k(n)$, with another randomly selected candidate solution, $\mathbf{x}_m(n)$, from the mating pool so that

$$\mathbf{v} = [\mathbf{x}_k(n) + \mathbf{x}_m(n)]/2. \tag{16}$$

To improve diversity, this recombination operator generates the another candidate solution by circularly shifting the elements of the newly formed candidate solution, $\mathbf{v}$, by a uniformly distributed integer and then randomly changing the signs of the elements. In Matlab, this new vector, $\mathbf{w}$, can be created by

$$w = sign(randi(2, N, 1) - 1.5).^{*}circshift(v, randi(N)). \tag{17}$$

Because this algorithm is an elitist algorithm, the best candidate solution, $\mathbf{x}_{K(n)}(n)$, is always selected for this recombination operator. The other candidate solutions are selected randomly with a probability of $P_{cr}(n)$. On average, this operator creates

$$(M(n) - 1)2P_{cr}(n) + 2 \tag{18}$$

new candidate solutions.

3.6 Solution space

A candidate solution is considered infeasible if it does not lie within the solution space. If a new candidate solution is infeasible, that solution is made feasible by one of two methods. If a convergence operator, such as the differential evolution for convergence or the recombination operator for convergence, creates an infeasible candidate solution, the infeasible solution vector is moved to the nearest edge of the solution space by changing the vector's elements that lie outside solution space to the nearest edge of the solution space. This method attempts to generate feasible solutions within the neighborhood of the original infeasible solution so that the intent of the convergence operator that created the infeasible solution is maintained.

If a diversity operator, such as the differential evolution mutation for diversity operator or the recombination operator for diversity, creates an infeasible solution, the infeasible solution vector is moved into the solution space by performing a spatially circular shift of the infeasible solution vector's elements. For example, if an infeasible solution, $\mathbf{v}$, is created by a diversity operator in a hyper-rectangular solution space, the infeasible solution vector is moved into the solution space using

$$\mathbf{v} = mod[\mathbf{v} - (\mathbf{X}_c - 0.5\mathbf{X}_s), \mathbf{X}_s)] + (\mathbf{X}_c - 0.5\mathbf{X}_s) \tag{19}$$

where $\mathbf{X}_c$ is a vector containing the center of the solution space in rectangular coordinates, and $\mathbf{X}_s$ is a vector containing the size of each dimension of the solution space in rectangular coordinates. Similarly, if an infeasible solution, $\mathbf{v}$, is created by a diversity operator in an elliptical solution space centered at the origin, the infeasible solution vector, $\mathbf{v}$, expressed in polar coordinates, $re^{j\theta}$, is moved into the solution space using

$$\begin{aligned} r_k &= rem(r_k, r_{k\max}) \\ \theta_k &= \theta_k + \pi \end{aligned} \tag{20}$$

where rem is the remainder function, r_k is a radius that places the candidate solution outside of the solution space, $r_{k\max}$ is the maximum value of r_k that keeps the candidate solution inside the solution space and θ_k is the angle associated with the radius, r_k. This method attempts to generate feasible solutions away from the neighborhood of the original infeasible solution so that the intent of the diversity operator that created the infeasible solution is maintained.

3.7 Taguchi crossover

A crossover operator is a recombination operator that combines the elements from two or more parent candidate solutions to generate a new offspring candidate solution. Taguchi crossover generates new candidate solutions by intelligently selecting elements from the two or more parent solutions vectors [11]. Taguchi crossover is a simple design of experiments method that creates a near optimal candidate solution from the parent candidate solutions. Consequently, Taguchi crossover can greatly increase an algorithm's rate of convergence [11, 18].

Before selecting candidate solutions for Taguchi crossover, all new candidate solutions created by the other operators are added to the mating pool. The mean number of candidate solutions in the mating pool at this stage can be obtained by summing

Eq. (14), Eq. (15) and Eq. (18) which implies that the mean number of candidate solutions in the mating pool at this stage is

$$M(n) + (M(n) - 1)P_3(n) + 4 \tag{21}$$

where $P_3(n) = P_{DE1}(n) + P_{DE2}(n) + 2P_{cr}(n)$.

Because this is an elitist algorithm, the best candidate solution is always selected for Taguchi crossover. The other candidate solutions from the mating pool are selected randomly for Taguchi crossover with a probability of P_{Tc}. For two level Taguchi crossover, crossover involving two parent solutions, one other candidate solution is selected randomly from the mating pool. For three level Taguchi crossover, crossover involving three parent solutions, two other candidate solutions are selected randomly from the mating pool.

On average, the Taguchi crossover operator creates

$$[(M(n) - 1)(1 + P_3(n)) + 4]P_{Tc} + 1 \tag{22}$$

new candidate solutions.

3.8 Managing population size

Because the selection operator, the differential evolution operators, the recombination operators and Taguchi crossover operator generate a random number of new candidate solutions, the population size and mating pool size vary each generation, or iteration of the algorithm. After the Taguchi crossover operator, the average number, $E[K(n)]$, of the candidate solutions can be calculated by adding Eq. (21) and Eq. (22) which results in

$$E[K(n)] = [(M(n) - 1)(1 + P_3(n)) + 4](1 + P_{Tc}) + 2. \tag{23}$$

To maintain the population's size, $K(n)$, at the population's initial size, $K(0)$, the probabilities of at least one of the operators must vary so that

$$E[K(n)] = K(0). \tag{24}$$

Substituting Eq. (23) into Eq. (24) and solving for $P_3(n)$,

$$P_3(n) = \frac{K(0) - 6 - 4P_{Tc}}{(1 + P_{Tc})(M(n) - 1)} - 1 \tag{25}$$

where P_{Tc} is assumed to be fixed and $P_3(n)$ varies. In this algorithm, the requirement in Eq. (25) is met by fixing $P_{DE1}(n)$ and $P_{DE2}(n)$, and letting

$$P_{cr}(n) = [P_3(n) - P_{DE1}(n) - P_{DE2}(n)]/2. \tag{26}$$

4. Optimization test function results

To evaluate this algorithm's ability to solve optimization problems, the algorithm was applied to 13 commonly used global numerical optimization test functions. **Table 1** lists these 13 cost functions, $J_1(\mathbf{x})$ through $J_{13}(\mathbf{x})$, where $\mathbf{x} =$

Function	Solution space $x_k \in [\bullet, \bullet]$
$J_1(\mathbf{x}) = \sum_{k=1}^{N} x_k^2$	[−5.12, 5.12]
$J_2(\mathbf{x}) = \sum_{k=1}^{N} k x_k^2$	[−5.12, 5.12]
$J_3(\mathbf{x}) = \sum_{k=1}^{N} [k(x_k - 5k)]^2$	[−500, 500]
$J_4(\mathbf{x}) = \sum_{m=1}^{N} \sum_{k=1}^{m} x_k^2$	[−65.536, 65.536]
$J_5(\mathbf{x}) = \sum_{k=1}^{N} \lvert x_k \rvert^{k+1}$	[−1, 1]
$J_6(\mathbf{x}) = 10N + \sum_{k=1}^{N} \left[x_k^2 - 10\cos(2\pi x_k)\right]$	[−5.12, 5.12]
$J_7(\mathbf{x}) = 418.9828872724338N - \sum_{k=1}^{N} x_k \sin\left(\sqrt{\lvert x_k \rvert}\right)$	[−500, 500]
$J_8(\mathbf{x}) = 1 + \sum_{k=1}^{N} \frac{x_k^2}{4000} - \prod_{k=1}^{N} \cos\left[\frac{x_k}{\sqrt{k}}\right]$	[−600, 600]
$J_9(\mathbf{x}) = \sum_{k=1}^{N-1} \left[100\left(x_k^2 - x_{k+1}\right)^2 + (x_k - 1)^2\right]$	[−5, 10]
$J_{10}(\mathbf{x}) = 39.16616570377142N + \sum_{k=1}^{N} \left(x_k^4 - 16x_k^2 + 5x_k\right)$	[−5, 5]
$J_{11}(\mathbf{x}) = 20 + e - 20e^{-0.2\sqrt{\frac{1}{N}\sum_{k=1}^{n} x_k^2}} - e^{\sum_{k=1}^{N} \frac{\cos(2\pi x_k)}{N}}$	[32.768, 32.768]
$J_{12}(\mathbf{x}) = 100\left(x_2 - x_1^2\right)^2 + \left[6.4(x_2 - 0.5)^2 - x_1 - 0.6\right]^2$	[−5, 5]
$J_{13}(\mathbf{x}) = 959.640662720851 - x_1 \sin\left(\sqrt{\lvert x_1 - x_2 - 47 \rvert}\right) - (x_2 + 47)\sin\left(\sqrt{\left\lvert \frac{x_1}{2} + x_2 + 47 \right\rvert}\right)$	[−512, 512]

Table 1.
Optimization test functions and their solution spaces.

$\begin{bmatrix} x_1 & x_2 & \dots & x_N \end{bmatrix}^T$, and their solution spaces. These functions include a spherical, three hyper-ellipsoid, the sum of different powers, Rastrigin's, Schwefel's, Griewank's, Rosenbrock's valley, Styblinski-Tang, Ackley's Path, Price-Rosenbrock, and Eggholder's functions. The first 11 functions, $J_1(\mathbf{x})$ through $J_{11}(\mathbf{x})$, are multidimensional functions and are tested for two dimensions ($N = 2$) and 35 dimensions ($N = 35$). Functions $J_{12}(\mathbf{x})$ and $J_{13}(\mathbf{x})$ are two dimensional functions and were only tested for $N = 2$. For all 13 functions, $J_{min} = 0$ where J_{min} is the global minimum value of the cost function. **Figure** 2 shows a plot of the two dimensional Schwefel function and **Figure 3** shows a plot of the two dimensional Eggholder function.

For all functions and dimensions, the initial population, $K(0)$, was set to 50, $\eta^- = 0.9$, $P_{DE1}(n) = 0.16$, $P_{DE2}(n) = 0.2$, $P_{Tc}(n) = 0.22$ and $P_{cr}(n)$ was set each iteration according to Eq. (18). The algorithm was applied 1000 times to each function, and the algorithm was assumed to converge when a solution, $\mathbf{x}_{opt}$, was determined so that $J(\mathbf{x}_{opt}) \le J_{tol}$ where J_{tol} for each function is listed in **Table 2**. **Table 2** lists the mean and standard deviation of the number of iterations that the algorithm required to converge for two level ($L = 2$) and three level ($L = 3$) Taguchi crossover for each function. **Table 2** also lists the means and standard deviations of the number of cost function evaluations that the algorithm required to converge for two level ($L = 2$) and three level ($L = 3$) Taguchi crossover for each function.

The number of cost function evaluations that the algorithm required to converge can also be calculated as a function of the algorithm's average population size, average mating pool size and operator probabilities. For example, 2-D functions require four

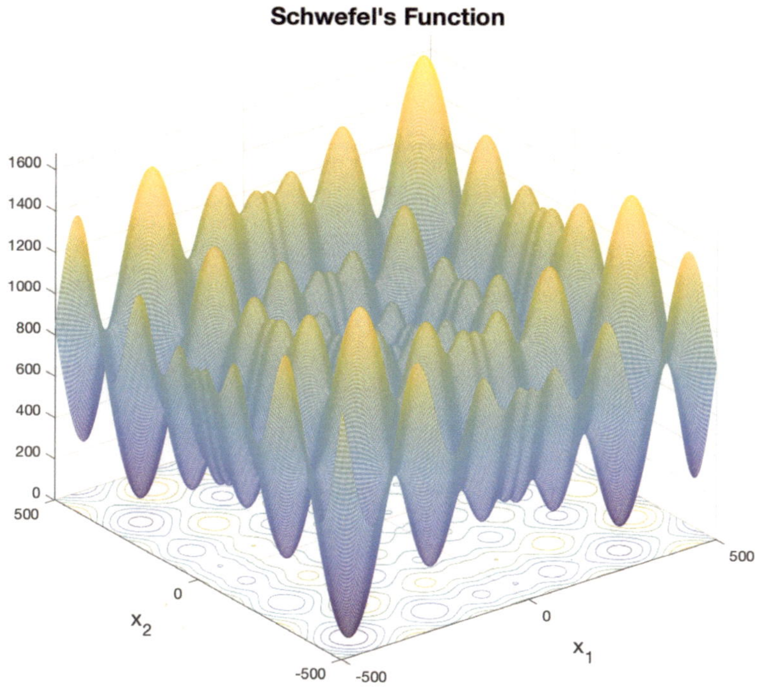

Figure 2.
A plot of the two dimensional Schwefel's function.

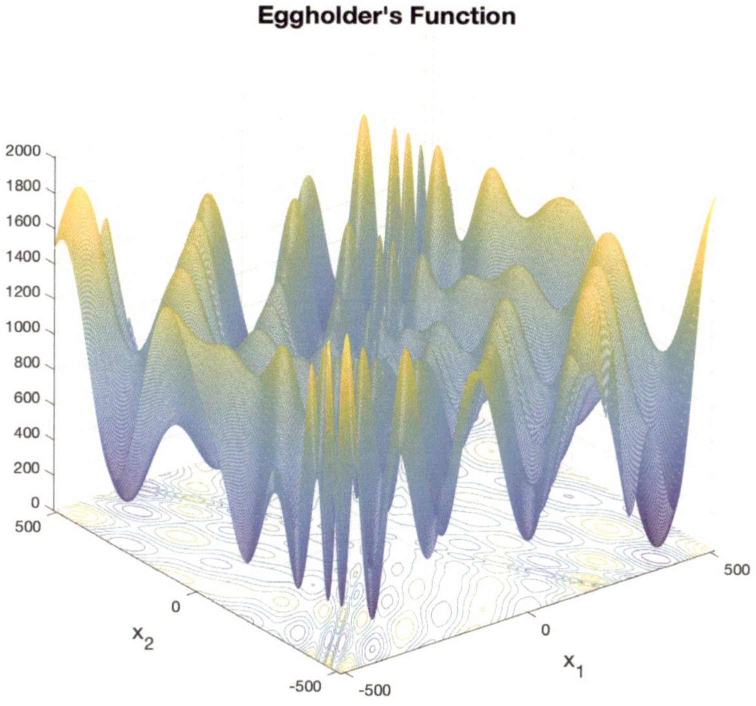

Figure 3.
A plot of the two dimensional Eggholder's function.

Cost Fn	J_{tol}	N = 2 Mean Iter St Dev Iter		N = 2 Mean J Evals St Dev Evals		N = 35 Mean Iter St Dev Iter		N = 35 Mean J Evals St Dev Evals.	
		$L=2$	$L=3$	$L=2$	$L=3$	$L=2$	$L=3$	$L=2$	$L=3$
$J_1(\mathbf{x})$	10^{-300}	43	30	3950	4250	130	105	58,000	90,300
		22	17	2000	2400	4	3	2600	4200
$J_2(\mathbf{x})$	10^{-300}	45	31	4150	4300	137	110	61,000	94,400
		22	17	2050	2400	4	3	2500	4300
$J_3(\mathbf{x})$	10^{-8}	44	39	4000	5450	1170	975	5.3e5	8.3e5
		15	20	1350	2800	1540	1650	7.0e5	1.4e6
$J_4(\mathbf{x})$	10^{-300}	68	71	6200	9950	6917	2990	3.1e6	2.5e6
		34	33	3150	4700	1520	765	6.9e5	6.6e5
$J_5(\mathbf{x})$	10^{-300}	42	33	3800	4700	922	343	4.1e5	2.9e5
		17	15	1600	2200	108	47	48,550	40,200
$J_6(\mathbf{x})$	10^{-300}	31	24	2800	3300	84	65	37,500	55,400
		12	10	1150	1450	4	3	2420	3450
$J_7(\mathbf{x})$	10^{-10}	40	33	3650	4500	155	100	69350	86,350
		6	5	550	650	12	7	6200	6600
$J_8(\mathbf{x})$	10^{-300}	39	35	3550	4900	90	77	40,300	65,700
		19	18	1750	2600	4	4	2500	4650
$J_9(\mathbf{x})$	10^{-10}	65	67	5950	9500	14,325	5776	6.5e6	4.9e6
		82	88	7500	12,500	6920	4804	3.1e6	4.1e6
$J_{10}(\mathbf{x})$	10^{-11}	31	26	2850	3650	105	70	47,000	60,000
		3	3	300	450	6	3	2650	3250
$J_{11}(\mathbf{x})$	10^{-15}	40	28	3700	3900	110	72	49,600	61,400
		22	16	2050	2250	17	16	7400	14,200
$J_{12}(\mathbf{x})$	10^{-2}	19	18	1750	2550	NA	NA	NA	NA
		24	19	2200	2700	NA	NA	NA	NA
$J_{13}(\mathbf{x})$	10^{-11}	869	881	7.9e4	1.2e5	NA	NA	NA	NA
		1068	1162	9.7e4	1.6e5	NA	NA	NA	NA

Table 2.
Results for the optimization of the 2-D and 35-D test functions where $K(0) = 50$, $\eta^- = 0.9$, $P_{DE1} = 0.16$, $P_{DE2} = 0.2$ and $P_{Tc} = 0.22$ for two level ($L = 2$) and three level ($L = 3$) Taguchi crossover. Results are averages over 1000 runs.

cost function evaluations for two level Taguchi crossover and nine cost function evaluations for three level Taguchi crossover. Therefore, the average number of cost function evaluations per algorithm iteration is

$$\overline{K} + 4 + 4P_{Tc}\left[\left(\overline{M} - 1\right)\left(1 + \overline{P}_3\right) + 4\right] \quad (27)$$

for two level Taguchi crossover and

$$\overline{K} + 9 + 9P_{Tc}\left[\left(\overline{M} - 1\right)\left(1 + \overline{P}_3\right) + 4\right] \tag{28}$$

for three level Taguchi crossover where $\overline{K}$ is the average population size, $\overline{M}$ is the average mating pool size after selection and $\overline{P}_3$ is the average of $P_3(n)$.

Similarly, for the 35-D functions, two level Taguchi crossover requires 40 cost function evaluations, and three level Taguchi crossover requires 81 cost function evaluations. Therefore, the average number of cost function evaluations per algorithm iteration is

$$\overline{K} + 40 + 40P_{Tc}\left[\left(\overline{M} - 1\right)\left(1 + \overline{P}_3\right) + 4\right] \tag{29}$$

for two level Taguchi crossover and

$$\overline{K} + 81 + 81P_{Tc}\left[\left(\overline{M} - 1\right)\left(1 + \overline{P}_3\right) + 4\right] \tag{30}$$

for three level Taguchi crossover.

Although no algorithm can solve all types of optimization problems [8, 9], the data in **Table 2** shows that the algorithm converged below the specified J_{min} for 100% of the 1000 runs for all the test functions. The data in **Table 2** also shows that this algorithm requires significantly more iterations to converge for Eggholder's function, J_{13}, and for Rosenbrock's valley, J_9 when $N = 35$ which implies that the algorithm has not been optimized for all types of cost functions. The data also shows that although the three level Taguchi crossover algorithm typically converges using few iterations than the two level Taguchi crossover algorithm, the two level Taguchi crossover algorithm typically requires fewer cost function evaluations than the three level Taguchi crossover algorithm.

5. Summary and conclusions

This chapter presents a hybrid genetic, differential evolution algorithm that represents the set of parameters being optimized in a vector. The algorithm uses an elitist, ranking, random selection method to generate a mating pool. Candidate solutions from the mating pool are randomly selected for two differential evolution operators, and two recombination operators. The new candidate solutions generated by these operators are added to the mating pool. Candidate solutions from this expanded mating pool are selected randomly for Taguchi crossover.

To evaluate this algorithm's ability to solve optimization problems, the algorithm was applied to 13 commonly used global numerical optimization test functions, including a spherical, three hyper-ellipsoid, the sum of different powers, Rastrigin's, Schwefel's, Griewank's, Rosenbrock's valley, Styblinski-Tang, Ackley's Path, Price-Rosenbrock, and Eggholder's functions. The algorithm was evaluated using two and three level Taguchi crossover. For both two and three level Taguchi crossover, the algorithm converged below the specified J_{min} for 100% of the 1000 runs for all the test functions. Although the three level Taguchi crossover algorithm typically converged using fewer iterations than the two level Taguchi crossover algorithm, the two level Taguchi crossover algorithm typically required fewer cost function evaluations than the three level Taguchi crossover algorithm.

Although this algorithm required significantly more iterations to converge for Eggholder's function and for 35-D Rosenbrock's valley function, ref. [19] shows that this algorithm has been successfully used to design digital infinite impulse response (IIR) filters with arbitrary magnitude responses. As a result, it can be expected that the simple optimization algorithm described in this chapter can be used successfully for similar engineering optimization applications.

Author details

Peter Stubberud
University of Nevada Las Vegas, Las Vegas, USA

*Address all correspondence to: peter.stubberud@unlv.edu

References

[1] Fogel DB. What is evolutionary computation? IEEE Spectrum. 2000;**37**(2):26-32. DOI: 10.1109/6.819926

[2] Goldberg D. Genetic Algorithms in Search, Optimization and Machine Learning. Reading, MA: Addison Wesley; 1989. p. 372. DOI: 10.5860/9780201157673

[3] Storn R, Price K. Differential evolution - a simple and efficient heuristic for global optimization over continuous spaces. Journal of Global Optimization. 1997;**11**:341-359. DOI: 10.1023/a:1008202821328

[4] Bonyadi MR, Michalewicz Z. Particle swarm optimization for single objective continuous space problems: A review. Evolutionary Computation. 2017;**25**(1):1-54. DOI: 10.1162/evco r 00180

[5] Chen S, Istepanian R, Luk BL. Digital IIR filter design using adaptive simulated annealing. Digital Signal Processing. 2001;**11**(3):241-251. DOI: 10.1006/dspr.2000.0384

[6] Karaboga D. An Idea Based on Honey Bee Swarm for Numerical Optimization Technical Report TR06. Computer Engineering Department: Erciyes University; 2005

[7] Niu B, Wang H. Bacterial colony optimization. Discrete Dynamics in Nature and Society. 2012;**2012**:1-28. DOI: 10.1155/2012/698057

[8] He Y, Yuen SY, Lou Y, Zhang X. A sequential algorithm portfolio approach for black box optimization. Swarm and Evolutionary Computation. 2019;**44**: 559-570. DOI: 10.1016/j.swevo.2018.07.001

[9] Wolpert DH, Macready WG. No free lunch theorems for optimization. IEEE Transactions on Evolutionary Computation. 1997;**1**(1):67-82. DOI: 10.1109/4235.585893

[10] Grosan C, Abraham A. Hybrid evolutionary algorithms: Methodologies, architectures, and reviews. Studies in Computational Intelligence. 2007;**75**:1–17. DOI: 10.1007/978-3-540-73297-6_1

[11] Tsai J-T, Liu T-K, Chou J-H. Hybrid Taguchi-genetic algorithm for global numerical optimization. IEEE Transactions on Evolutionary Computation. 2004;**8**(4):365-377. DOI: 10.1109/tevc.2004.826895

[12] Blickle T, Thiele L. A comparison of selection schemes used in evolutionary algorithms. Evolutionary Computation. 1996;**4**(4):361-394. DOI: 10.1162/evco.1996.4.4.361

[13] Goldberg DE, Deb K. A comparative analysis of selection schemes used in genetic algorithms. Foundations of Genetic Algorithms. 1991;**1**:69-93. DOI: 10.1016/b978-0-08-050684-5.50008-2

[14] Črepinšek M, Liu S-H, Mernik M. Exploration and exploitation in evolutionary algorithms. ACM Computing Surveys. 2013;**45**(3):1-33. DOI: 10.1145/2480741.2480752

[15] Reeves CR, Rowe JE. Genetic algorithms—principles and perspectives. In: Operations Research/Computer Science Interfaces Series. US: Springer; 2002. DOI: 10.1007/b101880

[16] Corus D, Lissovoi A, Oliveto PS, Witt C. On steady-state evolutionary algorithms and selective pressure: Why

inverse rank-based allocation of reproductive trials is best. ACM Transactions on Evolutionary Learning and Optimization. 2021;**1**(1):1-38. DOI: 10.1145/3427474

[17] Bäck T. Optimization by Means of Genetic Algorithms. In: Technical University of Ilmenau. 1989. p. 163-169. DOI: 10.1.1.40.5648. Available from: cite seer.ist.psu.edu/71967.html. [Accessed: 2022-06-01]

[18] Leung Y-W, Wang Y. An orthogonal genetic algorithm with quantization for global numerical optimization. IEEE Transactions on Evolutionary Computation. 2001;**5**(1):41-53. DOI: 10.1109/4235.910464

[19] Stubberud P. Digital IIR filter design using a differential evolution algorithm with polar coordinates. 2022 IEEE 12th Annual Computing and Communication Workshop and Conference (CCWC) [Internet]. IEEE; 2022; DOI: 10.1109/ccwc54503.2022.9720786

Chapter 3

A Big Data Analytics Architecture Framework for the Production and International Trade of Oilseeds and Textiles in Sub-Saharan Africa (SSA)

Gabriel Kabanda

Abstract

Among the most revolutionary technologies are big data analytics, artificial intelligence (AI) and robotics, machine learning (ML), cybersecurity, blockchain technology, and cloud computing. The project was focused on how to create a Big Data Analytics Architecture Framework to increase the production capability and global trade for Sub-Saharan Africa's oilseeds and textile industries (SSA). The infrastructure, e-commerce, and disruptive technologies in the oilseeds and textile industries, as well as global e-commerce, all demand large investments. The pragmatic paradigm served as the foundation for the research approach. This study employed a review of the literature, document analysis, and focus groups. For the oilseeds and textile sectors in SSA, a Big Data analytics architectural framework was created. The Hadoop platform was created as a framework for big data analytics. The open-source Hadoop platform offers the analytical tools and computing capacity needed to handle such massive data volumes. It supports E-commerce and is based on the Hadoop platform, which offers the analytical tools and computing power needed to handle such massive data volumes. The low rate of return on investments made in breeding, seed production, processing, and marketing limits the competitiveness of the oil crop or legume seed markets.

Keywords: big data analytics, machine learning, AI, cybersecurity, E-commerce, oilseeds, textile industry, Hadoop

1. Introduction

Massive amounts of data are produced in the Internet of Things (IoT) age from a number of heterogeneous sources, such as mobile devices, sensors, and social media. Among the most revolutionary technologies are big data analytics, artificial intelligence (AI) and robotics, machine learning (ML), cybersecurity, blockchain

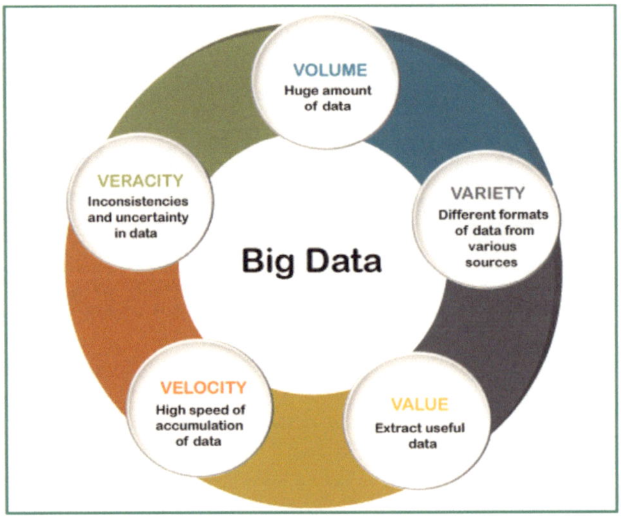

Figure 1.
Big data characteristics.

technology, and cloud computing. The two basic features of machine learning are the automatic analysis of large data sets and the creation of models for the broad relationships between data (ML). Analyzing large amounts of data to find information—such as hidden patterns, correlations, market trends, and customer preferences—that can assist organizations in making strategic business decisions is known as big data analytics [1, 2]. Volume, value, variety, velocity, and veracity are the five characteristics that define Big Data, as shown in **Figure 1**.

Legumes, shea butter, groundnuts, and soybeans are significant crops in Sub-Saharan Africa (SSA) because they offer a range of advantages in terms of the economy, society, and the environment. Sub-Saharan Africa contributes a relatively little amount to global agricultural output despite having over 13% of the world's population and about 20% of its land area being used for agriculture, claims the [3]. The research paper is purposed to develop a Big Data Analytics Architecture Framework for the Production and International Trade of Oilseeds and Textiles in Sub-Saharan Africa (SSA).

1.1 Background

More over 950 million people live in Sub-Saharan Africa (SSA), accounting for roughly 13% of the global population. Oilseed production in SSA is expected to increase by 2.3 percent per year to 11 Mt. by 2025, accounting for barely 2% of global production.

Although expected increase in Southern Africa is more modest at 16 percent, the base is significantly greater, and Southern Africa accounts for the largest proportion of additional protein meal use in absolute volumes. Southern (1.4 percent per year) and Eastern Africa (1.2 percent per year) are expected to grow at the quickest rates to 2025. Protein meal use is increasing across most of SSA as livestock industries strengthen in the future years, with Western Africa (43 percent) and Eastern Africa (43 percent) seeing the largest rise (32 percent). Oilseed production in SSA is expected to increase by 2.3 percent per year to 11 Mt. by 2025, accounting for barely 2% of global production. Nonetheless, total imports into SSA are expected to grow at a

	2017/18	2018/19	2019/20	2020/21	2021/22
Production					
Copra	5.78	5.82	5.7	5.59	5.86
Cottonseed	45.25	42.97	43.55	40.81	42.75
Palm Kernel	18.69	19.46	19.32	19.03	20.05
Peanut	47.15	46.71	48.14	50.25	50.29
Rapeseed	75.28	72.85	69.6	73.59	71.18
Soybean	343.74	362.44	340.15	368.12	349.37
Sunflowerseed	48.01	50.66	54.2	49.25	57.38
TOTAL	583.9	600.91	580.65	606.64	596.87
Imports					
Copra	0.13	0.2	0.15	0.08	0.08
Cottonseed	0.87	0.73	0.81	0.83	0.97
Palm Kernel	0.18	0.16	0.14	0.15	0.17
Peanut	3.08	3.53	4.34	4.31	4
Rapeseed	15.72	14.64	15.71	16.66	13.97
Soybean	154.11	146.02	165.12	165.47	154.46
Sunflowerseed	2.38	2.89	3.34	2.73	2.2
TOTAL	176.47	168.17	189.61	190.24	175.86
Exports					
Copra	0.16	0.18	0.28	0.1	0.13
Cottonseed	0.89	0.84	0.88	0.96	1.16
Palm Kernel	0.16	0.07	0.08	0.06	0.05
Peanut	3.51	3.83	4.95	4.89	4.64
Rapeseed	16.53	14.62	15.92	17.98	13.84
Soybean	153.27	148.97	165.21	164.51	155.57
Sunflowerseed	2.75	3.24	3.66	2.91	2.59
TOTAL	177.28	171.75	190.97	191.41	177.97
Crush					
Copra	5.67	5.83	5.56	5.52	5.71
Cottonseed	33.73	32.75	33.62	31.95	33.2
Palm Kernel	18.62	19.42	19.29	19.01	20.08
Peanut	18.15	18.05	19.24	19.86	20.1
Rapeseed	68.45	68.03	68.41	71.45	70.2
Soybean	295.44	298.61	312.31	315.08	313.68
Sunflowerseed	44.17	46.52	49.31	45.13	47.34
TOTAL	484.24	489.2	507.73	508	510.31
Ending Stocks					
Copra	0.12	0.1	0.05	0.05	0.07

	2017/18	2018/19	2019/20	2020/21	2021/22
Cottonseed	1.96	1.82	1.61	1.41	1.42
Palm Kernel	0.23	0.26	0.24	0.25	0.23
Peanut	5.16	5.08	4.67	4.89	4.33
Rapeseed	8.14	9.93	7.81	5.96	4.27
Soybean	99.84	114.19	94.66	99.91	85.24
Sunflowerseed	2.79	2.57	2.92	2.56	7.61
TOTAL	118.24	133.95	111.96	115.02	103.16

Source: https://apps.fas.usda.gov/psdonline/circulars/oilseeds.pdf

Table 1.
Major oilseeds world supply and distribution (2017–2022) [million metric tons].

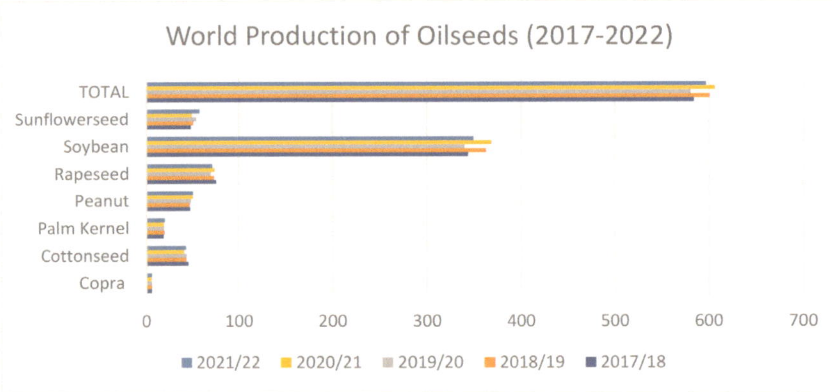

Figure 2.
World production of oilseeds (2017–2022).

3.7 percent annual rate, with Nigeria (4 percent per year), Sudan (5 percent per year), Ethiopia (6 percent per year), and Kenya (3 percent per year) accounting for the majority. Per capita consumption has grown at a rate of 2.1 percent per year, making it one of the fastest growing commodities in the region during the last decade. Over the next decade, Sub-Saharan Africa's net food imports are expected to rise, however productivity-boosting investments could counteract this trend. Despite the fact that agricultural productivity has increased significantly over the last decade, SSA remains the world's most food insecure region, with inconsistent progress toward hunger eradication. The world oilseeds supply and distribution in million metric tons for the period 2017 to 2022 is shown on **Table 1**.

The world production of oilseeds for the period 2017–2022 is shown on **Figure 2**.

The world oilseeds crush distribution for the period 2017–2022 is shown on **Figure 3**.

The focus of the researchers was on how to use and implement Big Data to improve production for both oilseeds and textile production and international trade for Sub-Saharan Africa (SSA).

The top 15 textile exporters in Sub-Saharan Africa (SSA) are shown on **Table 2** below and illustrated on **Figure 4**.

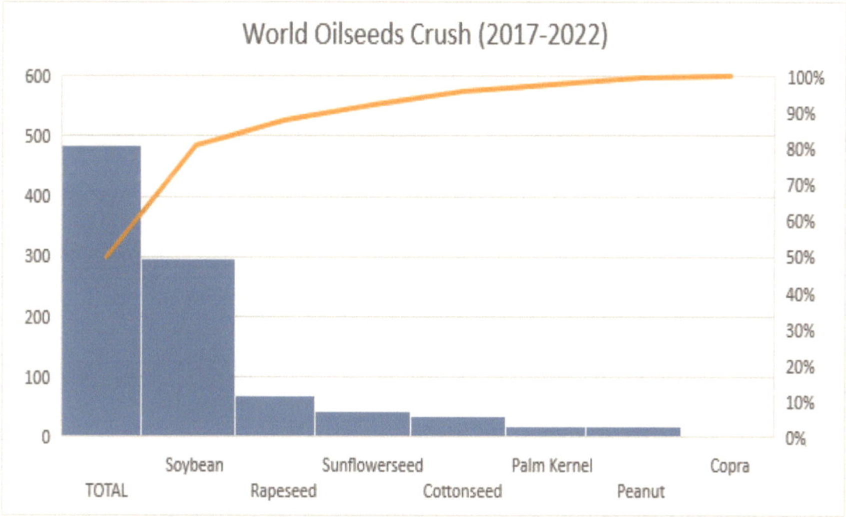

Figure 3.
World oilseeds crust distribution (2017–2022).

	1995	2000	2005	2010	2015	2016
Lesotho		146365.92	408337.98	293625.99	310412.35	304867.13
Kenya	40557.59	46921.64	286480.04	212267.49	381118.11	352218.08
Mauritius	201,844	259,609	175787.13	127105.49	221933.63	203340.45
Madagascar	7475.2	115429.39	293757.75	58139.23	54429.66	108345.99
South Africa	164868.09	187000.1	107985.72	23786.08	26942.7	25108.16
Swaziland		33407.42	168769.77	97887.4	2807.2	1067.87
Tanzania	6084.74	253.87	4437.83	2159.59	27999.56	37883.39
Botswana		9028.59	31459.14	12209.52	8685.86	4981.05
Ethiopia(excl. Eritrea)	971.4	30.98	3829.68	7113.17	18799.72	34457.11
Namibia		196.09	56050.93	47.06	230	122.43
Malawi	2509.89	7653.83	24018.24	10728.07	6437.02	1603.53
Zimbabwe	15484.16	21574.02	3086.21	87.37	130.48	99.08
Ghana	3216.37	718.84	5749.01	1071.03	9620.28	6631.52
Cameroon		2769.28	407.24	749.97	1003.44	342.41
Uganda		5.07	5143.94	461.64	73.47	78.62

Source: World Bank.

Table 2.
Top 15 SSA exporters of textiles and clothing to US (US$'000).

Many textile and apparel inputs now produced in SSA nations can be made more competitive by new or increased investment or other methods, especially as output of these inputs is restricted and diminishing in many cases. New or expanded investment, as well as other initiatives, could help the industry maintain or expand present

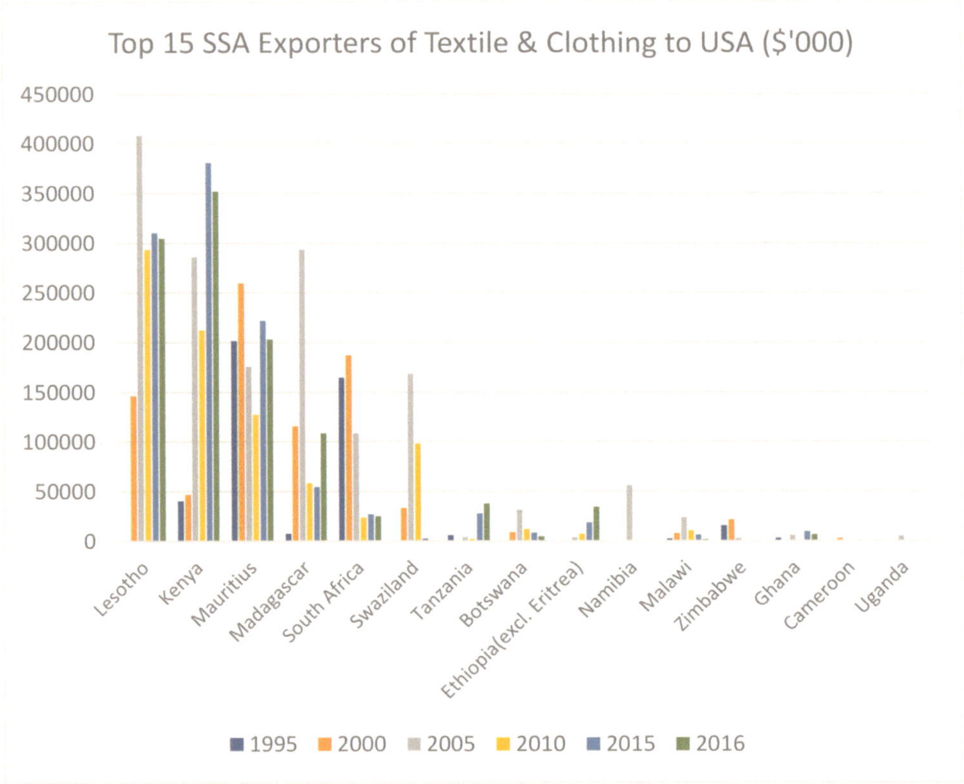

Figure 4.
The top 15 SSA exporters of textiles and clothing to US (US$'000).

production and export levels of these inputs, as well as extend the possibility for new product development.

This paper aims to develop a Big Data Architecture framework for oilseeds and textile industry production and international trade for SSA.

1.2 Statement of the problem

Organizations struggle to manage and track the growth of both new and old open-source big-data solutions, which are continually expanding. The considerable volume of data produced by a wide range of sources, including as information services, Internet of Things (IoT) devices, social media, and mobile devices, is not only too large but also moves too quickly and is too complex to be handled and stored by conventional techniques. The sector is driven by the data's exponential growth, which also draws researchers to create new models and scalable methods for handling big data. A well-known open-source framework for big-data analytics, Apache Hadoop is made to integrate with a number of other open-source technologies to allow for the storing and processing of large amounts of data using commodity hardware clusters. A distributed file system, cluster administration, storage, distributed processing, programming, data analysis, data governance, and data pre-processing tools are all included in the Hadoop Stack. The production and global commerce of oilseeds and the textile industries should take this into account.

The African Growth and Opportunity Act (AGOA), a non-reciprocal trade preference program, was established by the US Congress in 2000 to assist developing SSA nations in improving their economies through increased exports to the US. Notably, the "third-country fabric clause" in AGOA permits US clothing imports from specific SSA nations to qualify for duty-free treatment even if the clothing products use yarns and fabrics manufactured by non-AGOA members, such as China, South Korea, and Taiwan. Furthermore, AGOA trade preferences offer much bigger duty savings for manmade-fiber products, which are subject to higher U.S. tariffs, even though SSA nations generate largely cotton-based textile and garment inputs due to a plentiful availability of local cotton. Cotton yarn, cotton knit fabric, denim fabric, and to a lesser extent cotton woven shirting fabric appear to have the most potential for competitive production in SSA countries, either for direct export to or use in downstream apparel production for export to the United States, the EU, and similar markets. However, because the manmade-fiber textile and apparel sectors are underdeveloped in most SSA countries, it is not possible to produce these products. All of these products may be competitive in some local and regional markets because numerous SSA industry sources reported producing textile and garment inputs for both regional consumption and export beyond the region.

1.3 Research aim

This paper aims to develop a Big Data Architecture framework for oilseeds and textile industry production and international trade for SSA.

1.4 Research objectives

The objectives of the research include the following:

1. To identify areas of Big Data applications that can help the oilseeds and textile industries in SSA increase their production and worldwide commerce.

2. To develop a Big Data Analytics architecture framework for usage by organizations in the oilseeds and textile production industry, as well as international trade in SSA.

3. To determine the competitive challenges facing Sub-Saharan Africa (SSA) in the production of oilseeds and textile industry.

4. To evaluate yield production capacity and competitive variables across SSA for both oilseeds and textile industry.

1.5 Research questions

1. What are some Big Data applications that can help SSA boost its oilseed and textile output and international trade?

2. How do you create a Big Data Analytics architecture framework to assist and improve oilseed, textile, and international trade production?

3. What are the competitive issues in the oilseed and textile industries in Sub-Saharan Africa?

4. What has been the state of production capacity and competitive factors in the oilseeds and textile industries across SSA?

2. Critical context

2.1 Literature review

Big Data (Data Intensive) Technologies aim to process (1) highvolume, highvelocity, high-variety data (sets/assets) to extract intended data value and ensure high-veracity of original data and obtained information; this calls for cost-effective, innovative forms of data and information processing (analytics) for improved insight, decision-making, and process control; all of these call for (should be supported by) new data models (supporting all data states and stages during the whole data lifecyle) and infrastructure services and tools. Generally, the term "big data" refers to the rapidly expanding volume and velocity of data sets that are being accessible and connected. According to studies, big data may generally be defined using the four (4) V's of big data. The five properties of volume, value, diversity, velocity, and veracity are frequently used to describe big data, which is a collection of data from various sources. Big data analytics, which some academics define as the capacity to compile and analyze those fine-grained data sets, is already altering how insurers see sizable client bases, manage risks, and meet the diverse needs of their clients. Kabanda [4] defines big data analytics as the straightforward application of analytics approaches to significant data sets. The five properties of volume, value, diversity, velocity, and veracity are frequently used to describe big data, which is a collection of data from various sources. Many significant businesses employ software for machine learning, artificial intelligence, data mining, cybersecurity, and other big data. Big data analytics, which some academics define as the capacity to compile and analyze those fine-grained data sets, is already altering how insurers see sizable client bases, manage risks, and meet the diverse needs of their clients. OECD-FAO [4] defines big data analytics as the straightforward application of analytics approaches to significant data sets.

The types of analytics applicable in the oilseeds and textile industries are shown on **Figure 5** and are briefly explained below:

a. *Descriptive analytics* - Descriptive analytics aims at describing and analyzing historical data collected on students, teaching, research, policies and other administrative processes. The goal is to identify patterns from samples to report on current trends.

b. *Predictive analytics* - Predictive analytics can provide organizations with better decisions and actionable insights based on data. Predictive analytics aims at estimating likelihood of future events by looking into trends and identifying associations about related issues and identifying any risks or opportunities in the future. Predictive analytics could reveal hidden relationships in data that might not be apparent with descriptive models, such as demographics, etc.

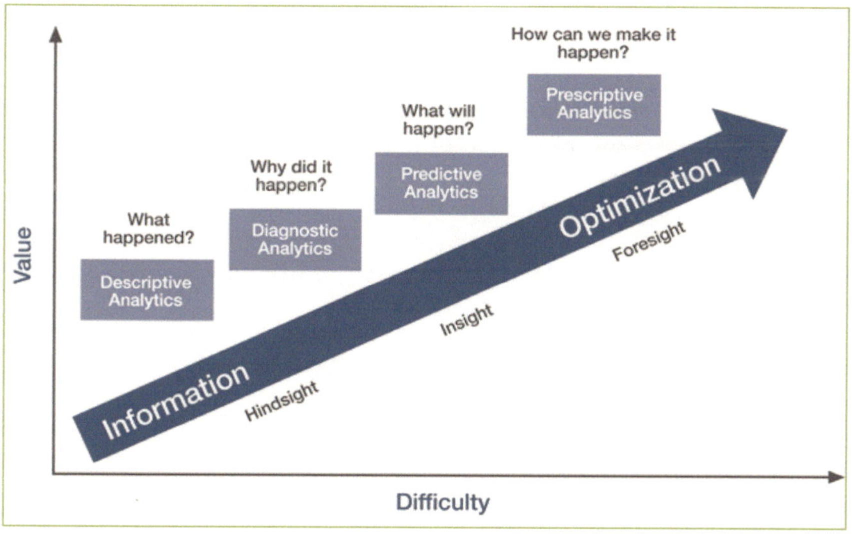

Figure 5.
Types of analytics.

c. *Prescriptive analytics* - Prescriptive analytics helps organizations assess their current situation and make informed choices on alternative course of events based on valid and consistent predictions. It combines analytical outcomes from both descriptive and predictive models to look at assessing and determining new ways to operate to achieve desirable outcomes while balancing constraints indicated that prescriptive analytics enables decision makers to look into the future of their mission critical processes and see the opportunities as well as presents the best course of action to take advantage of that foresight in a timely manner.

Machine learning is a method for instructing computers to learn (ML). Big data analytics is known to be automated using machine learning, which also creates models of the fundamental relationships in the data. The way we teach, learn, and study in the educational setting could be completely changed by machine learning (ML). Localization, transcription, text-to-speech, and personalisation are just a few of the ways that machine learning is expanding the reach and impact of online learning content [5]. Data mining can be handled through machine learning. According to Truong [6], there are three types of ML:

I. Supervised learning: where training examples are given to the methods in the form of inputs labeled with corresponding outputs;

II. Unsupervised learning: where unlabeled inputs are given to the methods;

III. Reinforcement learning: where data used is in the form of sequences of actions, observations, and rewards.

Machine Learning essentially includes programming analytical model construction and is a technique of big data analytics [7].

Data mining is the process of discovering anomalies, trends, and correlations in large data sets in order to predict outcomes [8]. Data mining is most usually characterized as the process of searching massive sets of data for patterns and trends using computers and automation, then translating those findings into business insights and predictions. Data mining is an important element of data analytics and one of the fundamental disciplines in data science, in which advanced analytics techniques are used to extract meaningful information from large data sets. While both are valuable for spotting patterns in enormous data sets, they work in quite different ways. The practice of detecting patterns in data is known as data mining. And, while data mining is sometimes used as part of the machine learning process, it does not necessitate continual human engagement (e.g., a self-driving car relies on data mining to determine where to stop, accelerate, and turn).

Computer systems that imitate human intellectual processes, such as learning, reasoning, and self-correction, are referred to as artificial intelligence (AI). The ability of AI to arrive at a solution based on facts rather than a predetermined series of procedures is what most closely mimics the human brain's thinking function. Artificial intelligence (AI) is defined by its ability to replicate human behavior and cognitive processes, to capture and preserve human expertise, to respond swiftly, and to manage large amounts of data quickly.

As a result, cyber security has become an important concept in everyday life, and cyber security knowledge is critical in preventing cyber attacks on people and systems. With the rise of a global and borderless information culture, the internet has brought and continues to present new opportunities to all countries globally, as technologies play a key role in social and economic development [9]. With the rise of a global and borderless information culture, the internet has brought and continues to present new opportunities to all countries globally, as technologies play a key role in social and economic development [9]. Cyber security refers to strategies used to secure sensitive data, computer systems, networks, and software applications from cyberattacks, according to [10]. The cyber security concept's main purpose is to protect data confidentiality and integrity while also providing data availability when it's needed. However, as the nature of cyber threats changes, so does public concern about cyber security issues like social engineering and phishing.

The foundation of Big Data architecture is infrastructure. In every Big Data project, having the correct tools for storing, processing, and analyzing your data is critical [11].

3. Oilseeds and textile production competitive challenges in SSA

Certain competitive challenges affected nearly all the SSA countries, as described below.

- *Insufficient demand from the apparel sector*

A healthy and thriving garment industry offers the stable market demand for textile and apparel inputs that is required to support capital expenditures that take longer to recover than apparel investments.

- *Lack of knowledge of regional and international market opportunities*

Many industry experts pointed to a lack of marketing and business contacts, both within the SSA region and in international markets. According to industry sources, the

USAID has aided in the development of regional and international market potential, but further assistance is needed.

- *Insufficient supply of reliable electricity at competitive rates*

Many nations in the SSA region have among of the highest electricity tariffs in the world, and many countries have an unstable electrical supply, which adds to producers' expenses. Electricity outages also diminish efficiencies and lower quality in yarn and fabric production.

- *Insufficient supply of clean water and wastewater treatment facilities*

Many countries lack access to clean water, which is required for the manufacturing of yarn and fabric, particularly for finishing and dyeing activities. Intraregional trade is further hampered by a lack of adequate transportation networks within SSA.

- *Lack of access to capital at competitive rates*

When capital is available, the high cost of capital not only discourages new investment in yarn, fabric, and other inputs, but it also raises the costs of existing production. The finished products created on this machinery, particularly woven textiles, are often not of adequate quality for export to the United States, the EU, or similar markets, or for use in downstream commercial garment production for export to these countries.

- *Scarcity of trained/skilled labour*

According to industry sources, there is a shortage of trained workers in the textile and garment industries, particularly in nations without a substantial manufacturing base.

4. Conceptual framework on adoption of big data analytics

The study is guided by the conceptual framework shown on **Figure 6** below:

4.1 Research methodology

The study's research philosophy, as well as the research design, research approach, data collection instruments, target population, sampling method, and data processing techniques, are all explained in the Research Methodology. The research philosophy, approach, strategy, choice, time horizon, and techniques and processes constitute the layers, as shown on **Figure** 7.

The Mixed Method Research and the Pragmatism paradigm utilized in this study are closely related on a philosophical level (MMR). A worldview or paradigm known as pragmatism ought to guide the majority of mixed-methods studies. It is a problem-focused attitude that holds that the best research techniques are those that contribute most significantly to the solution of the research topic. When conducting social science research, this frequently entails combining quantitative and qualitative

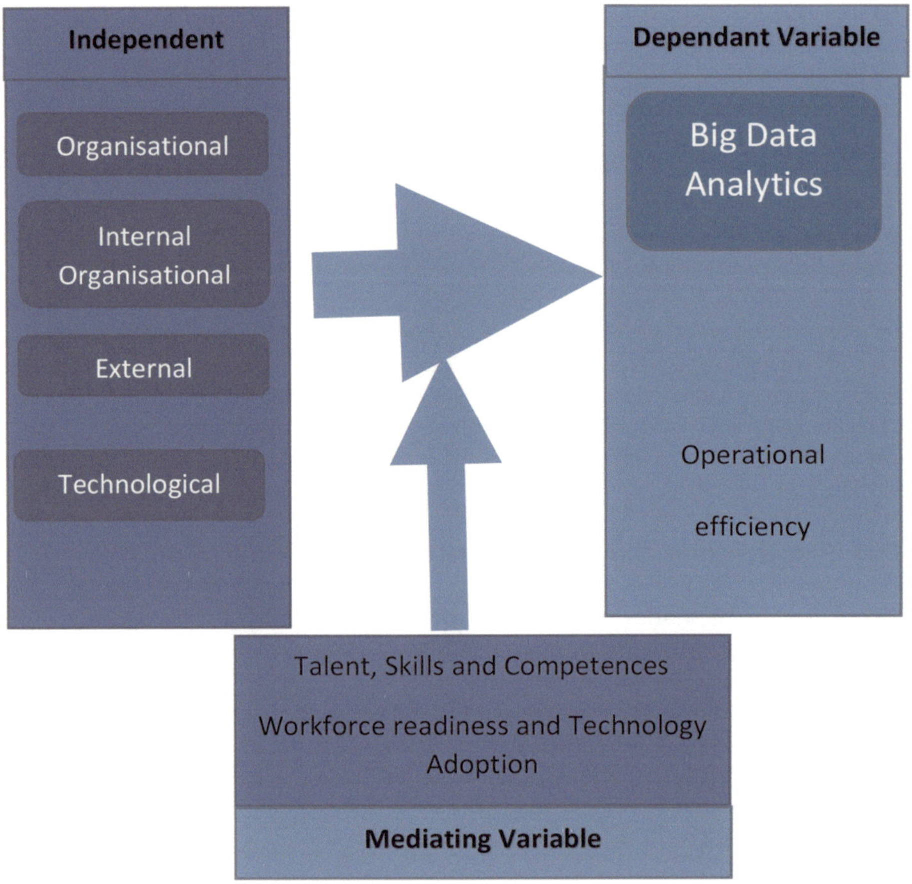

Figure 6.
Conceptual framework.

methodologies to assess various facets of a research subject. The pragmatic worldview served as the foundation for the Mixed Methods Research technique. A mixed-methods strategy was used in this study, combining qualitative (Focus Group discussions) and quantitative techniques (a questionnaire). System logs, document analysis, and a literature review were also utilized in this study.

The purpose for the Focus Group discussion was to research and determine on how to use and implement Big Data to improve production for both oilseeds and textile production and international trade for Sub-Saharan Africa (SSA). The Focus Groups were derived from 10 Groups of Masters students at the University of Zimbabwe in the 2021 cohort who then were tasked to conduct surveys and interview the management of various corporates in Zimbabwe and other nearby Southern African countries involved in the oilseeds and textile industries. Secondary data was collected form the World Bank, FAO [FAOSTAT, www.faostat.org] and US Department of Agriculture (https://apps.fas.usda.gov/psdonline/circulars/oilseeds.pdf) for analysis.

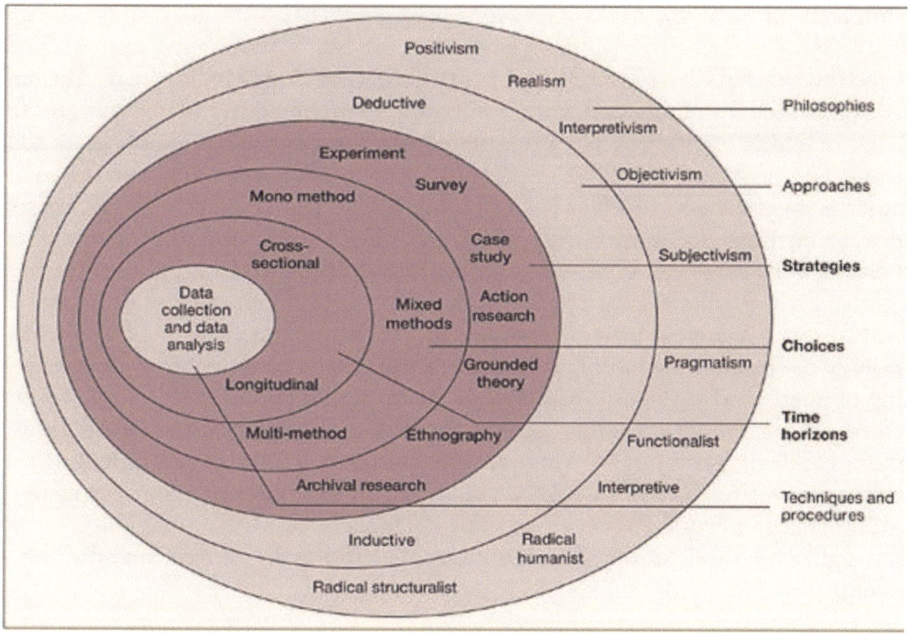

Figure 7.
Research onion (Saunders et al., 2009:138).

5. Results and analysis

5.1 Critical challenges around the application of big data

5.1.1 Analytics in the oilseeds and textile industries

The Critical challenges around the application of big data analytics in the oilseeds and textile industries as obtained from the participants of the focus group are:

- *Lack of Talent* - While there is a massive demand for experienced data experts, there simply is not enough supply. Unfortunately, this deficit has not yet been addressed by most top universities as data science programs are still lacking.

- *Storage and Scalability Issues* - The volume of data being generated exceeds the processing power of currently accessible Big Data tools. This can cause significant issues and force systems to crash or slow down, leading to a negative experience and a reduced quality of the analysis.

- *Security* - Security protocols were not built for a Big Data world and need to be reworked to account for the volume of data that Big Data uses in its analysis. The cybersecurity systems in most of the organizations in the oilseeds and textile industries is still in their infancy stages of development.

5.1.2 Implementation of an AI Chatbot and E-commerce

Huge investments are required in the infrastructure that is inclusive of AI Chatbots and E-Commerce for all the corporates and entities involved in the oilseeds and textile business. Machine learning is a key feature of AI chatbots since it allows them to learn and improve based on their experiences. Electronic business can allow an organization to implement cybercash, Electronic Data Interchange (IDE), electronic advertising, business to business and business to customer online transactions on a worldwide scale. Small businesses can compete with well-established and capital-rich businesses on a global level thanks to electronic commerce and sound strategy and policy methods. From a business process standpoint, electronic business is the application of technology to the automation of company transactions and workflow. Electronic trading of goods and services, on-line delivery of digital content, electronic fund transfers, electronic share trading, electronic bills of lading, commercial auctions, collaborative design and engineering, on-line sourcing, public procurement, direct consumer marketing, and after-sales services are all examples of transactions in the global information economy.

The eight Unique Features of E-commerce Technology required includes the following:

1. Ubiquity

2. Global reach

3. Universal standards

4. Information richness

5. Interactivity

6. Information density

7. Personalization/customization

8. Social technology

Each of the corporates involved in the oilseeds and textile industries is encouraged to invest extensively in AI Chatbots and E-Commerce in order to build a basis upon which to successfully implement a Big Data Analytics Framework.

5.1.3 Data analysis of oilseeds production in SSA

1. Soybean

   Soybean is a vital crop for at least one million African smallholder farmers. Other factors have contributed to rising soybean demand, such as the need for domestic processing to meet rising domestic demand for soybean meal,

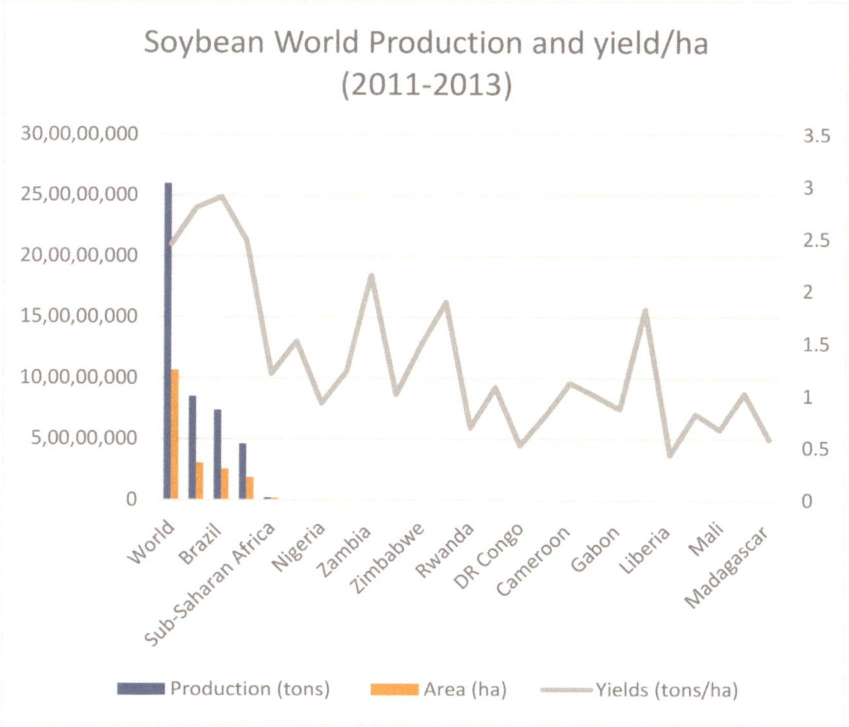

Figure 8.
Soybean world production and yield/ha.

especially for the poultry feed industry, and the favorable outlook for edible oil. The United States, Brazil, and Argentina, as the world's top three soybean exporters, will continue to account for approximately 90% of global soybean, soybean meal, and soybean oil exports in the coming decade. The soybean production levels and yield per hectare for the world, Sub-Saharan Africa (SSA) and other countries are shown on **Figure 8** below. Both area expansion and yield growth have contributed about equal amounts to the reported growth in soybean output in SSA, with yearly growth rates of 3% in area and 3.5 percent in yield.

2. Groundnuts

After oil palm, soybean, rapeseed, and sunflower, groundnut is the world's fifth most important oilseed crop. Groundnut is a major oil, food, and feed legume crop that is produced in over 100 countries, covering 25.44 million hectares and producing 45.22 million tons of pods in 2013. Despite Africa's declining share of the global groundnut market, the crop still accounts for a large portion of export revenues in several countries (for example, 8% in Senegal and over 84 percent in Gambia in 2002). Groundnut is a nutritious food that helps to improve the health of rural people. Groundnut haulms, which contain 8–15 percent protein, 1–3 percent fats, 9–17 percent minerals, and 38–45 percent carbs, are used as cattle feed in both fresh and dried form, as well as for making hay and silage.

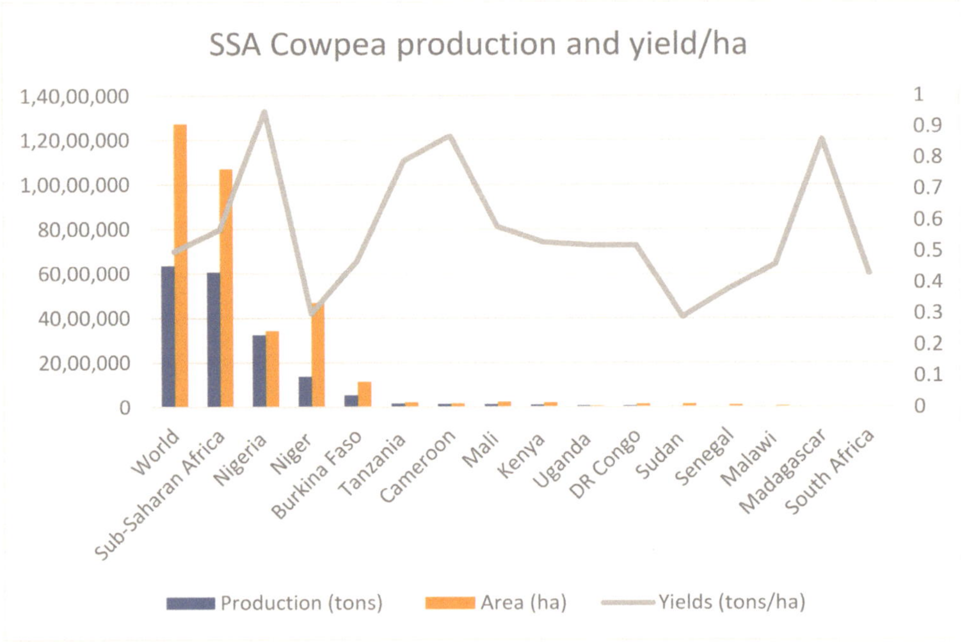

Figure 9.
SSA cowpea production and yield/ha.

3. Cowpea

About 95 percent of global cowpea production is produced in Sub-Saharan Africa (SSA), with West Africa producing over 80 percent of Africa's share. Over 65 percent of cowpea is produced by poor households in Nigeria, meaning that cowpea is primarily produced by the poor, who stand to benefit from cowpea research and extension. The basic analysis shows the production of cowpeas and yield production per ha shown on **Figure 9**.

Despite these encouraging signs, cowpea yields remain low due to a variety of production restrictions as well as a lack of adoption of improved varieties and agronomic approaches.

4. Shea Butter

Shea grows over an estimated 1 million km^2 between western Senegal and northwestern Uganda in the Sudan zone's dry savannas, woods, and parklands. According to OECD-FAO [3], Nigeria has the greatest potential for shea nut production, with high production zones in Benin, Burkina Faso, Cote D'Ivoire, Ghana, Mali, and Nigeria. Because producers, particularly women, and the private sector in nations where production capacity is not fully utilized, the potential of production capacity is not fully realized. Because producers, particularly women and the private sector in countries where shea trees grow, are not completely participating in the value addition sales of the nuts or butter, the potential of the production capacity is not fully realized. When Ghana's shea production potential is completely realized, this amount is predicted to quadruple.

6. The key recommendations for the oilseeds and textile industries is the need to attend to the problems for each of the following areas

1. Poor access to improved seeds

   A multitude of issues contribute to the existing seed system's failure to offer improved varieties of oil crop and legume seeds to smallholder farmers. Many farmers have grown accustomed to receiving free seed from non-governmental organizations (NGOs) and are unappreciative of the investment necessary. Based on lessons learned in other regions of the world, establishing a Foundation Seed Enterprise committed to the production and distribution of foundation/basic seed can aid seed companies interested in commercializing enhanced publically developed varieties.

2. *Lack of farm machinery*

   Despite the development of yield-enhancing technologies over the last three decades, labor-intensive farming practices continue to prevail, and crop products are still processed manually at home. However, due to poor input marketing arrangements, inorganic amendments are rarely available in cheap quantities to farmers.

3. *Low soil fertility*

   However, due to poor input marketing arrangements, inorganic amendments are rarely available in cheap quantities to farmers.

4. *Input market constraints*

   Improved seed, fertilizers, crop protection products, and novel agronomic practices are all examples of science and technology that can help accelerate agricultural growth. Because of a lack of oversight, pesticides that are old or contaminated are widely used.

5. *Output market constraints*

   Because of a number of structural and institutional obstacles that impede market participation, smallholders have not been able to respond effectively to potential soybean market possibilities. Low quality grain, insufficient supply, and high cleaning costs restrain processors and traders, whilst market intermediaries suffer high assembly costs, high market risk, and cash flow issues. Improving smallholder farmers' market access and competitiveness would necessitate new types of market institutions that allow contract formulation and enforcement, as well as vertical and horizontal coordination of production and marketing tasks. Farmers' awareness and access to new information, expected benefits and local availability of new technologies, market access and opportunities, and access to credit and other policies that enable farmer investment in new technologies have all been shown to be major drivers of research product dissemination and adoption.

6. *Low levels of technology adoption*

   A number of socioeconomic and targeting studies (http://www.icrisat.org/impi-tl-2.htm) demonstrate that new variety acceptance has been slow and sluggish, with old varieties launched 15–20 years ago still occupying much of the production area. Farmers' awareness and access to new information, expected benefits and local availability of new technologies, market access and opportunities, and access to credit and other policies that enable farmer investment in new technologies have all been shown to be major drivers of research product dissemination and adoption.

7. Textile production capacity and competitive factors

The textile production capacity and competitive factors for each top country is summarized on **Table 3**, indicating the competitive advantages and disadvantages of each country.

Group 1 Countries	Textile and apparel input production	Competitive factors
Ethiopia	The Ethiopian textile sector includes eight vertically integrated textile mills, along with stand-alone spinning mills for yarn and thread production. Most of the yarn spun in Ethiopia is used in the production of woven cotton fabric. In addition to cotton yarn and woven fabric, Ethiopia's textile sector also produces acrylic yarn, nylon fabric, woolen and waste-cotton blankets, bedsheets, and sewing thread. Ethiopia currently produces cotton and silk yarn for domestic hand-loomed production of niche products, such as home furnishings, for export to the United States, Canada, and Europe.	Competitive advantages: • large potential domestic apparel market • domestic production of raw materials (cotton, silk) • stable political and business environment • access to Ethiopian government-supported investment incentives and financial assistance Competitive disadvantages: • import competition from used clothing • low cotton production; cotton contamination • poor transportation infrastructure • underutilized industrial capacity • outdated machinery and equipment • low labor productivity • lack of skilled labor
Kenya	The Kenyan textile industry has contracted since the 1990s and currently consists of three vertically integrated firms and a few smaller, nonintegrated firms. Kenya's vertically integrated firms produce cotton (including organic) and synthetic yarn, and knitted and woven fabric for use in apparel exported to the United States and the EU. Some yarn and fabric is also sold regionally.	Competitive advantages: • export-oriented apparel industry • relatively skilled labor Competitive disadvantages: • poor roads • high-cost electricity • limited and high cost of financing for new equipment
Lesotho	Lesotho has one vertically integrated denim textile mill that spins cotton yarn, dyes the yarn, weaves the fabric, and cuts and sews the finished denim jeans. The mill reportedly produces 10,800 tons of openended ring-spun cotton yarn, and 18 million yards of denim fabric a year for regional apparel manufacturers producing for the export market. Lesotho primarily exports woven fabric to other apparel-producing African countries. The vast majority of Lesotho's apparel exports are to the U.S. market.	Competitive advantages: • export-oriented apparel industry • government investment support for plant acquisitions Competitive disadvantages: • poor water/wastewater and internal transport infrastructure • low labor productivity • high HIV/AIDS prevalence rates • lack of skilled labor

Group 1 Countries	Textile and apparel input production	Competitive factors
Madagascar	The Malagasy textile industry consists of one large vertically integrated woven textile and apparel firm that consumes most of its own fabric production, two small knit apparel firms that produce their own knit fabric, and another firm that weaves fabric for blankets. The Malagasy apparel sector is geared to supply the U.S. and EU markets.	Competitive advantages: • export-oriented apparel industry • availability of skilled and productive labor • government investment incentives and support Competitive disadvantages: • diminishing supply of domestic cotton • high-cost, unreliable electricity • political instability • high cost of capital • poor road infrastructure
Mauritius	The Mauritian industry is concentrated among 10 large textile and apparel groups that collectively account for 75 percent of total textile and apparel exports. The textile and apparel input industry in Mauritius produces yarn and knit fabric mostly for vertical operations, but also for local and regional apparel manufacturers. Mauritius exports textile and apparel inputs to the region and finished apparel primarily to the EU.	Competitive advantages: • export-oriented apparel industry • market linkages with EU apparel buyers • favorable business environment • government support in product and market diversification • relatively modern machinery and equipment • shorter lead times to the region and to some EU customers • availability of skilled labor Competitive disadvantages: • small domestic apparel market • increased labor costs due to labor shortages • long lead times to the United States and to some EU customers • increasing land and energy costs • additional costs associated with geographic isolation
Nigeria	The Nigerian textile industry has contracted since the 1990s and currently consists of 20 or fewer factories. Some larger textile firms are vertically integrated from cotton ginning to spinning, weaving, dyeing, printing, and finishing. The major textile firms produce a variety of products, including polyester staple fiber and filament, yarn, greige cloth, and wax prints. Nigerian printed fabric is sold as loose cloth, rolls, or pieces to the domestic market. Nigerian textile exports are focused on the EU market.	Competitive advantages: • large potential domestic apparel market • history of cotton and integrated textile production • availability of skilled labor Competitive disadvantages: • lack of a developed apparel industry • increased import foreign competition (ethnic cloth and used clothing) • cotton quality issues • poor infrastructure, particularly electricity
South Africa	The South African textile sector is relatively large and encompasses the full range of manufacturing operations, including production of fiber, thread, yarn, knit and woven fabric, nonwovens, trim and accessories, and dyeing and finishing operations. There are currently 11 firms in South Africa producing yarn. Five firms manufacture nonwovens, and reportedly seven firms produce trim, including elastic, buttons, zippers, and similar items. Approximately 16 firms produce woven fabric, while 15 companies produce knit	Competitive advantages: • large domestic apparel industry • developed infrastructure (transport, power, water) • favorable and stable business environment • large and developed textile industry Competitive disadvantages: • high labor costs • inflexible labor market • lack of skilled labor in the industry • lack of management, marketing, and technical skills • lack of investment

Group 1 Countries	Textile and apparel input production	Competitive factors
	fabric. Of the country's textile producing firms, nine are vertically integrated, manufacturing either yarn through fabric, yarn through finished apparel, or yarn through household textiles. Cotton, wool, mohair, manmade fibers, and natural fibers are used in the domestic textile industry.	• long lead times from order to delivery • highly volatile exchange rate
Swaziland	Swaziland has one integrated textile producer that dyes, spins, and knits cotton fabric (including organic), and then sews the fabric into apparel for export. The firm produces yarn for internal consumption and for export to the region and the EU. Swaziland has an internationally branded zipper producer that supplies local and regional apparel manufacturers.	Competitive advantages: • export-oriented apparel industry • government incentives for foreign direct investment in the textile and apparel industry • reliable electricity supply Competitive disadvantages: • small domestic apparel market • limited amount of local raw materials • labor unrest • high HIV/AIDS prevalence rates
Tanzania	The Tanzanian textile sector consists of one independent spinning mill and several integrated firms. The industry spins mostly cotton yarns for both knit and woven fabric. A few fabric mills also blend cotton with polyester or other synthetic fibers; however, all synthetic fibers must be imported. Tanzanian textile mills sell these textiles regionally, or minimally process and print fabric to be sold locally as final products.	Competitive advantages: • availability of good-quality domestic cotton • history of cotton yarn exports to the EU • stable political and economic environment Competitive disadvantages: • lack of a developed apparel industry • unreliable and costly electricity • port delays and congestion • lack of skilled labor • lack of market knowledge • low labor productivity
Zambia	The Zambian textile sector consists of an estimated four knitting/weaving firms and four vertically integrated firms that spin their own yarn for use in finished textile and apparel production. Zambia's textile sector produces primarily 100 percent cotton yarn, along with small quantities of manmade-fiber yarn, including poly/cotton and acrylic yarn. Most of the yarn produced in Zambia is exported, but a small share is used domestically in the production of woven fabric used to manufacture niche apparel articles such as uniforms and mining work wear, primarily for the local or regional market.	Competitive advantages: • domestic availability of high-quality cotton • open trade regime Competitive disadvantages: • small domestic apparel market • insufficient access to affordable credit • outdated machinery and equipment • lack of skilled labor • low labor productivity • high transportation costs and time • unreliable electricity supply

Table 3.
Summary of selected SSA textile and apparel input producers.

Changes in the volume by country are illustrated graphically on the **Figure A1** on Appendix 1.

The African Value Chain is highly fragmented and is illustrated by **Figure 10** below.

The 4 leading countries on imports of apparels from SSA to USA under AGOA are Kenya, Lesotho, Madagascar and Ethiopia. Opportunities for development of the

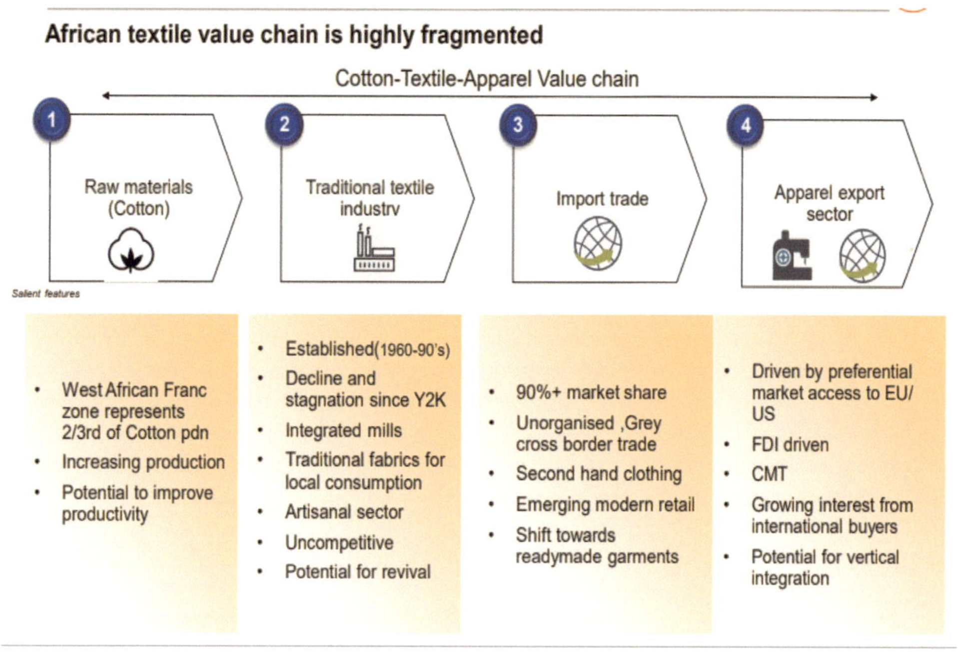

Figure 10.
The African textile value chain.

textile-cotton industry in SSA depend on the following critical success factors. African countries face 5 key opportunities to develop the cotton-textile sector and these are:

1. Restructuring (Shift of industry from China to other developing and LDC's; consolidation and upgradation; economic imperative, etc.)

2. Endowment (Availability of abundant raw material; Africa's labour pool; Land; Water, etc.)

3. Market access (Preferential market access to the EU and US; RTA's/ AfCFTA; etc.)

4. Global initiatives (Belt & Road Initiative; other international projects, etc.)

5. Sustainability (Guidance from the 17 SDGs).

These opportunities require policy actions in the following areas:

1. Enabling environment

2. Market access

3. Raw material

4. FDI

5. Capacity building

The textile industries of Ghana, Nigeria, Uganda, and other nations have been destroyed by cheap Chinese imports. According to the Industrial and Commercial Workers Union in Ghana, only four out of thirty textile enterprises are still active (ICU). The organization claims that the country used to produce yarn for garments marketed domestically and in Sub-Saharan Africa, but that this is no longer the case.

8. Conclusion and recommendations on the cotton and textile industry in SSA

Apparel manufacturing is particularly labour-intensive, with minimal start-up costs and readily transferable technologies. As a result, several nations with low labour costs, particularly in South and East Asia, have gained significant market share in the recent four decades.

Main policy recommendations for LIC governments, industry associations and clothing firms can be summarized as follows:

1. Improve productivity, skills, and capabilities within fi rms and develop from cutmake-trim (CMT) to full package suppliers.

2. Increase backward linkages and reduce lead times.

3. Improve physical and bureaucratic infrastructure.

4. Improve labour and environmental compliance.

5. Diversify end markets to fast-growing emerging markets.

6. Increase regional integration.

7. Build locally embedded clothing industries.

8.1 Big data analytics framework model for oilseeds and textile production in SSA

From the concept of a Big Data strategy to the technical tools and capabilities that a company should have, there's a lot to consider. The following are the key advantages of using a Big Data framework:

1. The Big Data Framework provides a framework for businesses looking to get started with Big Data or improve their Big Data capabilities.

2. The Big Data Framework encompasses all aspects of an organization's structure that must be considered in a Big Data environment.

3. The Big Data Framework is not tied to any particular vendor. You can expand the data storage by adding more nodes.

The Big Data Framework's Structure.

When establishing a Big Data organization, organizations should consider the Big Data framework, which is a structured approach that comprises of six basic

DOI: http://dx.doi.org/10.5772/intechopen.107225

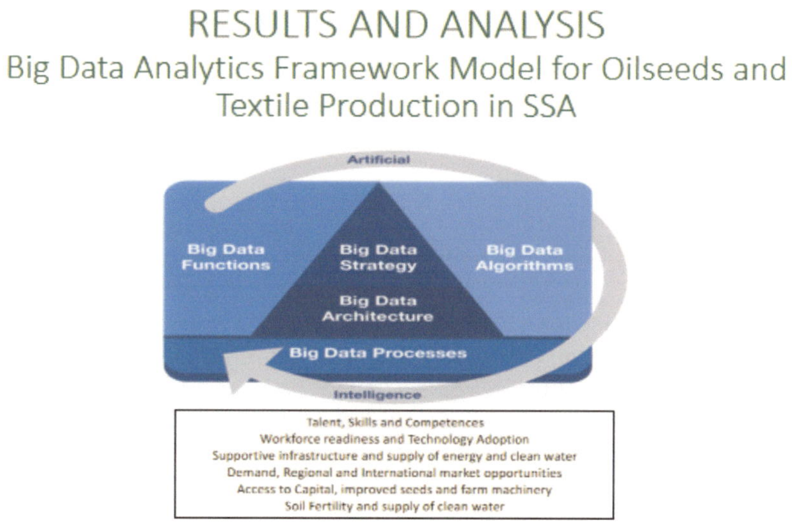

Figure 11.
Big data analytics framework model for oilseeds and textile production.

capabilities. The following is a diagram of the Big Data Framework shown on **Figure 11**. The Hadoop Architecture layout is shown on **Figure 12**.

When establishing a Big Data organization, organizations should consider the Big Data framework, which is a structured approach that comprises of six basic capabilities. It's a people business when it comes to big data. Even with the world's most modern computers and processors, businesses will fail if they lack the necessary knowledge and skills. As a result, the Big Data Framework strives to broaden the expertise of everybody interested in Big Data. The modular method, as well as the supporting certification scheme, attempts to create Big Data knowledge in a similar

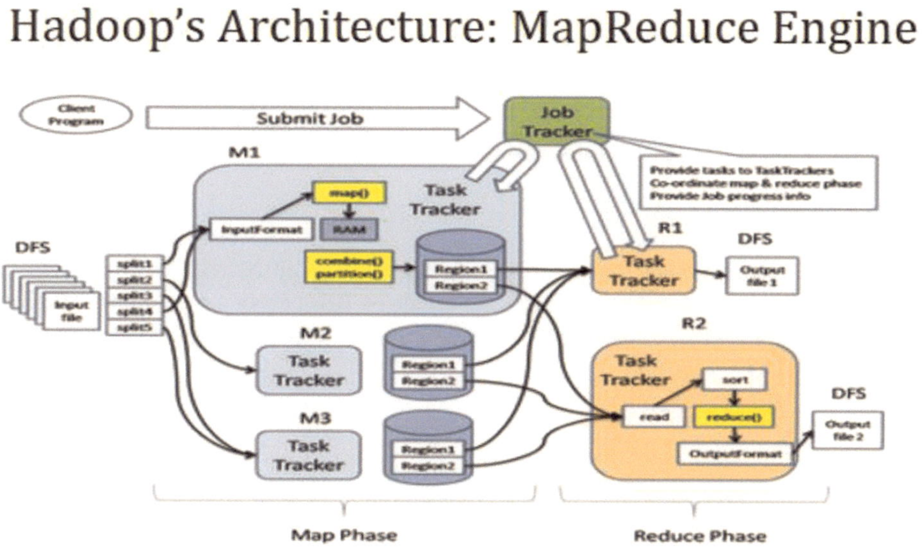

Figure 12.
Hadoop's architecture.

organized manner. The Big Data framework is a comprehensive approach to Big Data. It examines the numerous elements that businesses should consider when establishing a Big Data company. Every component of the framework is as important, and organizations can only progress if they give all components of the Big Data framework similar attention and effort.

9. Conclusion

The Hadoop platform was created as a framework for big data analytics. The open-source Hadoop platform offers the analytical tools and computing capacity needed to handle such massive data volumes. The Hadoop Distributed File System (HDFS) and the MapReduce parallel processing engine are the two primary parts of Apache Hadoop. Apache Hadoop has been successfully established as an open source option for distributed systems in the fields of Big Data, cluster, and cloud computing. Scalability, availability, and fault tolerance to a great degree are promised by the master/slave design. By simply adding existing hardware, it is possible to obtain cost-effectively extra memory, increased I/O capacity, and improved performance. A technology called Map-Reduce allows for the concurrent processing of sizable data sets across many nodes in sizable clusters. Map-Reduce at the level of "Distributed data processing" coupled with the database "HBase" can be taken into consideration since the processing and management of data are two things that are naturally in direct connection.

Because they are self-pollinated crops and farmers can keep and recycle grain from past harvests, the competitiveness of oil crop or legume seed markets is limited by the poor rate of return on investments in breeding, seed production, processing, and marketing. One way to do this is to persuade commercial seed companies to invest in seed production of publicly developed varieties, and to work with them and other stakeholders to improve coordination along the value chain in order to provide farmers with the necessary incentives to invest in improved seed and other complementary inputs to increase productivity and improve quality. The major textile firms produce a variety of products, including polyester staple fiber and filament, yarn, greige cloth, and wax prints.

Acknowledgements

Great appreciation is expressed to the University of Zimbabwe Business School Masters students who studied the Applied Business Informatics module taught by the author from April to July, 2022 and who participated in the Focus Group discussions.

Appendix

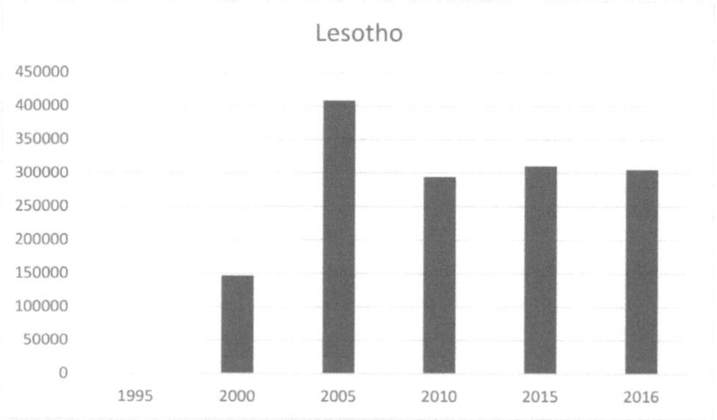
Lesotho
450000
400000
350000
300000
250000
200000
150000
100000
50000
0
1995
2000
2005
2010
2015
2016

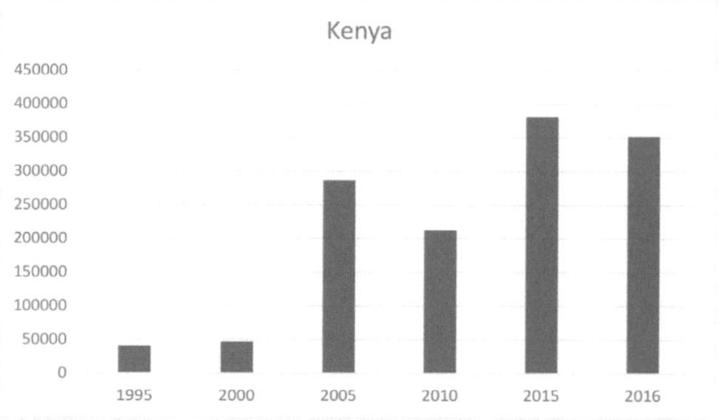
Kenya
450000
400000
350000
300000
250000
200000
150000
100000
50000
0
1995
2000
2005
2010
2015
2016

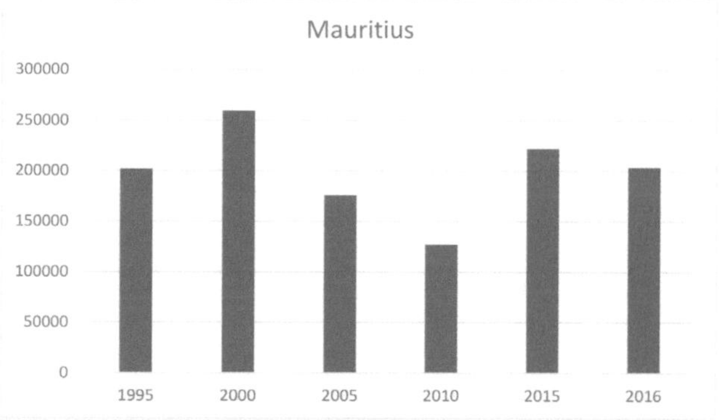
Mauritius
300000
250000
200000
150000
100000
50000
0
1995
2000
2005
2010
2015
2016

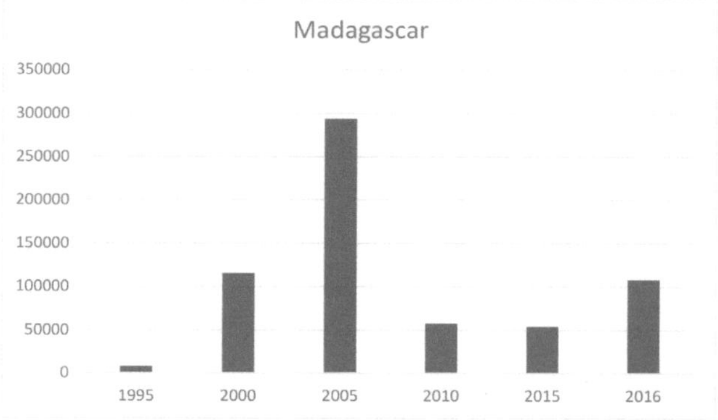
Madagascar
350000
300000
250000
200000
150000
100000
50000
0
1995
2000
2005
2010
2015
2016

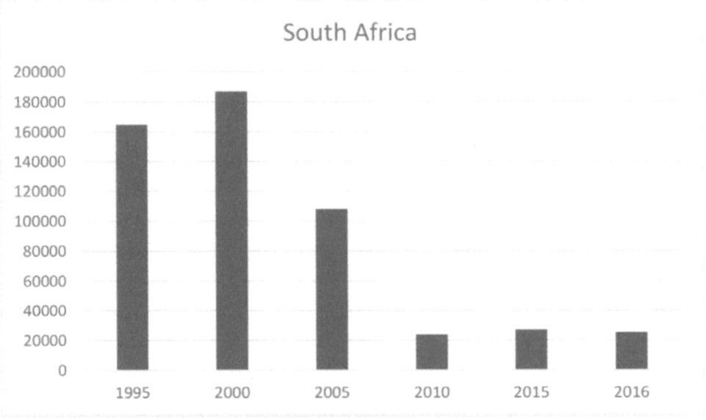
South Africa
200000
180000
160000
140000
120000
100000
80000
60000
40000
20000
0
1995
2000
2005
2010
2015
2016

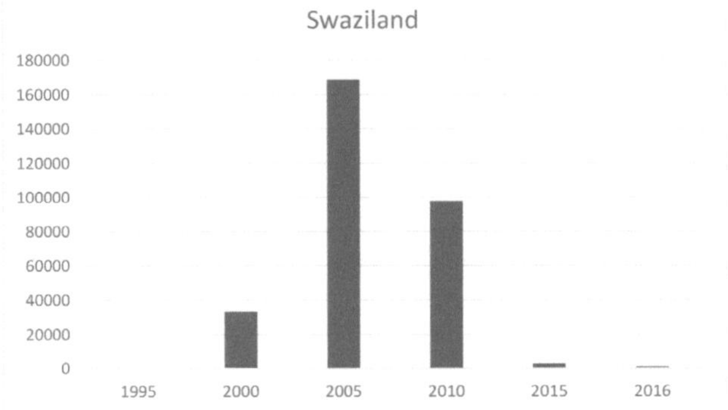
Swaziland
180000
160000
140000
120000
100000
80000
60000
40000
20000
0
1995
2000
2005
2010
2015
2016

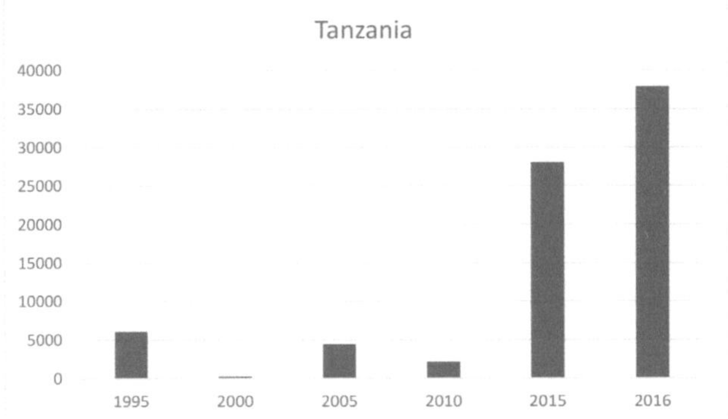
Tanzania
40000
35000
30000
25000
20000
15000
10000
5000
0
1995
2000
2005
2010
2015
2016

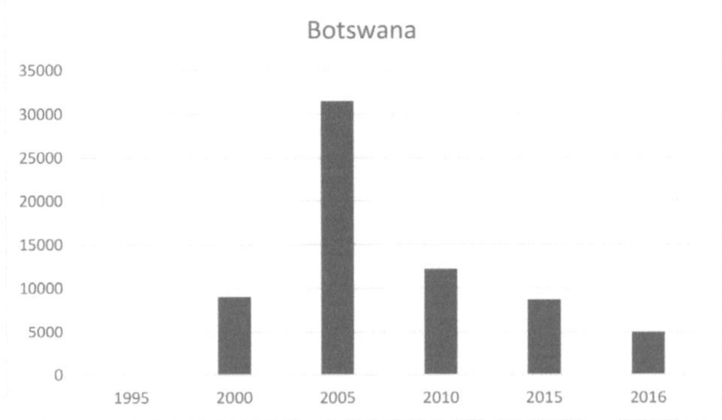
Botswana
35000
30000
25000
20000
15000
10000
5000
0
1995
2000
2005
2010
2015
2016

DOI: http://dx.doi.org/10.5772/intechopen.107225

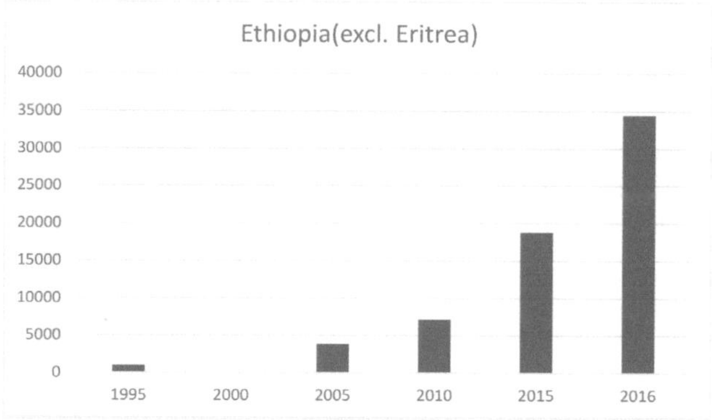

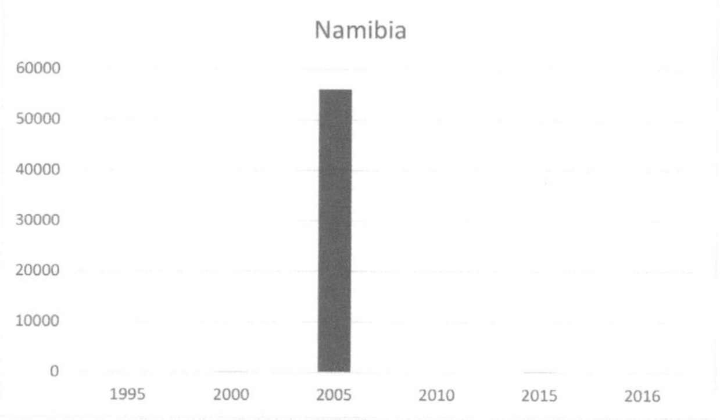

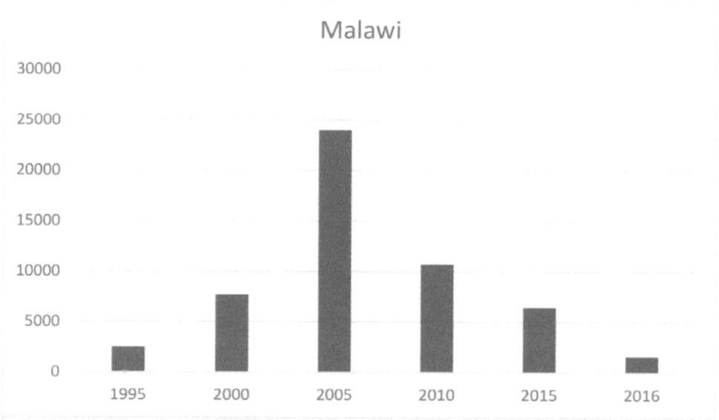

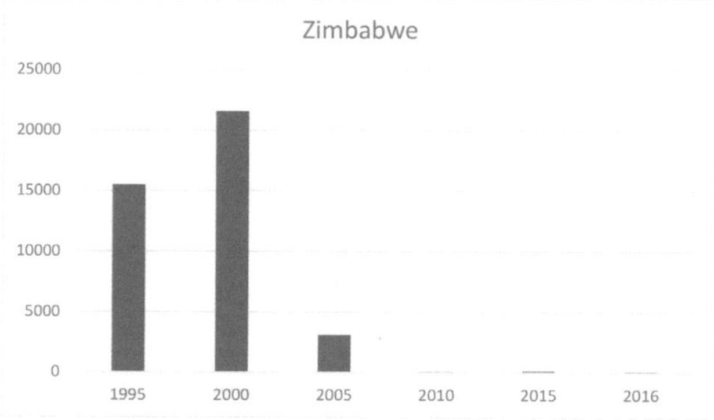

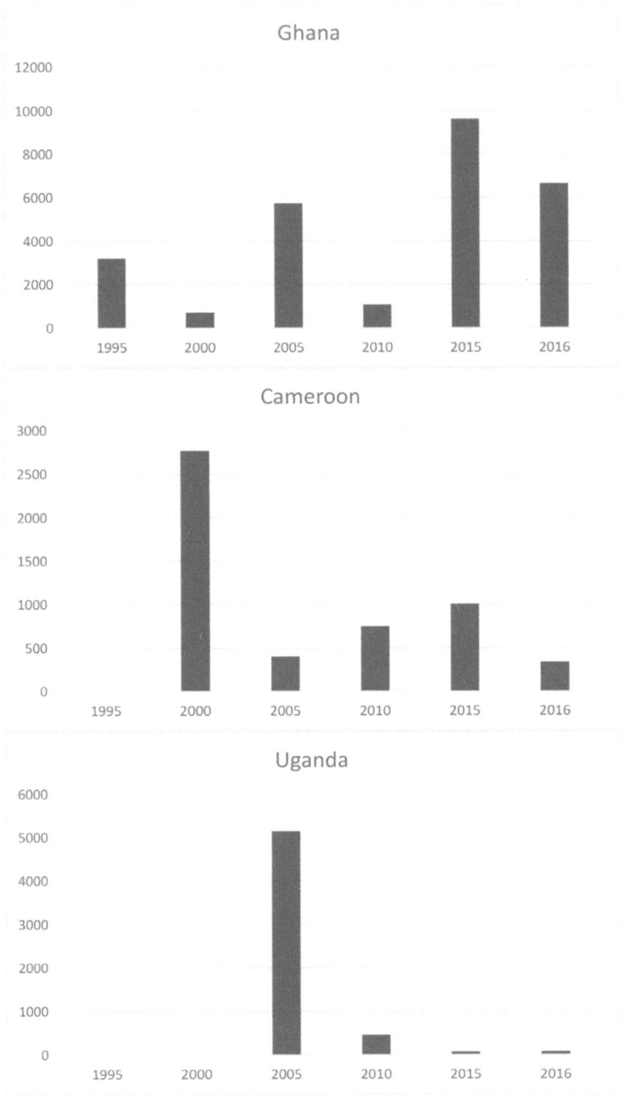

Figure A1.
Changes in the volume of production by country.

Author details

Gabriel Kabanda
Adjunct Professor of Machine Learning, Woxsen School of Business, Woxsen University, Hyderabad, India

*Address all correspondence to: gabriel.kabanda@woxsen.edu.in; gabrielkabanda@gmail.com

References

[1] Sun J, Reddy CK. Big data analytics for healthcare. In: Proceedings of the 19th ACM SIGKDD International Conference on Knowledge Discovery and Data Mining 2013 Aug 11. ACM; 2013. pp. 1525-1525

[2] Kwon T, Chung MI, Gupta R, Baker JC, Wallingford JB, Marcotte EM. Identifying direct targets of transcription factor Rfx2 that coordinate ciliogenesis and cell movement. Genom Data. 2014; **2**:192-194

[3] OECD/FAO. OECD-FAO Agricultural Outlook. Paris: OECD Publishing; 2016

[4] Kabanda G. Bayesian network model for a Zimbabwean cybersecurity system. Oriental journal of computer science and technology. 2020;**12**(4):147-167

[5] Alpaydin E. Machine Learning. The MIT Press Essential Knowledge Series. London, England: MIT Press; 2016

[6] Truong TC, Qb D, Zelinka I. Artificial intelligence in the cyber domain: Offense and defense. Symmetry. 2020;**2020**(12): 410

[7] NAPANDA K, Shah H, Kurup L. Artificial intelligence techniques for network intrusion detection. International Journal of Engineering Research & Technology (IJERT). 2015;**4**(11)

[8] Adriaans P, Zantinge D. Data mining. Addison-Wesley Longman Publishing Co., Inc.; 1997

[9] International Telecommunication Union (ITU). Global Security Report. ITU; 2017. p. 2017

[10] Shambhoo K. Predicting and Accessing Security Features into Component-Based Software Development: A Critical Survey. Singapore: Springer; 2019

[11] Bakshi K. Considerations for big data: Architecture and approach. In: 2012 IEEE aerospace conference. IEEE; 2012. pp. 1-7

Section 2

Smart Environments

Chapter 4

How Is the Internet of Things Industry Responding to the Cybersecurity Challenges of the Smart Home?

Sara Cannizzaro and Rob Procter

Abstract

In this article, we investigate the privacy and security challenges of the smart home as perceived by the industry, with findings relating to cybersecurity awareness, transparency on legal data use, malicious data use, regulation issues, liability, and market incentives for cybersecurity; we also reveal how the industry has been responding to these challenges. Based on survey findings, we outlined a series of socio-technical challenges to smart home adoption. To understand these findings in more depth, we investigated qualitatively how these challenges were perceived and responded to by organizations in the Internet of Things (IoT) sector. We interviewed seven experts from six organizations involved in the design, development, or review of consumer IoT devices and services including both businesses and NGOs. Thematic analysis focused on two main themes, that is, responses to privacy and responses to security challenges of smart home adoption. Our study revealed that industry stakeholders are looking to address these adoption challenges by providing new technical solutions to mitigate the privacy and security risk of the smart home, producing new standards and influencing regulation, as well as building up communities of learning surrounding common issues. With this knowledge, industry stakeholders can take steps toward increasing smart home acceptability for consumers.

Keywords: IoT, smart home, industry stakeholder, acceptability, adoption, thematic analysis, privacy, security

1. Introduction

Smart home technologies are marketed to enhance consumers' home life. The "smart home" can be defined as the integration of the Internet of Things (IoT, i.e., Internet-enabled, digital devices with sensors) and machine learning in domestic environments. The aim of smart home technologies is to provide enhanced entertainment services, easier management of the home, domestic chores, and protection from domestic risks. They can be found in devices such as smart speakers and hubs, lighting, sensors, door locks and cameras, central heating thermostats, and domestic appliances. The European market for smart home devices is expected to boom in the next 5 years [1], but amid such positive expectations, there looms the productivity paradox identified by scholars of social informatics—that technology alone, even good technology, is not sufficient to create social or economic value and strategies of computerization do not readily produce expected economic and social benefits in a vast number of cases [2].

Currently, businesses are actively promoting positive visions of what the smart home means for consumers (e.g., convenience, economy, and home security). However, at the same time, consumers are actively comparing their smart home experiences against these visions and some are coming up with different interpretations and meanings from those that business is promoting [3, 4]. Hence, if the expected growth of the smart home market is to be realized, it is important for smart home device manufacturers and service providers to understand consumer reactions and thereby reduce the chance that the technology may not be valuable or meaningful to consumers.

Previous studies have found that UK consumers are not convinced that they can trust the privacy and security of smart home technologies [3, 5]. Cannizzaro et al. [3] predicted that the potential for security incidents happening through smart home devices would be a significant obstacle to smart home adoption. They also showed that consumers are unconvinced that their privacy will not be at risk. Consumers' perceived risk of using the Eco-friendly smart home (ESHM) reduces their intention to adopt IT [6]. This means that there are issues with the acceptability of smart home technologies; hence, it is highly likely that privacy and security concerns will impact negatively on their future adoption [7]. Proof of robust cybersecurity and low risk of privacy breaches will be key in smart home technology companies persuading consumers to invest in their products. Businesses and policymakers need to work together in order to increase consumers' trust [3] and ensure consumers' safety and well-being while using these devices. However, the smart home business community is not likely to act speedily to address consumers' concerns without a strong regulatory incentive. However, other incentives for businesses, other than regulation, would clearly include the reputation of having products that do not violate users' privacy. At the same time, some argue that the rapid pace of IoT development militates against effective policy interventions [8]. The UK government has produced the Code of Practice for Consumer Internet of Things Security [9] with 13 voluntary recommendations, but debate is currently open as to whether to enforce some of these on the UK market [10].

When it comes to understanding the implications of issues, such as the privacy and security risks of smart home devices, it is important to consider the views of a full range of stakeholders [11]. In this article, we report the findings of our IoT industry stakeholder study, which was conducted as part of the Petras research programme, the UK's Research Hub for IoT[1]. In addition to representing the voices of consumers, we sought to discover the opinions of industry stakeholders (such as small and large businesses), as well as NGOs (including community and IoT interest groups), to understand how these stakeholders influence the smart home development in the UK and respond to the challenges that have been reported. Our aim is to enrich our understanding of the socio-technical context in which the technology is being promoted. We argue that this can help businesses to harness the economic opportunities of the smart home, while increasing the technology's acceptability for consumers.

[1] https://petras-iot.org/.

2. Literature review

2.1 Technology adoption and acceptability

Social informatics studies the relationships between people, digital technologies, and their contexts of use [12]. In this approach, the focus is on the relationship between technology and society from a perspective that does not privilege either [2] but examines, as they put it, the hyphen in the "socio-technical" expression. Adoption studies can be a practical application of social informatics approaches because, to be able to study and promote adoption, an understanding of the possibilities harnessed by the materiality of the technology—as well as the value that the technology brings into people's lives—is necessary. It is an approach that contrasts with an *a priori* promotion of technologies that occasionally work well for people, occasionally are valuable, are sometimes abandoned, are sometimes unusable, and thus incur predictable waste and inspire misplaced hopes [13].

Adoption is a process "starting with the user becoming aware of the technology, and ending with the user embracing the technology and making full use of it" [14]. Awareness has been seen as the key to developing new ICT infrastructures [15] and as a key determinant of consumers' adoption behavior [16]. Lack of awareness was identified as an obstacle to mobile phone adoption [17] and in the IoT landscape, our survey showed that the less aware people are of the expression "Internet of Things," the higher the odds (1.3 times) that they will not want to use the technology in the future [3]. Furthermore, security and privacy can influence the adoption of smart home technologies. For example, in their investigation of trust in the cybersecurity-preserving capabilities of smart home devices, Cannizzaro et al. [3] revealed how anxiety about the likelihood of a security incident in IoT for the home, emerged as a statistically significant factor influencing the adoption of smart home technology. Lipford et al. [18] outlined how IoT technologies introduce challenging privacy issues that may frustrate their widespread adoption, whereas Guhr et al. [19] emphasize how privacy concerns directly and indirectly influence the intended smart home usage.

Adoption studies are typically carried out by what Rogers [20] calls "change agencies," whose short-term goal is to facilitate the adoption of innovations and who often follow a segmentation strategy of least resistance to innovations. This logic of pursuing economic gain and sidelining wider societal interests also appears in recent key IoT adoption studies (e.g., [21–24]), which justify adoption purely through economic arguments and do not mention the societal risks that the technology may raise. The underlying economic model of the new wave of digital innovations has been dubbed "surveillance capitalism" [24], defined by the harvesting of data and its analysis for the commodification of human activity. In response, Helbing [25] states that we must ensure the ethical use of new digital technologies. Hence, acceptability is a way to mitigate this one-sided approach to adoption and can help to understand the impact of unintended consequences, for example, the erosion trust in technology, privacy [12], or the rate of acceptance of the smart home in older adults [6, 26] Technology acceptability is "the degree of primary users' predisposition to carry out daily activities using the intended device" [27]. Philosophically, technology acceptability is a judgment that prescribes the way in which the technology examined ought to be desirable [28]. Acceptability is a popular perspective in health and assistive technology-related IoT services and products, where, for example, Shahrestani [29] defines acceptability as "guidelines to evaluate how a particular approach or technology is working for the elderly or people with disability," thus relating acceptability to the general process of *evaluation*. In regard to the IoT, Taylor et al. [30] define acceptability in conjunction with "attitudes," for example, "Policymakers need to investigate the *attitudes* of the public if *acceptability* of IoT is to be understood" ([30], emphasis added). Hence, "acceptability" feeds on evaluations, predispositions, and attitudes toward a given technology, foregrounding the user in the user-technology relation. As such, acceptability has the potential to give consumers a voice and thus rebalance the business-consumer relationship. The socio-technical approach intrinsic in acceptability can encourage a discovery process that helps designers effectively understand the relevant life worlds and work worlds of the people who will use their systems [2].

Outside of academia, acceptability-related studies are rather popular and are often carried out by interest groups [31, 32] or organizations defending consumers' rights (e.g., [5]). Trust is fundamental to consumer technology where the transmission of personal and sensitive information is involved.

De Poel and Verbeek note how science and technology scholars have shied away from explicit normative or ethical discussions [33], but with the advent of the IoT, and the smart home being marketed to the wider population, ignoring technology ethical-acceptability concerns and disregarding consumer trust is no longer possible.

Trust in privacy and security are key factors affecting the acceptability of the smart home [3, 34]. To date, there have been few nontechnical studies of security and privacy concerns of smart home device users [35].

3. Methodology

3.1 Interviews as survey follow-up

In previous work [3], we confirmed one of the social informatics' key lessons, that is, the effects of technology are always unequal, in other words, "that some social groups will benefit more than others from the uses of digital technologies" [12]. We also found that the privacy and security-preserving capability of devices are the most significant challenges to smart home adoption. Hence, we further investigated how organizations in the sector perceive and respond to these challenges. This study involving Human Subject Research received full approval by the University of Warwick ethics committee on May 29, 2019 (ref. no BSREC 51/18-19). The methodology consisted of a series of semi-structured interviews: seven experts from six organizations involved in the design, development, or review of smart home devices and services (**Table 1**)[2]. We adopted a semi-structured interview format as this is more likely to ensure that valid and reliable data can be obtained from interviewees [36]. Also, semi-structured interviews provide respondents with enough flexibility to build and expand on the initial guiding topic, which, in turn, allows the researcher to analyze the dataset with different degrees of depth.

In order to achieve a balance of views, a broadly equal proportion of business and nonbusiness organizations were included in the sample with four experts from NGOs and three experts from businesses. Respondents from interviews [2, 3, 7] are business respondents, whereas those from interviews [4, 5, 8] are NGO respondents. Interview [5] includes two NGO experts from the same organization (see **Table 1**).

[2] Ethical approval for the study was secured from the Biomedical and Scientific Research Ethics Committee (BSREC) at the University of Warwick on 29 May 2019.

	Organization type	**Location**	**Type of IoT product/ approach developed**	**Target represented**	**Respondent role within the organization**
Interview (ref. 1)	Business	UK	Telecommunication products		Innovation consultant
Interview (ref. 2)	Business	UK	Developing innovative solutions, advisory, and management activities		CEO
Interview (ref. 3)	NGO	UK	Social purpose corporation	Consumers	Advisor
Interview (ref. 4)	NGO	Worldwide	Online community	Smart home industry business leaders	Co-founder
Interview (ref. 4)	NGO	Worldwide	Online community	Smart home industry business leaders	Chief operations officer
Interview (ref. 5)	Business	Germany (UK office)	Auditing, testing services, and product certification		Business development manager
Interview (ref. 6)	NGO	Worldwide (UK office)	Consumer group	Consumers	Digital advocacy manager

Table 1.
Details of sample composition consisting of business (product provided and respondent role) and NGO (target represented and respondent role) organizations.

We sought to include policy-side views on the security threats in smart home adoption. The majority of our respondents were from large organizations but we sought to include at least one small business among them.

The sample of interviewees arrived through suggestions made by Petras project colleagues. Interviews were conducted face-to-face and by video conference call and lasted between 30 min and 1 h.

To ensure rigorous data collection, we followed the guidelines set by Braun and Clarke [37] concerning planning thematic analysis. Hence, in devising the interview questions, we first clarified the scientific method upon which the analysis would rest and opted for a broadly deductive approach, constrained by the survey findings and adoption challenges of the smart home identified in Cannizzaro et al. [3] and listed below:

i. Overall, fairly low levels of trust.

ii. Overall, levels of satisfaction are still uncertain despite the prolonged presence of IoT in society.

iii. Younger respondents' low-risk awareness.

iv. Older respondents' resistance to IoT.

v. Less-educated respondents' resistance to IoT.

Our questionnaire was developed based on these challenges that allowed us to formulate a question guide. Each question topic was formed of guiding questions as well as some follow-up questions [38] (see Appendix A). The interviews were transcribed and a thematic analysis via coding was conducted on the transcripts. The thematic analysis was based on Braun and Clarke's [37] principle of *realism*. These questions were rotated according to the background of the respondents, particularly whether they were businesses or NGO organizations. Topics forming the questions guide included general background questions to allow participants to respond to questions about their roles within the organization and break the ice; followed by the topics pertaining to the most significant factors affecting IoT adoption, as previously explored quantitatively in [3, 39], such as IoT and smart home *awareness*, *risks and benefits* of IoT for both organizations and consumers, *trust, digital* divide in IoT adoption, *future and change* in the sector, including *responses to IoT challenges* (see Appendix A). The interviews were transcribed and a thematic analysis via coding (based on the topics above) was conducted on the transcripts. In order to reach the saturation point, we then examined the transcripts further using Social Construction of Technology (SCOT), a mid-ground theoretical framework, which is outlined below.

3.2 Theoretical framework: SCOT's interpretive flexibility

Within innovation studies, approaches to understanding meanings range from technological determinist (e.g., [40]) to social constructivist (e.g., [41]). Occupying a conceptual middle ground is the SCOT framework [42]. In SCOT, a key concept is "interpretive flexibility" [43], which recognizes that the "meaning" of an innovation may be initially contested by different stakeholders or social groups before "closure"—and hence its use-value—is reached [44]. According to Orlikowski [43], interpretive flexibility is an attribute of the relationship between people and technology, a function of the material artifact, the characteristics of the human agents, and the institutional context in which technology is being introduced [45]. The social groups involved in interpreting the meanings of the technology include producers, engineers, designers, marketers, and investors; those who have a direct relationship with technology and develop an artifact—advocates—policymakers, lobbyists, and academics; those who are indirectly related with technology and work on policy-making, lobbying, and research; and also, users and bystanders [46]. Elle et al. [47] contend that, in most cases, interpretive flexibility diminishes when the social groups reach an agreement on an interpretation.

Initially, SCOT perspectives originated in studies of organizational innovation processes. Unsurprisingly, Rowland [48] argues that SCOT emphasizes the role of large business corporations, whereas Burns et al. [49] see innovation within a context of receptivity and institutionalization. However, some argue that in the current context where digital innovation is a largely available consumer commodity, SCOT needs to be translated to the consumer digital technology marketplace, and hence it requires a new framework variant, Social Construction of Digital Technologies (SCODT). The SCODT framework posits that dimensions of innovation ought to be considered in light of digital advances [50, 51]. This implies that the social groups involved interact in different ways from those involved with technological innovation—traditional employees-employers' hierarchies typical of the workplace are replaced by consumer-seller relationships, where power relationships occur in an always connected, and competitive, digital context. Wellman et al. [52] argue that digital technology users are connected in a specific way, that is, by means of networked individualism: fragmented, opportunistic, fast connecting individuals, and organizations forming temporary relevant social groups. Furthermore, SCODT posits that interaction switches from interpersonal to interpersonal, person-technology, technology-technology, and technology-physical environment interactions [50], where it is also artificial agents (*sensu* [53]) in addition to human agents that take decisions within such relationships.

4. Findings

Through thematic analysis, we identified three key themes in the dataset: (1) IoT awareness, including both industry and perceived public awareness; (2) trust in privacy and trust in security as industry challenges; (3) responses to privacy and security challenges of the IoT. **Table 2** shows how the challenges and the responses map.

	Challenges	Industry responses to the challenges
Privacy	Data collection is always on • uncertainty and insecurity surrounding data use • transparency of the smart device in regard with how it collects data and uses Illegal, malicious data use • impact of a privacy breach	Trials to find new ways to protect people's privacy • working on a safety program involving the practice of obscuring personal data Public campaigns • "Trust by Design for IoT products" • designing a new standard for "Privacy by Design" in smart home devices and services as part of the ISO PC 317 standard
Security	Lack of security awareness in the public • average person does not understand the security risks associated with IoT devices • difficulty in gauging which device has more security at the point of making a purchase • lack of education on how to make security judgments • Not understanding the impact of security breaches on smart home devices Regulation issues • Lack of regulation • lack of focus and fragmentation of government's efforts and responsibility • regulatory efforts not being sufficient since they rely on voluntary compliance Liability for the consumer Problem at the market level • security not being a priority because it lacks a sufficient market incentive	Security as a default setting Companies to develop standards and guidelines with the support of consumer organizations Security labeling to help consumers make informed choices Regulation enforcement to be made clear for consumers Developing specific technical security solutions External review and independent testing of devices Governments to take responsibility for the security of smart home devices Responsibility for the security of smart home devices should be transnational

Table 2.
Summary of the cybersecurity challenges of the smart home as perceived by the IoT industry, and of the industry's responses to these challenges.

4.1 Awareness

4.1.1 IoT awareness: connectedness and the problems IoT can solve

Businesses tended to provide general definitions of IoT—one in terms of the shape of communication it entails, its abstract structure, that is, IoT stands for "connected to everything everywhere" [3], and another in terms of its material structure, or "bare bones" [7], that is, "a piece of electronic equipment with a radio in it, in a box" [7]. NGO organizations, instead, defined the IoT less in terms of its shape and structure but more in terms of its function:

> *For most people it is the smart speaker, it's the home hub, it's the thing that does lots of tasks, which don't really add much – remove much friction from your daily life but they're nice to have. I don't really think they think about the more advanced areas that do actually remove friction. [4]*

In this case, the function of IoT, "not removing much friction" points at consumers' IoT identity coinciding with something superfluous—perhaps a luxury product of a consumeristic society.

The case of IoT being purely functional was made even stronger by this NGO respondent, who explained that a "true" IoT is "the problem that that device or that product is trying to solve" [5]. Also, the respondent elaborated on the idea of IoT as benign primarily represented by its function:

> *We're purists as an organisation, we want to see IoT for the real purpose of IoT rather than it being IoT washed if you like, where everyone is just putting a sensor on something or connecting something to call it IoT. I think that's the false IoT. [5]*

In this view, definitions of IoT simply based on structure, shape, network, and connections, do not fully represent the "real" IoT. Furthermore, both business organizations and NGOs point to privacy and security being issues that are intrinsic to IoT's identity.

4.1.2 Perceived public awareness

Business respondents were in agreement that public awareness of IoT was low: "I'd imagine there's still some people who won't know what IoT stands for" [3]. Also, they thought that while the public may be familiar with services such as Alexa (introduced in 2016 in the UK) they did not connect them with IoT, for example, "lots of people have got Alexa, lots of people have got Google Home, but they don't know that that's actually part of the IoT" [7]. Furthermore, the lack of awareness is also related to the need to have specific knowledge and skillset to be able to grasp IoT identity: "I don't think anybody I know that is not an engineer works for this industry understands what the IoT is or have heard of it" [7].

Regarding awareness of privacy and security issues, a business respondent stated that "I don't think people understand exactly what privacy is and what it means as a consumer." This view was echoed by an NGO respondent:

> *You see the stories of murder cases that use a small bit of audio from an Amazon Echo recording or how someone has been able to play a song in someone else's room when*

> *they shouldn't have. And they're funny, they're intriguing, they're engaging, but as I mentioned earlier, it's not tangible until it happens to you. [4]*

The "Stories" mentioned by the respondent point to the role of media reports of security incidents potentially shaping risk perception. However, these may be insufficient for the public to understand the risks more fully. The respondent explained that direct experience of working with IoT gives a more realistic idea of the extent to which security is an intrinsic aspect of IoT's identity:

> *there are much more concerning areas to it that I in my job are fully aware of and I would never have a smart home hub in my house, ever, and I wouldn't let my house mate bring his into my house because I just didn't like the idea of that thing being on. [4]*

4.2 Privacy

A prominent challenge pertaining to the smart home industry was privacy. Industry respondents pinpointed some examples of privacy issues pertaining to the smart home and also provided responses to these challenges.

4.2.1 Privacy challenges perceived by the IoT industry

In general, the context surrounding privacy issues was defined as a tradeoff between privacy versus productivity and a response concluded that "We're in a bit of a catch 22 scenario." Zubiaga et al. [4] explained the NGO respondent representing consumers. Smart home privacy issues were raised in unison across the industry spectrum since there was not a marked distinction between business organizations and NGOs in the kind of privacy issues being recollected.

Both NGO and business respondents referred to a privacy-problematic aspect of smart home devices, that is, data collection being always on: "Alexa, for example, has had a bad rep to the fact she's always listening" [3] and "every single word, every single tone, every single character is being referenced and archived for the evolution of AI for Alexa" [5]. This creates uncertainty and insecurity surrounding data use. The business respondent providing consultancy and design solutions, highlighted the central role of trust in the transparency of the smart device in regard to how it collects data and uses it, in other words, its integrity: "Not only the collection of data, what are you going to do with that data? Are you going to do what you're saying? And even if you do what you're saying, what does that mean for me?" [2]. This industry view displays awareness of how key a concern trust is in systems' integrity for successful smart home adoption.

Illegal, malicious data use is also a concern according to a respondent who reported the example of remote control wireless plugs used to control an appliance that was then discovered to be sending data to a server in China. A business respondent outlined the general lack of awareness in regard to the meaning and consequences of privacy breach: "People are not bothered if somebody can see their light going off" [7]. However, the respondent suggested that public attitudes can change when they become aware of the potential impact of a privacy breach:

> *It's when people understand what that privacy data that's getting out there means in a different context, and it starts to worry them. [...] what happens if somebody breaks into your system and there's a guy there with the crowbar that knows that when the light's turned off you've gone to bed, and then he comes and breaks your back door? [7]*

4.2.2 Responses to privacy challenges

In order to respond to the privacy challenges of the smart home, business respondents reported experimenting with trials to find out the extent to which data can be collected and used. A business organization respondent providing services and products explained how they were having to be cautious of problems that are raised with the smart home in terms of what data can be shared and that they are experimenting with "workaround" trials to find new ways to protect people's privacy [3]. Specifically, they were working on a safety program involving the practice of obscuring personal data, thereby relying on partial data use: "what we've done is for that particular trial, we would hide parts of their journey so they can't actually be identified" [3].

An NGO respondent representing smart home consumers described two initiatives aimed at protecting privacy: the campaign "Trust by Design for IoT products" to make consumers aware of security risks in products such as IoT baby monitors, and principles and recommendations to make consumer rights, privacy, safety, and security key features of smart home devices; and designing a new standard for "Privacy by Design" in smart home devices and services as part of the ISO PC 317 standard [8], "Consumer protection: privacy by design for consumer goods and services" [54].

A service and product provider business respondent outlined that there are others in the sector, like service providers, who bear responsibility for protecting privacy: "providers, like the voice assistants like Google and Amazon, I think people are quite wary of. [...] So, I think they have a certain level of responsibility to reassure people and let people know where that data is going" [3]. The importance of integrity for increasing consumer trust is underlined by the business respondent who argued that it is service providers that have the greatest responsibility toward data integrity:

> *They need to do more and at least be open and honest what that data is being used for, because obviously the cases where you see an advert has been personalised for them from what it's heard in the home, then the data is being used for other purposes than what it stated. So, it does need to be more honest. [3]*

NGOs take responsibility for improving industry practices in regard to protecting privacy, while also calling for collaboration with external, noncommercial, and nongovernmental players as academic institutions and researchers:

> *there is certainly better than evil being done with AI. It is up to folks like us as a community, you all with your research, to participate in trying to help create this balance or expose the risk but expose the value of the technology. So that we don't have binary decisions. We want to make adjustments to ensure privacy that don't hinder the ongoing development and capability of things like AI. [5]*

In other words, the NGO respondent clearly declared their own responsibility but also the need to work alongside other players "as a community" to improve industry practices, persuade businesses to be more transparent about data use, and increase consumers' trust.

4.3 Security

4.3.1 Security challenges perceived by the IoT industry

Both NGO and business respondents believe there is a general lack of public awareness of smart home security issues. An NGO respondent representing the business community reported not feeling confident that the average person understands the risks associated with the security of IoT devices [5][3]. A business respondent providing testing and certification also agreed that the public lacks security awareness and that "the consumer doesn't really understand [...] how important it is to have a secure device..." [7]. The NGO respondent recollected a famous case of a hack of a smart home device in a Las Vegas casino, one of the most commercially secure areas as there can be, which allowed hackers to gain entry into their entire network and download its "high roller" database [5]. The underlying problem here is that the consumer finds themselves in a difficult position when having to gauge which device has more security at the point of making a purchase: "the end user ends up trying to make a decision, 'do I want to buy this for twenty dollars a person or do I want to buy this for fifty dollars a person?'" [5]. A business respondent pointed to a lack of a communication strategy to help the consumer make their choices in regard to the security of devices: "The way of explaining to them [the consumers] how secure a device is, is secure or isn't, there's no real way of demonstrating that by say a cybersecurity mark" [7]. An NGO respondent outlined how this lack of awareness of security issues of smart home devices coupled with a lack of education on how to make security judgments, creates a "ticking timebomb" situation: "[if] we put a whole bunch of IoT devices out there that are not secure, we're just creating a botnet army for the cyber guys" [5].

Furthermore, as with privacy, there may be a gap in regard to understanding the impact of security breaches of smart home devices. As a business respondent put it: "some people just don't even care. I know a number of people that have these cameras at home and they say they don't care... But I would hazard a guess that they would care if they were to find that their camera was livestreaming on the internet and they could see it themselves" [7].

Another key problem for both NGO and business respondents is the lack of regulation. For one NGO respondent, security standards are difficult to implement because of a lack of focus and fragmentation of the government's efforts and responsibility, for example, "security, for example, it's fragmented across government [...] it's with the National Security Secretariat, it's with DCMS, it's with Cabinet Office" [4]. For a business respondent, there was a sense that existing regulatory efforts are not sufficient, since they rely on voluntary compliance. This business respondent stated that businesses are slow to take action: "But the biggest problem I've noticed when I speak to customers is that cyber security is not yet mandated in products and because of that, people will not pay for that work to be done" [7].

An NGO-specific security concern is a liability for the consumer, for example, "I don't know about the UK but in the United States... If the hack goes through your network, known or unknown to you, you have a level of legal liability" [5].

---

[3] This reference number refers to the interview reference code used to preserve the businesses' anonymity in **Table** 1.

From a business perspective, however, security may not be a priority, as this business respondent stated: "When I speak to customers [product makers] their idea of security is, well, it's something we want and something we're thinking about, but it's not a priority" [7]. Furthermore, there is a sense in the industry that security is not a priority because it lacks a sufficient market incentive: "Whether [cybersecurity] it's a marketing point I'm not really sure. And I would even be not as sure to go towards a no."

4.3.2 Responses to security challenges

Responses to security challenges differ between NGO and business respondents. An NGO respondent representing the business community stressed the importance of security being a default setting of devices that prevents security issues rather than reacts to them: "we want to see secure by design IoT devices out there rather than people thinking about security as an afterthought when it comes to just getting the product to market" [5]. Another NGO respondent representing consumers stated that standards and guidelines developed by companies with the support of consumer organizations can provide transparency of how IoT products should be developed [8]. As for a consumer-centered approach, a respondent stressed the need for security labeling that could help consumers to understand what kind of levels of privacy, security, and trust they could have in that product [5] and help them to make more informed choices. Also, in response to the challenge of fragmented regulation and lack of regulation enforcement, an NGO respondent stated that clarity about enforcement needs to be made clear for consumers: "regulation should be designed with consumers at the heart... [and] clear guidance needs to be set out on how policy and regulation will be enforced, and the measures need to be clear" [8].

Business respondents, on the other hand, reported working on specific technical security solutions such as blockchains in security and quantum key distribution and were "confident that the smart home will be protected through the use of these security technologies" [3]. Another business respondent providing consultancy and design solutions also stressed the need for external review and independent testing of devices to ensure security:

> *we would provide information about how secure we believe their product is, and then they would take that information and through some kind of dialogue work out some kind of solution on what they want to do to make the actual product more secure. [2]*

NGO respondents representing consumers stressed that, ultimately, the responsibility for ensuring the security of smart home devices lay with the government:

> *I think it's really up to the government to think more broadly about how you change the discourse around security, about preparing for things that go wrong, rather than just reacting to them. [4]*

That smart home security is seen as the government's responsibility is significant because it is unlike privacy, where responsibility seems to be down to the user to consent to data collection and use: "it really shouldn't necessarily be solely down to the consumer to become security-savvy, to have to be the one that protects their device. The device should have some adequate level of protection to the consumer from the get-go" [5] stated the respondent representing the business community.

DOI: http://dx.doi.org/10.5772/intechopen.106012

Another NGO respondent representing consumers stressed that such responsibility toward ensuring the security of smart home devices is transnational:

> *The responsibility for ensuring that consumers' rights are protected online, and autonomy and personal freedom are upheld, cannot be managed by one country alone. It requires international collaboration across governments, international organisations and businesses. [8]*

For this respondent, given the cross-border nature of data flows and the size of technology companies that are major market leaders in the development of smart home devices, national efforts should link to international approaches.

5. Discussion

The discussion of results centers on revealing the interpretive flexibility and closure of meaning that characterizes smart home devices. When technology is interpretively flexible, it means that the "interaction of technology and organizations is a function of the different actors and socio-historical contexts implicated in its development and use" [43].

In terms of awareness, business respondents tended to provide definitions of IoT in terms of its structural properties, that is, connectedness. NGO respondents, instead, defined the IoT more in terms of its function and the problems the IoT can solve. In this view, the IoT's identity is intrinsically connected to its pragmatic aspect, that is, its role in a context or "situatedness." This might explain why the wider UK population awareness is greater for the expression "smart home" (90% of people are aware of "smart home") than for the expression IoT (47% of people are aware of "IoT") [3], since "smart home" indicates a recognizable context for use of these devices.

Business respondents are uncertain about the public awareness of IoT. This finding was also reflected in [3]. A deeper awareness of IoT examples and functions may be crucial. Zeng and Roesner [55] point out in fact some of the limitations of current smart home devices design, for example, in regard with the management of multiple users and sometimes lacking basic access control. Hence, promoting awareness of functionalities of this kind may also stimulate adoption in the home, and different players in the industry may need to act in concert to stimulate this functional awareness.

The lack of awareness is also related to the need to have specific technical knowledge and skillsets to be able to grasp both the connectedness and functionality of IoT. This requirement for a technical mindset and expertise could place adopting the IoT beyond the reach of the layperson, particularly those who are less well-educated since usually, it is the "more highly educated individuals who tend to adopt innovations sooner" [56]. Also, [3] survey showed how those with high and medium levels of education were early adopters of smart home devices, though those with less education were catching up.

Business and NGO respondents feel privacy and security issues are not sufficiently part of IoT awareness for the wider public, which is consistent with the finding that 59% of the wider population are not aware of media reports of security incidents involving smart home devices [57].

Previous research [58] showed that the smart home industry is insufficiently emphasizing measures to build consumer confidence in data security and privacy. The industry respondents we recruited, felt they possessed the skillset to judge the security-preserving capacity of smart home devices, but were unsure about the public possessing adequate skillsets. This suggests there is a perceived need to educate the population in regard to security issues pertaining to IoT. This is consistent with the survey finding that consumers' security concerns are likely to impact negatively on IoT adoption. In regard to privacy, both business and NGO respondents raised privacy issues as an industry-wide IoT concern. Hence, privacy as an obstacle to the adoption of the smart home emerges as a stable and established meaning of the smart home. The specific issues respondents raised concern data collection being always on, the uncertainty of data use, illegal malicious data use, and legal but harmful data use. Particular emphasis was placed on the importance of trusting smart home systems' integrity—the belief that the entity is honest and will fulfill its promise to the client [59]—for successful smart home adoption; this view reflects the finding that public trust in companies *not* using data produced by smart home devices without consumers' explicit consent, was fairly low [3]. Significantly, the issue of the influence of friends and experts may have on Privacy Decision Making (e.g., allowing or denying data collection) was not mentioned by any of the participants but this was shown to be an important factor for IoT adoption [60].

One respondent outlined what was perceived to be the neutral position of the public in regard to the likelihood of privacy breach, which was also reflected in our survey [3]. However, in our survey, the public's neutrality changed when the emphasis was placed on understanding the impact or consequences of a privacy breach. Again, this emerging feeling was consistent with our survey finding that the UK public tends to agree that the impact of privacy-related incidents is high [3].

Actions in the form of responses to privacy challenges revolved mainly around taking responsibility for mitigating privacy-related risks. This is key because it has been shown that even when users do indeed trust device manufacturers to protect their privacy, they do not verify that these protections are in place [61]. For business respondents taking responsibility to address privacy-related risks involved taking direct action and experimenting with the technology in order to find new ways to protect privacy. Business respondents felt that a big part of the responsibility toward guaranteeing data integrity was with big service providers. On the other hand, NGO respondents responded to privacy challenges by emphasizing standards, applying pressure to improve industry practices toward data use, and persuading consumers that their data is properly curated and looked after. They also called for collaboration with external, noncommercial, and nongovernmental players, such as academic institutions and researchers. Synergy among industry or industry-relevant stakeholders emerges in this view as the key mechanism toward responding to the privacy challenges of the smart home. When it came to security, both NGO and business respondents associated security issues with the public's lack of awareness of security and uncertainty over making security judgments about a device, which is consistent with the survey finding that people seem to be more concerned about the likelihood of a security incident rather than its impact [3] (unlike for privacy, where it is the other way round), suggesting that there is an education gap in regard to the practical consequences of security breaches.

NGO and business respondents alike thought that security risks were exacerbated by problems at the level of regulation. Specifically, NGO respondents felt that the issue is with a fragmented security-regulation effort, with security being too thinly spread as an issue across government, which is therefore unable to provide a solid answer to this challenge. Steps have been made toward providing a unified approach, with the UK government producing the Code of Practice for Consumer Internet of Things Security [9]. However, this effort may not be sufficient to unify security improvement practice in the sector. Brass et al. [62] point to the proliferation of non-governmental *de facto* standards for smart home cybersecurity produced by businesses, trade associations, and interest groups, as well as NGOs themselves. For businesses, the issue with regulation is felt through a lack of enforcement.

Addressing a specific security concern, one NGO respondent felt that liability may be exacerbated through the public-wide lack of awareness of security issues of smart home devices. Businesses felt that a key security issue is the lack of a marketing incentive for smart home cybersecurity, a feeling that reflects a wider trend with cybersecurity in the private sector in general. Gordon et al. [63] underline how, in general, firms invest in cybersecurity activities at a level below what would be optimal. The issue is particularly significant in regard to small to medium enterprises (SMEs), which are deemed to be potentially the ones most at risk [64], as they often neglect cybercrime prevention [65] and do not possess adequate knowledge in cyber security [66].

In terms of actions, we found NGOs to be leading with the range of responses to the security challenges posed by smart home devices, as they primarily aim to make security a default positioning of devices. They stressed the key role of government in changing the *discourse* around smart home security. The choice of the socio-philosophical term "discourse" refers to the fact that it is both ideas and actions [67] around security that should be promoted and performed, a task for which the government is held to be both capable and responsible for. This perception underlines how it is important that the consumer does not feel he or she is solely responsible for smart home security. However, this feeling contrasts with the attitudes of the public, who ranked the service provider (e.g., Google, Amazon, and Apple) as the main actor responsible for the security of smart home devices, followed by the consumer and the manufacturer, with the government ranking fifth only [57]. This misalignment of perception across NGO experts and consumers may represent an opportunity for intervention for a number of players in the smart home ecosystem. Finally, the global marketplace for smart home devices reminds us that responsibility toward ensuring the security of smart home devices requires an international effort.

6. Conclusions for adoption and acceptability of the smart home

The aims of this project were to investigate smart home adoption from a socio-technical perspective that holds that people and the technologies they use are "co-constitutive" [12]. To this end, we qualitatively interrogated the survey findings pertaining to the most significant factors affecting smart home adoption, as previously flagged up quantitatively in [3]. Our objective was to understand how industry stakeholders interpret and influence smart home's development in the UK and respond to the socio-technical challenges that smart home adoption flags up. The following findings reflect the different levels of interpretive flexibility regarding the challenges of smart home adoption

- Businesses are uncertain about the level of public awareness of IoT, particularly about privacy and security issues.

- Industry-wide concerns surrounding the privacy issues of smart home, concern data collection being always on, the uncertainty of data use, illegal malicious data use, and legal—yet harmful—data use.

- To respond to smart home privacy challenges, businesses are providing new technical solutions, whereas NGOs are producing standards and encouraging synergy amongst industry stakeholders at various levels and academia.

- Industry-wide concerns surrounding key security issues of a smart home are public uncertainty over how to make security judgments when purchasing a device, fragmented regulation for NGOs, and lack of regulation enforcement for businesses; an NGO-specific security concern is a liability; a business-specific concern is the lack of marketing incentive for security.

- In terms of actions, NGOs were found to be leading businesses in regard to the variety of responses to smart home security challenges as they aim to make security a default positioning of devices by underlining the need to change the discourse around security, to make the effort transnational, and to not make the consumer feel solely responsible for the security of smart home devices.

Overall, the smart home industry is responding to the smart home adoption challenges by providing new technical solutions to mitigate the privacy and security risk of smart homes, producing new standards and influencing regulation and building up communities of learning. These findings reveal that there is awareness in the industry of the need to improve sector practices by mitigating privacy and security risks of smart homes in order to increase consumers' trust and promote sector growth.

In terms of implications for the management of smart home adoption, this stakeholders' picture of smart home adoption in the UK and worldwide may help influence future business models and regulatory frameworks. Our study contributes to building awareness of obstacles to adoption and of ethics of data so that new, adaptable, and ethical business models can be proposed; policymaking by providing evidence of stakeholders' opinions toward regulation for common security or data interchange standards. With this knowledge, an open challenge for the smart home is the ethical concerns it may raise, in regard, among other things, cybersecurity. Hence future directions for this work may include the identification and specification of ethical principles relevant to assessing the ethical impact of the smart home and steps that can be taken toward increasing smart home acceptability—that is, the ethical and instrumental desirability for consumers of adopting new technologies.

The study has some limitations that can provide avenues for further research. We strived to achieve a balance of businesses and NGOs in our sample, and included one SME among the business respondents quota. Despite efforts taken to ensure a balanced sample, the small number of interview participants may still introduce bias in the results. Hence, to improve the approach taken in this work, the sample size could be increased in order to include: (1) a higher number of SMEs as these provide new ideas for products and services which can disrupt the sector's business models yet can also exacerbate security and privacy risks; also, this work does not address the voice of non-Western organizations involved in the development and management of the smart home. Hence future work could include the voice of more non-Western organizations to balance and achieve a more culturally diverse sample on the cybersecurity of the smart home. Of particular importance would be to also include representatives from developing countries, for whom the cybersecurity challenges of the smart home will be no less prominent, if not more, in the years to come.

DOI: http://dx.doi.org/10.5772/intechopen.106012

Appendix A. Interview questions guide

Awareness

1. What do you think the IoT means to the public?

2. What do you think "smart home" means to the public?

Risks and benefits of IoT

For the organization

3. Can you summarize the business opportunity that these products and/or services represent for your company? What is your company's business model? (BUSINESS)

4. How easy has it been to promote IoT products and/or related services to the British public? (BUSINESS)

5. How big do you expect the market for your company's products and/or services to be in the future a) 5 years, b) 10 years' time? (BUSINESS)

6. How easy has it been for your organization to achieve your objectives in the IoT sector? (NGO)

For consumers

7. Why should consumers adopt a smart home device? What do you think are the key benefits of your product and/or service that make it desirable to adopt?

8. Why might they not adopt it?/What do you think are the main issues that might make people reluctant to adopt your company's products and/or services?

9. Is your organization taking any steps to deal with these issues? Which ones?

10. Are there new risks for the public specifically related to (your) IoT (products)?

Trust

11. Should consumers trust smart home devices?

12. Do you think the risks for privacy and security posed by smart home devices are acceptable?

13. What kind of actions would be necessary to improve public trust in smart home devices?

Digital divide/technology rejection

14. Are you aware of which groups are less likely to adopt smart home technology? What can your organization do about it?

15. These are some of the results of our survey. Do any of these come as a surprise? If so, why?

    i. Overall fairly low levels of trust

    ii. Overall, levels of satisfaction are still uncertain despite the prolonged presence of IoT in society

    iii. Younger respondents' low-risk awareness

    iv. Older respondents' resistance to IoT

    v. Less-educated respondents' resistance to IoT

16. Would these results be a concern for your company/organization and, if so, how might it respond?

Future and change

17. Do you think your company's business model/organization's strategy may need to adapt to deal with any of the challenges of IoT adoption?

18. If your organization was in charge of the whole sector, what would you change?

19. Are there any actions that the IoT industry as a whole should take to be able to encourage the adoption of IoT products and services?

20. Does your company welcome new policies and regulations for IoT products and services?

Author details

Sara Cannizzaro[1]* and Rob Procter[2]

1 Department of Computer Science and WMG, University of Warwick, Coventry, UK

2 Department of Computer Science, University of Warwick, Coventry, UK

*Address all correspondence to: sara.cannizzaro@warwick.ac.uk

References

[1] Armstrong, M. The Market for Smart Home Devices Is Expected to Boom over the Next 5 Years, 2022, Available from https://www.weforum.org/agenda/2022/04/homes-smart-tech-market/

[2] Kling R, Rosenbaum H, Hert C. Social informatics in information science: An introduction. Journal of the American Society for Information Science. 1998;**49**(12):1047-1052

[3] Cannizzaro S, Procter R, Ma S, Maple C. Trust in the smart home: Findings from a nationally representative survey in the UK. PLoS One. 2020;**15**(5):e0231615

[4] Zubiaga A, Procter R, Maple C. A longitudinal analysis of the public perception of the opportunities and challenges of the internet of things. PLoS One. 2018;**13**(12):1-18

[5] Consumers International. The Trust Opportunity: Exploring Consumers' Attitudes to the Internet of Things, 2019. Available from https://www.consumersinternational.org/media/261950/thetrustopportunity-jointresearch.pdf

[6] Zhang W, Liu L. How consumers' adopting intentions towards eco-friendly smart home services are shaped? An extended technology acceptance model. The Annals of Regional Science. 2022;**68**(2):307-330

[7] Jalali MS, Kaiser JP, Siegel M, Madnick S. The internet of things promises new benefits and risks: A systematic analysis of adoption dynamics of IoT products. IEEE Security & Privacy. 2019;**17**(2):39-48

[8] Tanczer L, Brass I, Elsden M, Carr M, Blackstock JJ. The United Kingdom's emerging internet of things (IoT) policy landscape. In: Ellis R, Mohan V, editors. Rewired: Cybersecurity Governance. New Jersey: John Wiley & Sons; 2019. pp. 37-56

[9] DDCMS Guidance. Code of Practice for Consumer IoT Security. 2018. Available from https://www.gov.uk/government/publications/secure-by-design/code-of-practice-for-consumer-iot-security

[10] DDCMS and Warman, M. Policy Paper: Proposals for Regulating Consumer Smart Product Cyber Security—Call for Views, 2020. Available from https://www.gov.uk/government/publications/proposals-for-regulating-consumer-smart-product-cyber-security-call-for-views

[11] Taebi B. Bridging the gap between social acceptance and ethical acceptability. Risk Analysis. 2017;**37**(10):1817-1827

[12] Meyer ET, Shankar K, Willis M, Sharma S, Sawyer S. The social informatics of knowledge. Journal of the Association for Information Science and Technology. 2019;**70**(4):307-312

[13] Kling R. What is social informatics and why does it matter? The Information Society. 2007;**23**(4):205-220

[14] Renaud K, Van Biljon J. Predicting technology acceptance and adoption by the elderly: a qualitative study. In: Proceedings of the 2008 Annual Research Conference of the South African Institute of Computer Scientists and Information Technologists on IT Research in Developing Countries: Riding the Wave of Technology. 2008. pp. 210-219.

DOI: 10.1145/1456659.1456684. Available from: https://dl.acm.org/

[15] Oye ND, Aiahad N, Abrahim N. Awareness, adoption and acceptance of ICT innovation in higher education institutions. International Journal of Engineering Research and Applications. 2011;**1**(4):1393-1409

[16] Velmurugan MS, Velmurugan MS. Consumer behaviour toward information technology adoption on 3G Mobile phone usage in India. The Journal of Internet Banking and Commerce. 1970;**19**(3):1-8

[17] Sudhir K, Pandey M, Tewari I. Mobile Banking in India: Barriers and Adoption Triggers, 2012. Available from https://som.yale.edu/news/news/mobile-banking-india-barriers-and-adoption-triggers

[18] Lipford HR, Tabassum M, Bahirat P, Yao Y, Knijnenburg BP. Privacy and the internet of things. In: Modern Socio-Technical Perspectives on Privacy. Cham: Springer; 2022. pp. 233-264

[19] Guhr N, Werth O, Blacha PP, Breitner MH. Privacy concerns in the smart home context. SN Applied Sciences. 2020;**2**(2):1-2

[20] Rogers EM. Diffusion of Innovations. New York: Free Press; 1983

[21] Hsu CW, Yeh CC. Understanding the factors affecting the adoption of the internet of things. Technology Analysis & Strategic Management. 2017;**29**(9):1089-1102

[22] Hsu CL, Lin JC. Exploring factors affecting the adoption of internet of things services. Journal of Computer Information Systems. 2018;**58**(1):49-57

[23] Kim Y, Park Y, Choi J. A study on the adoption of IoT smart home service: Using value-based adoption model. Total Quality Management & Business Excellence. 2017;**28**(9-10):1149-1165

[24] Zuboff S. The Age of Surveillance Capitalism: The Fight for a Human Future at the New Frontier of Power: Barack Obama's Books of 2019. New York: PublicAffairs, Profile books; 2019

[25] Helbing D, Caron H. Towards Digital Enlightenment. Cham, Switzerland: Springer International Publishing; 2019

[26] Sorwar G, Aggar C, Penman O, Seton C, Ward A. Factors that predict the acceptance and adoption of smart home technology by seniors in Australia: A structural equation model with longitudinal data. Informatics for Health and Social Care. 2022:1-5

[27] Cavallo F, Aquilano M, Arvati M. An ambient assisted living approach in designing domiciliary services combined with innovative technologies for patients with Alzheimer's disease: A case study. American Journal of Alzheimer's Disease & Other Dementias®. 2015;**30**(1):69-77

[28] Poel IV. A coherentist view on the relation between social acceptance and moral acceptability of technology. In: Philosophy of Technology After the Empirical Turn. Cham: Springer; 2016. pp. 177-193

[29] Shahrestani S. Internet of Things and Smart Environments. Cham: Springer International; 2018

[30] Taylor P, Allpress S, Carr M, Lupu E, Norton J, Smith L, et al. Internet of Things: Realising the Potential of a Trusted Smart World. London: Royal Academy of Engineering; 2018

[31] Porch.com. Swearing by Smart Homes. Analysing Trust in Smart Home Technology. 2017. Available from https://porch.com/resource/smart-home-trust

[32] TechUK. The State of the Connected Home. Edition 2 ed2018 Available from https://www.techuk.org/connected-home/our_report

[33] Van de Poel I, Verbeek PP. Ethics and engineering design. Science, Technology, & Human Values. 2006;**31**(3):223-236

[34] Misra S, Maheswaran M, Hashmi S. Vulnerable features and threats. In: Security Challenges and Approaches in Internet of Things. Cham: Springer; 2017. pp. 19-38

[35] Zeng E, Mare S, Roesner F. End user security and privacy concerns with smart homes. In: Thirteenth Symposium on Usable Privacy and Security (SOUPS 2017). USENIX Association; 2017. pp. 65-80

[36] Hove SE, Anda B. Experiences from conducting semi-structured interviews in empirical software engineering research. In: 11th IEEE International Software METRICS Symposium (METRICS'05). Como, Italy: IEEE; 2005. p. 10

[37] Braun V, Clarke V. Using thematic analysis in psychology. Qualitative Research in Psychology. 2006;**3**(2):77-101

[38] Khastgir S, Birrell SA, Dhadyalla G, Jennings PA. The science of testing: An automotive perspective. In: SAE World Congress Experience, WCX 2018, Detroit, United States; 10-12 April 2018. SAE Technical Papers; 2018. ISSN: 0148-7191. DOI: 10.4271/2018-01-1070

[39] Pliatsikas P, Economides AA. Factors influencing intention of Greek consumers to use smart home technology. Applied System Innovation. 2022;**5**(1):26

[40] Freeman C. Technology, Policy, and Economic Performance: Lessons from Japan. London: Pinter Pub Ltd; 1987

[41] Grint K, Woolgar S. The machine at work. Technology, Work and Organization. Cambridge, UK: Polity Press; 1997:65-94

[42] Pinch TJ, Bijker WE. The social construction of facts and artefacts: Or how the sociology of science and the sociology of technology might benefit each other. Social Studies of Science. 1984;**14**(3):399-441

[43] Orlikowski WJ. The duality of technology: Rethinking the concept of technology in organizations. Organization Science. 1992;**3**(3):398-427

[44] Williams R, Stewart J, Slack R. Social Learning in Technological Innovation: Experimenting with Information and Communication Technologies. Cheltenham: Edward Elgar Publishing; 2005

[45] Yousefikhah S. Sociology of innovation: Social construction of technology perspective. AD-minister. 2017;**30**:31-43

[46] Humphreys L. Reframing social groups, closure, and stabilization in the social construction of technology. Social Epistemology. 2005;**19**(2-3):231-253

[47] Elle M, Dammann S, Lentsch J, Hansen K. Learning from the social construction of environmental indicators: From the retrospective to the pro-active use of SCOT in technology development. Building and Environment. 2010;**45**(1):135-142

[48] Rowland W. Recognizing the role of the modern business corporation in the "social construction" of technology. Social Epistemology. 2005;**19**(2-3):287-313

[49] Burns TR, Machado N, Corte U. The sociology of creativity: Part I: Theory: The social mechanisms of innovation and creative developments in selectivity environments. Human Systems Management. 2015;**34**(3):179-199

[50] van Baalen PJ, van Fenema PC, Loebbecke C. Extending the social construction of technology (SCOT) framework to the digital world. In: ICIS Thirty Seventh International Conference on Information Systems. 2016

[51] Burns TR, Corte U, Machado N. The sociology of creativity: PART III: Applications–The socio-cultural contexts of the acceptance/rejection of innovations. Human Systems Management. 2016;**35**(1):11-34

[52] Wellman B, Quan-Haase A, Boase J, Chen W, Hampton K, Díaz I, et al. The social affordances of the internet for networked individualism. Journal of Computer-Mediated Communication. 2003;**8**(3):JCMC834

[53] Sharov AA. Functional information: Towards synthesis of biosemiotics and cybernetics. Entropy. 2010;**12**(5):1050-1070

[54] ISO. ISO/PC 317. Consumer protection: Privacy by Design for Consumer Goods and Services, 2018. Available from https://www.iso.org/committee/6935430.html

[55] Zeng E, Roesner F. Understanding and improving security and privacy in {multi-user} smart homes: A design exploration and {in-home} user study. In: 28th USENIX Security Symposium (USENIX Security 19). 2019. pp. 159-176

[56] Bartel AP, Lichtenberg FR. The comparative advantage of educated workers in implementing new technology. The Review of Economics and statistics. 1987;**69**:1-1

[57] Cannizzaro, S. Procter, R. Ma, S., Maple, C., Trust in the Smart Home Dataset. 2020. Available from https://figshare.com/articles/Trust_in_the_smart_home_findings_from_a_nationally_representative_survey_in_the_UK_dataset_/12068379

[58] Wilson C, Hargreaves T, Hauxwell-Baldwin R. Benefits and risks of smart home technologies. Energy Policy. 2017;(103):72-83

[59] Mayer RC, Davis JH, Schoorman FD. An integrative model of organizational trust. Academy of Management Review. 1995;**20**(3):709-734

[60] Emami Naeini P, Degeling M, Bauer L, Chow R, Cranor LF, Haghighat MR, et al. The influence of friends and experts on privacy decision making in IoT scenarios. Proceedings of the ACM on Human-Computer Interaction. 2018;**2**(CSCW):1-26

[61] Zheng S, Apthorpe N, Chetty M, Feamster N. User perceptions of smart home IoT privacy. Proceedings of the ACM on Human-Computer Interaction. 2018;**2**(CSCW):1-20

[62] Brass I, Tanczer L, Carr M, Elsden M, Blackstock J. Standardising a moving target: The development and evolution of IoT security standards. Living in the Internet of Things: Cybersecurity of the IoT—2018;**2018**:1-9. DOI: 10.1049/cp.2018.0024

[63] Gordon LA, Loeb MP, Lucyshyn W, Zhou L. Increasing cybersecurity investments in private sector firms. Journal of Cybersecurity. 2015;**1**(1):3-17

[64] Bell S. Cybersecurity is not just a 'big business' issue. Governance Directions. 2017;**69**(9):536-539

[65] Vakakis N, Nikolis O, Ioannidis D, Votis K, Tzovaras D. Cybersecurity

in SMEs: The smart-home/office use case. In: 2019 IEEE 24th International Workshop on Computer Aided Modeling and Design of Communication Links and Networks (CAMAD). IEEE; 2019. pp. 1-7

[66] Kent C, Tanner M, Kabanda S. How south African SMEs address cyber security: The case of web server logs and intrusion detection. In: 2016 IEEE International Conference on Emerging Technologies and Innovative Business Practices for the Transformation of Societies (EmergiTech). Balaclava, Mauritius: IEEE; 2016. pp. 100-105. Available from: https://ieeexplore.ieee.org/document/7737319

[67] Fairclough N. Language and Power. Edinburgh: Routledge; 2001

Chapter 5

On Defining and Deploying Health Services in Fog-Cloud Architectures

Rodrigo da Rosa Righi, Bárbara Canali Locatelli Bellini, Fernanda Fritsch, Vinicius Facco Rodrigues, Madhusudan Singh and Marcelo Pasin

Abstract

Infrastructures based on fog computing are gaining popularity as an alternative to provide low-latency communication on executing distributed services. With cloud resources, it is possible to assemble an architectub re with resources close to data providers and those with more processing capacity, achieved through internet links. In this context, this book chapter presents the first insight regarding fog-cloud architecture for the healthcare area. In particular, we address vital sign monitoring in sensor devices and provide intelligent health services that reside both in the fog and the cloud to benefit the end-users and the public government. The preliminary results show the advantages of combining fog and cloud and critical applications and highlight some points of attention to address system scalability and quality of service.

Keywords: healthcare, architecture, smart services, smart city, fog computing, cloud computing

1. Introduction

Over the last few years, the health sector has understood that the internet can be an essential support instrument in searching for a better quality of life and conditions for patient care [1]. Among other advantages associated with using the internet in the health field, the analysis, and processing of data in real-time through remote servers have been highlighted. A smart model that provides storage and processing of applications over the internet refers to the idea of cloud computing. The cloud can be described as a collection of software and hardware services that are delivered through the network to end-users. The users will have resources (both from hardware and software perspectives) with increasing capacity without requiring significant financial capital investments to acquire, maintain, and manage such resources.

Cloud computing acts as a support to enable the Internet of Things (IoT) applications. IoT environments are composed of hundreds or thousands of devices that constantly generate requests for collected data to be later analyzed. This process

 IntechOpen

naturally generates heavy requests that would be sent to a central processing server, flooding that server's network, and requiring computational power that a single computer would often not be able to supply. Here, cloud computing can be used as a processing medium for IoT scenarios to leverage its scalability and pay-as-you-go business model. However, sending requests from an IoT device to a cloud server adds network latency overhead to the communication that cannot be accepted in some cases. For example, we can cite some e-health scenarios, such as those addressing remote electrocardiogram (ECG), where data collecting and processing times are critical to the correct system functioning. We often cannot wait for a message to be sent, processed in the cloud, and returned, as the time involved in these procedures is prohibitive and can influence essential aspects such as a person's life or death. Furthermore, even with a highly scalable cloud computing environment, scaling it to serve many requests would result in additional power consumption.

To allow better scalability of IoT systems, it is necessary to design new architectures and solutions that simultaneously handle many devices and requests, maintaining the Quality of Service (QoS). Aligned with this sentence, fog computing expands the services the traditional cloud model offers to be closer to the data generators. Also, edge computing enters here to enable some processing and decision support precisely on the network's border, that is, close to the IoT device itself. Computing in fog or edge has as its main characteristics low latency, better support to collect the geographic distribution of data, and mobility over many nodes in the network. Thus, with predominantly wireless access, we have the execution of applications in real-time and more significant support for device heterogeneity. Data read by the sensors is collected, processed, and stored in a temporary database instead of delivered to the cloud, avoiding round-trip delays in network traffic.

A combination of cloud, fog, and the edge is especially pertinent to provide an architecture to answer pandemic research such as the case of COVID-19. More significantly, we are entering a period where long-COVID-19 research is mainstream, where the purpose is to continuously monitor the vital signs of those who were contaminated by the virus beforehand [2]. Most vital sign monitoring systems follow a generalized three-tier architecture composed of sensing devices, a gateway, and a cloud. By analyzing the current initiatives in the literature, they do not address all issues concomitantly as follows: (i) person's traceability, both in terms of historical view of vital signs or places visited in a smart city; (ii) artificial intelligence to execute health services proactively, generating value for end-users, in addition to hospitals and public sector; and (iii) state-of-the-art mechanisms to address QoS, elastic processing capability and an efficient and scalable message notification system.

In this context, this book chapter:

- We introduce an architecture that combines edge, fog, and cloud to address healthcare services.

- We also show how we can deploy health services over this architectural organization.

Our idea is to show details of the proposed architecture, detailing the modules and how multiple edge instances interact with fog nodes. In particular, we will offer vital signs-based services in the fog nodes and the cloud. These services can target a single person, generating personal insights and notifications, and multiple persons. In this last case, we provide health information regarding a community or district of a city [3]. Thus, we capture data from the citizens and process them in the edge and fog nodes, generating appropriate notifications. Finally, we show future directions regarding healthcare services (in particular to monitor long COVID-19 situations), which will execute in a combination of edge and fog resources depending on person priority and service priority (for example, teens and older people, and critical services like ECG or non-critical services like fever detection). We understand the new era of 5G communication will burst and favor scalable IoT data collection, bringing pertinent issues such as reliability, performance, and scalability to the assembly of the proper digital health in intelligent cities.

2. Vital signs remote monitoring

This section details some vital signs and how they are captured from the body. Vital signs monitoring is essential to observe how healthy a person is. Logically, we have lower and upper thresholds for each vital sign, that is, limits that a particular metric should operate. Also, these thresholds variate in accordance with the age of the person, their health status, if they have chronic diseases, and so on. The vital signs discussed here are relevant to give us insights sequels regarding the long COVID-19, which is especially important for patients with chronic diseases. The literature shows us that five health parameters are essential vital signs to detect the evolution of COVID- 19. **Figure 1** depicts them appropriately. They are: (i) heart rate; (ii) heart rate variability; (iii) body temperature; (iv) peripheral oxygen saturation; and (v) respiratory rate.

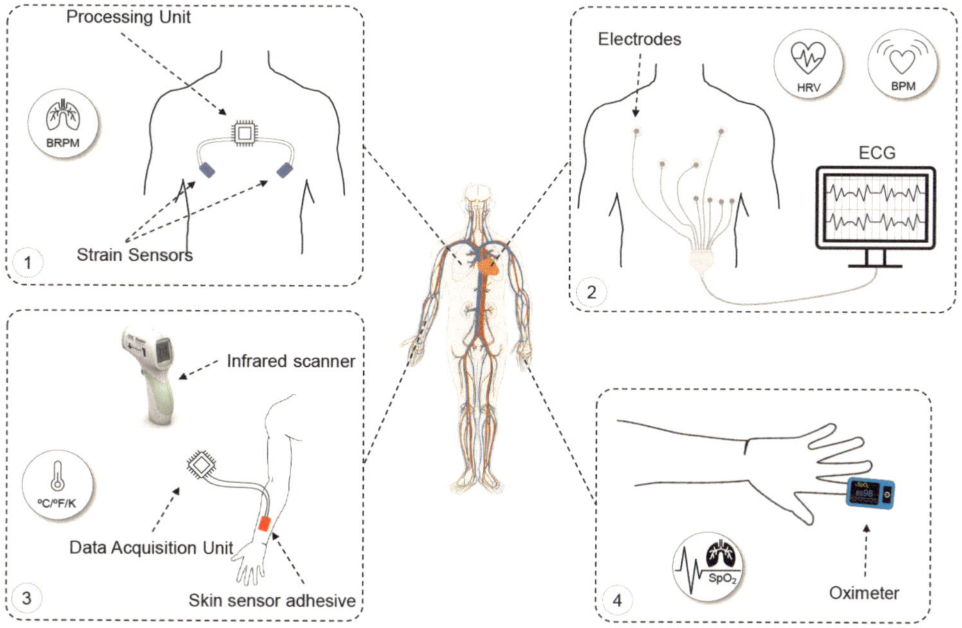

Figure 1.
Five vital signs are captured: (1) respiratory rate; (2) heart rate and heart rate variability; (3) body temperature; and (4) peripheral oxygen saturation.

2.1 Vital sign 1: respiratory rate

This vital sign analyzes the breathing rate per minute (BRPM). The literature states that an expected respiratory rate is between 12 and 20 BRPM. Regarding the idea of reducing the BRPM, there is a more significant change that a particular person has COVID-19. This occurs because COVID-19 attacks the lungs, turning challenging to breathe well and regularly. A wearable device collection can monitor BRPM through piezoresistive and inertial sensors [4]. Moreover, when analyzing the literature, we observe that most approaches require sensors in the patient's chest, abdomen, neck, or nose. We also observe the growth of new solutions that explore algorithms to derive the respiratory rate from optic sensors embedded in smartwatches and wristbands.

2.2 Vital sign 2: temperature

Body temperature is one of the most used signals to understand a person's health. The temperature is primarily used to observe that a person has an inflammation process, the starting of a disease, or particle reactions against viruses or bacteria [5]. Thus, fever is the second most common symptom of a COVID-19 infection. Usually, a body temperature over 37.3°C characterizes fever. As said, this could indicate that the body is trying to fight an illness or infection. Body temperature is captured in different ways: axillary, orally, and rectally using traditional thermometers.

Recent solutions use technologies that can measure skin temperature too. The skin temperature frequently varies to regulate and stabilize the core temperature. The use of imaging and infrared devices became common to fastly check the body temperature of individuals in a touchless manner. Other strategies apply skin carbon nanotube (CNT) printed adhesives that provide more precise temperature detection. However, CNT-based sensors require a computing unit to acquire data from them to make them available for processing.

2.3 Vital sign 3: heart rate

Heart rate measures the beats per minute (BPM) of an individual's cardiac cycle [6]. It varies throughout the day physiologically in a healthy individual, according to physical activity, consumption of caffeinated foods, and emotions, for example. However, the appropriate heart rate range for an individual at rest is from 50 to 90 BPM, which may be lower in people who practice physical activities [7]. Segundo [8] with a 1°C rise in body temperature, there is approximately the same amount as an 8.5 BPM increase in heart rate. For example, traditional methods for measuring heart rate include the electrocardiogram (ECG) and radial pulse palpation. However, such methods, in addition to depending on a professional to be measured, also have little mobility for access and difficulty monitoring daily activities. The ECG is an accurate method, but it needs to be in a specific place to perform it since the measurement through the radial pulse can be imprecise. Thus, current initiatives seek to explore different strategies of bioelectric sources to measure heart rate accurately. Smart bands often use photoplethysmography (PPG) to measure heart rate [9]. When the heart beats, capillaries expand and contract based on changes in blood volume. PPG is a non-invasive optical technique capable of measuring blood volume variations in the capillary structure [10]. Thus, continuous monitoring can predict some pathologies, such as arrhythmias, anemia, and hyperthyroidism. In the context of COVID-19, the heart is one of the organs affected by the virus. It can attack the organ of someone who already has a previous cardiac pathology or even an acute form of a healthy heart [11]. Thus, some pathologies such as myocarditis, arrhythmias, and cardiac arrest may be present in infected patients [12]. Thus, early detection of heart rate can help in the perception of a sign of severity in patients with the disease, in addition to facilitating the early detection of symptoms at home and in hospitals.

2.4 Vital sign 4: heart rate variability

Heart rate variation (HRV) is the variation between the time interval between two beats in the cardiac cycle and is one of the main ways to assess the proper functioning of the heart and the regulation of the autonomic nervous system [13], so it is a relevant measure to identify and assist in the prognosis of various pathologies. It has a large interpersonal variation, and a high value represents a more significant resistance to stress, while a low value may indicate illness, stress, depression, or anxiety, and low values may provide an early indication that the individual is suffering from infection [14]. In the context of COVID-19 infection, it is a relevant parameter to indicate how the patient's prognosis will be. Recent studies carried out with patients over 70 years old showed that those with high HRV had greater survival and low HRV showed greater survival. Intensive care unit admission rate [15]. The main way to detect HRV is through continuous monitoring in the hospital or the ward through the electrocardiogram. Hence, the lack of mobility is the main difficulty in continuous monitoring. In this way, wearable smart bands that rely on heart rate measurements, calculating the root mean square of successive differences between normal heartbeats (RMSSD), it is possible to determine and measure HRV using heart rate measurements, and thus help to monitor patients both in hospital and domestic environments, mitigating the problem of mobility [16].

2.5 Vital sign 5: oxygen saturation

Blood oxygen saturation (SpO_2) level measures the percentage of oxygen carried by hemoglobin molecules in an individual's peripheral blood. It may be decreased when an infection occurs, such as COVID-19, in which inflammatory cytokines prevent the efficient gas exchange from occurring in the respiratory membranes. Rates below 95% of oxygenated blood indicate a warning that the individual may be starting to become short of breath. Oxygen levels commonly remain at the same rate during all daily activities. Standard approaches to compute SpO_2 use PPG signals composed of red and infrared light sensors applied to the extremities of the body [17].

3. Fog-cloud architecture to monitor vital signs in smart cities

Employing several sensor devices to monitor the health parameter of people daily is crucial to track and monitor the spread of new diseases. We developed a monitoring infrastructure for intelligent cities to enhance public health topics. **Figure 2** depicts our vision of an innovative city architecture, where we focus on mobile health, vital signs collection, and artificial intelligence services. In the considered architecture, citizens use wearable devices (such as smart bands or standalone sensors) to send their vital sign parameters into the public health data center in real time. By combining fog and cloud computing, we offer a collection of health services to patients/users in a

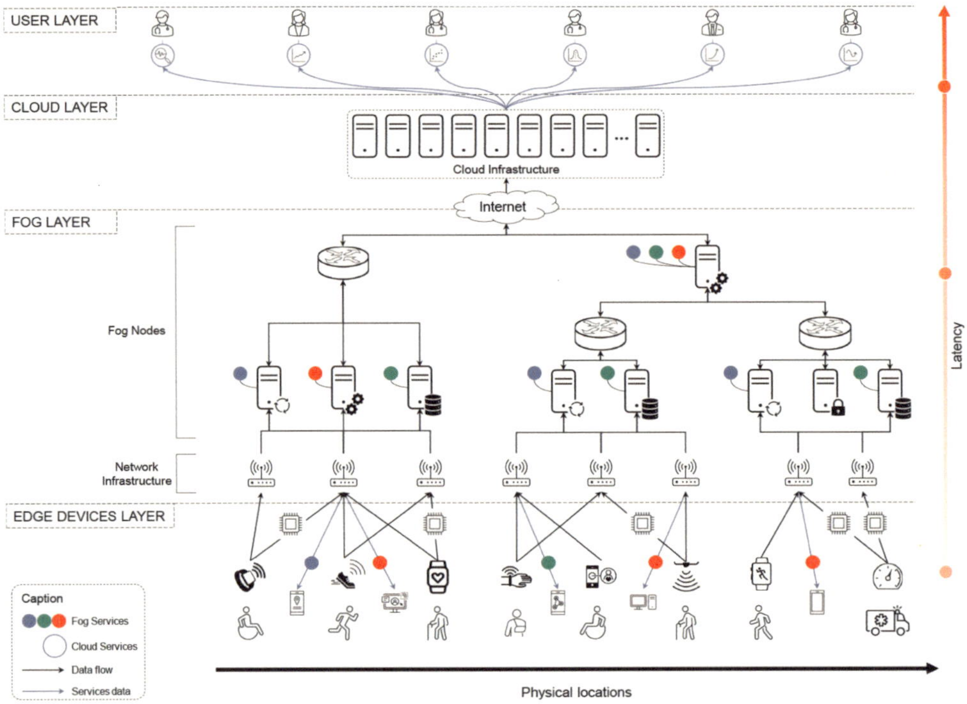

Figure 2.
Smart city architecture focuses on monitoring patients' health parameters. People wear sensors that transmit health parameters to a fog-cloud infrastructure that provides health services.

new paradigm. Here, the public health system provides intelligent services in proactive and on-demand services.

We envisage the functioning of the services by using both artificial intelligence and inferential statistics. The main idea is to enable a set of capabilities for end-users. The most used functionality is event prediction, which analyzes a collection of data in the past (where each element represents a vital sign data and a timestamp), employs a prediction engine, and presents as output a forecast of an event for the future. We can implement event prediction using logistic and linear regression, ARMA, ARIMA, random forest, or neural networks. The second type of event refers to correlations. For example, they can be implemented using confusion matrices, cosine's rule, and Pearson's coefficient. The third type of service uses data classification. Here, we have a learning process that helps build a learning model, enabling us to classify health situations. Classification is commonly deployed with Support Vector Machine and k-nearest neighbors.

Yet, pattern recognition is another type offered in the proposed architecture of health services. The main idea is to analyze raw data to perceive clusters with standard features. To implement pattern recognition, at this moment, we plan to use Neural Networks and K-means clustering. For example, a health surveillance system can forecast the health disorders of a person wearing smart bands. Thus, the system can proactively call an ambulance and schedule appropriate human resources in hospitals to support a patient. Using pattern recognition, we can identify sections of a city with a more considerable risk of a particular disease. Moreover, by blending vital signs and a geolocation system, we architecture can analyze the efficiency of lockdown policies.

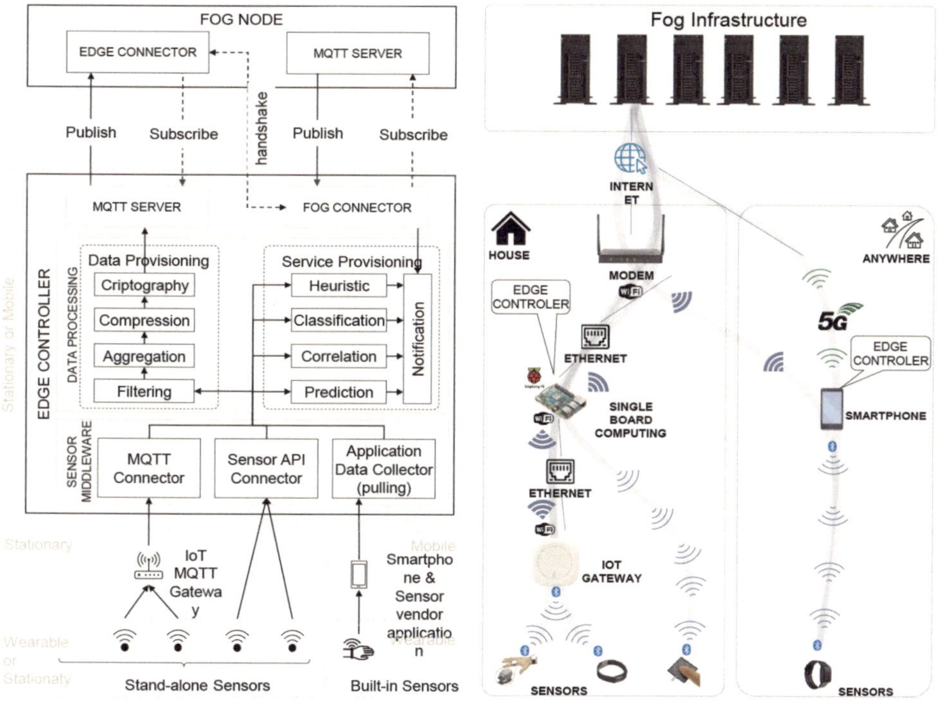

(a) Edge Controller (b) Local deployment

Figure 3.
Edge architecture and deployment proposal.

In addition, in the case of a pandemic scenario, we can generate cost-efficient procedures to reopen cities in a secure and timely way.

Our architecture can support different wearable devices, each functioning with a particular IoT protocol. In this way, we present in the Edge Controller a middleware to support device heterogeneity. It acts as a gateway, receiving different types of inputs and outputting a uniform protocol for the upper layers. We can consider a collection of factors that need to be considered when deploying health monitoring devices for remote patients. For example, some topics that should be considered are user authentication, data regulations, data privacy, API availability, data extraction mechanism, data processing system, and information transmission (including direct and indirect communication directives and intermediary brokers).

In our architecture, an Edge Controller is placed near the patient to collect, process, and transmit data to the Fog infrastructure. Also, the architecture envisages a mobile Edge Controller, enabling a user to change effortlessly from one Fog Node to another. **Figure 3a** illustrates the Edge Controller architecture and possible deployments at the patient's site. **Figure 3a** presents a collection of components and their communication to process sensor data. In addition, a viable deployment is depicted in **Figure 3b**.

4. Data processing in fog and cloud instances

To execute the health services, we plan to use two functionalities: (i) serverless computing; and (ii) vertical elasticity. In serverless computing, the user is in charge of submitting a collection of functions to the cloud using the HTTP protocol. Thus, the cloud, in its turn, is responsible for allocating an adequate number of virtual instances (containers or virtual machines) to execute the functions correctly. The name "Serverless," therefore, refers to the ability of the user does not take care of the number and configuration of resources to execute their demands. Vertical elasticity is used to reconfigure the resources with resizing. Taking as a starting point the physical resources, we can slice them into virtual parts (vCPU, vDisk, vMem, for example). The main with vertical elasticity is to adapt this virtual slice at runtime, allocating more or fewer resources by the demand. This strategy is pertinent to use the resources better, enabling us to pass resources from one health service to another (for example, from one that does not require so much processing power to another that is CPU hungry).

In addition to serverless computing and vertical elasticity, our architecture also uses data compression. Here, we employ two types of compression. First, we perform the following tasks: dynamic tune the interval for data collection for each person and each observed vital sign; adapt the changes on captured values to postpone data acquiring, so saving network latency. For example, the times to take data from an older adult could be different from a mid-age one. Also, if a person has a particular chronic disease or is passing through a health treatment, the time interval to analyze their vital signs should be reduced compared to that of healthy people. In addition to this first type of compression, we employ traditional lossless data compression. This compression is taken at the border to the Edge Controller. Considering that we are encapsulating vital sign data in JSON format, which is ASCII-based clear text, it is possible to use either LWW or Huffman Code algorithm to reduce the number of bytes transmitted through the network. These last two examples are known in the literature as being very efficient in dealing with text messages.

Privacy is another concern handled in the project. Our architecture deals with privacy by using federated learning and homomorphic cryptography concepts. With federated learning, data always stays close to the users. The user is in charge of training the ML algorithm, and only the gradients (the result of the ML model) are passed through the network. We can tune and update a global machine-learning model by collecting all user gradients. Homomorphic cryptography, in its turn, helps perform some action with a vector of data without exposing names or character data inside the vector. Homomorphic encryption can only be used over integer data by performing a particular arithmetic formula (for example, mean, maximum, and minimum, standard deviation). Thus, we can create insights into a specific district of a city. For instance, we can verify the number of people with fever, the mean temperature of a collection of people, and if they have heart disorders.

Our organization for information data flow is presented in **Figure 3b**. We can use a single board computer (such as Arduino or Raspberry Pi) to collect data from a family or people that work in a company. Also, the own smartphone can act as a gateway since it is commonly employed to collect that from smart bands. Employing an SBC or a smartphone depends on the use case. An SBC sends data to the internet via connectivity or an ISP provider and can interact with as many sensors as available at the patient's house. The smartphone has the advantage of online monitoring no matter where the patient is. At any moment, the user can receive notifications regarding their health status. The main idea here is to enable a proactive architecture, where we can alert the users about an eventual problem in the future, allowing them to seek timely treatment.

5. Proposal of health services

A health service can be understood as a computing service that inputs one or more vital signs from one or more persons. The output of a health service refers to insights regarding a particular person or a collection of persons (common health conditions of citizens of a city district or community). Thus, the heart rate sensors can detect and predict whether this rate is increasing or decreasing and whether it is falling to the point of causing heart failure [18, 19]. Under normal conditions, a person's heart rate varies between 60 and 100 bpm. Critical situations are considered when the heart rate is less than 40 bpm or greater than 150. In this case, the sensors can be used on patients in the hospital emergency room and patients with chronic cardiorespiratory diseases who want to monitor at home, using historical data from a single user over time. It is possible to trigger an alarm warning that the heart rate is decreasing so that doctors can verify the cause and possibly prevent a cardiac arrest. Not only that but an alert can be sent to the nearest emergency station, automatically triggering an ambulance to where the person is. Moreover, the same system can perform an alert network in the hospital environment, whether during observation, hospitalization, or in the ICU, generating a specific signal to the nearest infirmary, alerting that the patient is in cardiorespiratory arrest.

Besides, the sepsis prediction could be made too. It is characterized by a dysregulation of the inflammatory and their stems in response to a microbial invasion that produces body injury. During sepsis, tachypnea, tachycardia, and the high temperature usually occur. According to [20], two or more of these signs indicate sepsis temperature >38°C, heart rate >90/min, and respiratory rate >20/min. From the detection by the sensors, it can be predicted whether the patient is experiencing a worsening of his condition and getting septic. So, historical data from a single user to monitor over time can be used. This way, the hospital staff can be notified, and the patient should receive proper care.

In addition, from the measurement of individuals' vital signs, it is possible to follow the progression or regression of the chronicity of disease through the analysis of baseline reference values of the analyzed vital signs [21]. In chronic diseases such as cardiac diseases, chronic obstructive pulmonary diseases (asthma, emphysema, bronchitis), and renal diseases, all vital signs are usually monitored, as any of them can worsen and lead to decompensation of the disease. Data from the elderly would be monitored in a home for the elderly with chronic diseases or homes of an older population. This data could be saved for them or their caregivers to follow up. In this case, historical data from a single elderly user is used to monitor over time, and the underlying disease of the elderly can be followed over time.

Monitoring oxygen saturation in patients with Chronic Obstructive Pulmonary Disease (COPD) to help decrease respiratory function can be done. Patients with COPD are more likely to experience a drop in peripheral blood oxygen saturation (hypoxia) because oxygen entry into the lungs is impaired [22]. This way, neighborhoods, and cities could be monitored to predict a worsening clinical picture. Analysis of this vital sign can be sent to the hospital caring for that patient. It may indicate the need for mechanical ventilation or oxygen for the patient or additional treatment.

By measuring oxygen saturation, hypoxemia can be identified. It is characterized by a decrease in partial pressure of oxygen in the blood, leading to impaired blood perfusion and cyanosis in more critical cases [23, 24]. It can be measured through arterial oxygen saturation, characterized by the percentage of hemoglobin saturated with oxygen. Oxygen levels below 90% describe severe hypoxemia in peripheral blood

[25]. Some causes of hypoxemia are asthma, chronic obstructive pulmonary disease, idiopathic pulmonary fibrosis, pulmonary embolism, and COVID-19. Thus, measuring the arterial oxygen saturation becomes helpful in the hospital environment because once the oxygen saturation level of a patient who has entered the hospital or even who is already hospitalized is detected as low, it can be predicted whether the patient should be in an alert or critical state, and should or should not be intubated due to the need for interventions for mechanical ventilation.

Preeclampsia is a gestational disorder characterized by increased blood pressure and proteinuria during the third trimester of pregnancy. It is one of the leading causes of maternal and infant mortality. The diagnosis is based on the presence of hypertension, with measurements performed at two different times, with systolic blood pressure >140 mmHg and diastolic blood pressure at >90 mmHg, in previously normotensive patients and proteinuria at >300 mg. Thus, the measurement of blood pressure in gestational patients through a device can help diagnose the pathology in pregnant women, with measurement both in the residential and in the hospital or clinic. The device can send an alert to the hospital or pregnant patient, warning that the blood pressure is increasing. With this, the doctor who takes care of the patient can provide adequate treatment to avoid eventual problems.

6. Conclusion

We have presented an idea of a smart city organized in edge and fog nodes to manage vital signs-based healthcare services. In the future, each citizen will wear a smart band or smartwatch, which will help monitor vital signs, and input data into the architecture. With data from the whole city, public sectors can proactively address healthcare problems in particular districts or develop public strategies destinated to a particular aging interval. We are confident that the future will combine edge, fog, and cloud resources with supporting critical and non-critical services. The term critical here can be understood that services must be executed with high priority, for example, when involving older people with diseases or chronic problems or when addressing health services where the latency time is crucial, like ECG.

Acknowledgements

The authors would like to thank to: CAPES Financial Code 001), CNPq (Grant Numbers 309537/2020-7, 305263/2021-8) and FAPERGS(Grant Number 21/2551-0000118-6).

Author details

Rodrigo da Rosa Righi[1]*, Bárbara Canali Locatelli Bellini[1], Fernanda Fritsch[1], Vinicius Facco Rodrigues[1], Madhusudan Singh[2] and Marcelo Pasin[3,4]

1 Applied Computing Graduate Program, Universidade do Vale do Rio dos Sinos, São Leopoldo, RS, Brazil

2 School of Engineering, Management, Technology (EMT), Oregon Institute of Technology (Oregon Tech), Klamath Falls, Oregon, USA

3 Université de Neuchâtel, Institut d'informatique, Neuchâtel, Switzerland

4 Haute Ecole Arc - HES-SO University of Applied Sciences and Arts of Western Switzerland

*Address all correspondence to: rrrighi@unisinos.br

References

[1] Kamruzzaman MM, Alrashdi I, Alqazzaz A. New opportunities, challenges, and applications of edge-ai for connected healthcare in internet of medical things for smart cities. Journal of Healthcare Engineering. 2022:2022

[2] Raveendran AV, Jayadevan R, Sashidharan S. Long covid: An overview. Diabetes & Metabolic Syndrome: Clinical Research & Reviews. 2021;**15**(3):869-875

[3] Prokhin E. The concept of "smart city" as a main element for improving the efficiency of urban infrastructure. In: 2022 13th International Conference on E-Business, Management and Economics, ICEME 2022. New York, NY, USA: Association for Computing Machinery; 2022. pp. 617-626

[4] De Fazio R, Stabile M, De Vittorio M, Velázquez R, Visconti P. An overview of wearable piezoresistive and inertial sensors for respiration rate monitoring. Electronics. 2021;**10**(17)

[5] Chow EJ, Schwartz NG, Tobolowsky FA, Zacks RLT, Huntington-Frazier M, Reddy SC, et al. Symptom screening at illness onset of health care personnel with SARS-CoV-2 infection in King County, Washington. The Journal of the American Medical Association. 2020;**323**(20):2087-2089

[6] Qureshi F, Krishnan S. Wearable hardware design for the internet of medical things (iomt). Sensors. 2018; **18**(11):3812

[7] Nanchen D. Resting heart rate: what is normal? Heart. 2018;**104**(13):1048-1049. DOI: 10.1136/heartjnl-2017-312731. Epub 2018 Jan 30. PMID: 29382691

[8] Karjalainen J, Viitasalo M. Fever and cardiac rhythm. Archives of Internal Medicine. 1986;**146**(6):1169-1171

[9] Castaneda D, Esparza A, Ghamari M, Soltanpur C, Nazeran H. A review on wearable photoplethysmography sensors and their potential future applications in health care. International Journal of Biosensors & Bioelectronics. 2018;**4**(4): 195

[10] Sun Y, Thakor N. Photoplethysmography revisited: From contact to noncontact, from point to imaging. IEEE Transactions on Biomedical Engineering. 2015;**63**(3):463-477

[11] Shaha KB, Manandhar DN, Cho JR, Adhikari A, Man Bahadur KC. Covid-19 and the heart: What we have learnt so far. Postgraduate Medical Journal. 2021; **97**(1152):655-666

[12] Magadum A, Kishore R. Cardiovascular manifestations of covid-19 infection. Cell. 2020;**9**(11):2508

[13] Taralov ZZ, Terziyski KV, Kostianev SS. Heart rate variability as a method for assessment of the autonomic nervous system and the adaptations to different physiological and pathological conditions. Folia Medica. 2015;**57**(3/4):173

[14] Cohen S, Janicki-Deverts D, Turner RB, Doyle WJ. Does hugging provide stress-buffering social support? A study of susceptibility to upper respiratory infection and illness. Psychological Science. 2015;**26**(2):135-147

[15] Mol MBA, Strous MTA, van Osch FHM, Jeroen Vogelaar F, Barten DG, Farchi M, et al. Heart-rate-variability (hrv), predicts outcomes in covid-19. PLoS One. 2021;**16**(10):e0258841

[16] Shaffer F, Ginsberg JP. An Overview of Heart Rate Variability Metrics and Norms. Frontiers in Public Health. 2017; **5**:258. DOI: 10.3389/fpubh.2017.00258.

PMID: 29034226; PMCID: PMC5624990. Available from: https://pubmed.ncbi.nlm.nih

[17] Jagadeesh Kumar V, Ashoka K, Reddy. Pulse oximetry for the measurement of oxygen saturation in arterial blood. In: Studies in Skin Perfusion Dynamics. Singapore: Springer; 2021. pp. 51-78

[18] Wung S-F. Bradyarrhythmias: Clinical presentation, diagnosis, and management. Critical Care Nursing Clinics. 2016;**28**(3):297-308

[19] Mehrab Z, Adiga A, Marathe MV, Venkatramanan S, Swarup S. Evaluating the Utility of High-Resolution Proximity Metrics in Predicting the Spread of COVID-19. Vol. 8. No. 4. New York, NY, USA: Association for Computing Machinery; 2022. DOI: 10.1145/3531006

[20] Singer M, Deutschman CS, Seymour CW, Shankar-Hari M, Annane D, Bauer M, et al. The third international consensus definitions for sepsis and septic shock (sepsis-3). The Journal of the American Medical Association. 2016;**315**(8):801-810

[21] Lin R, Ye Z, Wang H, Budan W. Chronic diseases and health monitoring big data: A survey. IEEE Reviews in Biomedical Engineering. 2018;**11**:275-288

[22] West JB. Causes of and compensations for hypoxemia and hypercapnia. Comprehensive Physiology. 2011;**1**(3):1541-1553

[23] MacIntyre NR. Tissue hypoxia: Implications for the respiratory clinician. Respiratory Care. 2014;**59**(10): 1590-1596

[24] McMullen SM, Patrick W. Cyanosis. The American Journal of Medicine. 2013; **126**(3):210-212

[25] Bach J. A quick reference on hypoxemia. Veterinary Clinics of North America: Small Animal Practice. 2017; **47**(2):175-179. Advances in fluid, Electrolyte, and Acid-base Disorders.

Chapter 6

Mapping of Social Functions in a Smart City When Considering Sparse Knowledge

Oded Zinman and Boaz Lerner

Abstract

In recent years, technological advances, specifically new sensing and communication technologies, have brought new opportunities for a less expensive, dynamic, and more accurate mapping of social land use in cities. However, most research has featured complex methodologies that integrate several data resources or require much prior knowledge about the examined city. We offer a methodology that requires little prior knowledge and mainly relies on call detail records, which is an inexpensive available data resource of mobile phone signals. We introduce the Semi-supervised Self-labeled K-nearest neighbor (SSK) algorithm that combines distance-weighted k-nearest neighbors (DKNN) with a self-labeled iterative technique designed for training classifiers with only a small number of labeled samples. In each iteration, the samples (small land units) that we are most confident of their classification by DKNN are added to the training set of the next iteration. We perform neighbor smoothing to the land-use classification by considering feature-space neighbors as in the regular KNN but also geographical space neighbors, and thereby leverage the tendency of approximate land areas to share similar social land use. Based only on a few labeled examples, the SSK algorithm achieves a high accuracy rate, between 74% without neighbor smoothing, and 80% with it.

Keywords: call detail records, classification, computational social science, k-nearest neighbors, land use, machine learning, mobile phone data, smart cities, urban computing

1. Introduction

A city is a complex ecosystem and, as such, it is not the sum of its components; each component contributes but does not form the behavior of the whole [1]. The modern city is characterized by a sophisticated structure and zones of diverse urban social function, that is, residential neighborhoods, commercial areas, and industrial areas [2]. Functional city parts enable better orientation and support people's different needs [3, 4]. Rapid urban development has led to larger cities with more complex social dynamics, and this creates a great challenge for the accurate mapping of urban land use [5], for example, to promote social equity [6].

A smart city is a platform to facilitate technological and social innovation that enhances productivity, sustainability, and livability [7]. It opens the door for research designated for dynamic and automated identification of social function land use—understanding and classifying city lands of different social functions. Mapping of urban land use can be utilized for urban planning and designing of better urbanization strategies [8–10], urban air quality management [11], promotion of sustainable eco-cities [12, 13], and green utilization efficiency of urban land [14]. Knowledge of the function of city parts and their management can help govern a city [15] and contribute to a better understanding of mobility patterns and interconnections between city parts, which is crucial for efficient planning decisions within cities, for example, planning of highways. Moreover, it can serve businesses looking for the right spot for their business, advertisers choosing a location for enhanced advertisement, and social recommendations [3].

The digital revolution has brought a great opportunity for social sciences research in cities; the emergence of enhanced computing power and mobile phones with built-in sensors and location technologies has created an enormous amount of data for understanding and monitoring urban life [16]. Data sources, such as remote sensing imagery, social media data, taxi trajectories, and mobile phone patterns of usage, have been utilized for cheaper and enhanced social land-use identification research.

Most research in recent years has offered complex methodologies that require the integration of several data resources of different types or substantial prior knowledge about the examined city. The motivation for conducting this research is to offer a method that requires only sparse knowledge of the examined land and relies on an inexpensive data resource. Previous works have yet to achieve high accuracy in such conditions; therefore, research and creative solutions are needed to solve this problem. Although incorporating several data resources can definitely improve the identification rate, in this work, we aim to achieve solid land-use mapping with a simple and efficient methodology that requires one data resource. Our main assumption is that sparse prior knowledge about the examined city's functional zones can be obtained by a local or domain expert at a low cost. We mainly rely on call detail records (CDR), an inexpensive and available data source routinely collected by telecom operators, and assume that areas of different social functions cause different typical cellular communication behavior [17]. For example, one can expect the communication pattern in a residential neighborhood to have different characteristics than that used for industry; perhaps at night and in the early morning, there will be more communication in a residential neighborhood. We utilize this behavior to identify different area categories with different functions.

This paper presents a semi-supervised algorithm, denoted as SSK (Semi-supervised Self-labeled K-nearest neighbor), which requires only sparse prior knowledge of the examined urban area, meaning it assumes we possess only a small number of land-use labeled areas. SSK combines both the distance-weighted k-nearest neighbor (DKNN) with a self-labeled iterative technique aimed to enlarge the training set in an iterative manner. We also perform a neighbor smoothing approach that offers a unique interpretation of neighbors in the context of the KNN process. In addition to considering feature-space neighbors as in the regular KNN, we also consider the geographical space neighbors, and thus we utilize the geographical homogeneity of social functions in urban areas.

The contributions of this work are as follows:

1. We offer a simple methodology that relies solely on one data resource (CDR). Previous works dedicated to this problem used more than one data resource and complex methodologies that integrate them.

2. We offer a method designated to perform in a condition of sparse prior knowledge about the social functions of the lands in the examined city. Most works assumed substantial prior knowledge about the examined lands, while others, such as Pei et al. [18], offered a semi-supervised method that requires relatively little knowledge about the examined city; however, the accuracy rate achieved in their work is yet not satisfactory.

3. SSK offers methodological innovations as it combines self-labeling techniques aimed at the condition of sparse knowledge and a fresh perspective on KNN–a KNN that considers not only the feature-space neighbors as in regular KNN but also the geographical space neighbors.

4. The presented methodology although relying only on few labeled samples and only one data resource, achieves a high accuracy rate, between 74% without neighbor smoothing, and 80% with it.

The rest of this paper is organized as follows: Section 2 presents recent developments and research on land-use mapping, Section 3 describes the methodology and SSK land-use classification algorithm, Section 4 evaluates the efficiency of SSK and compares its performance with other algorithms that require more prior knowledge about the examined area, Section 5 presents the neighbor smoothing integrated into SSK, Section 6 evaluates the usage of neighbor smoothing in SSK and discusses its merits and drawbacks, and Section 7 summarizes the work, presents conclusions, and offers directions for further research.

2. Related works

Several techniques have been developed for identifying social land-use functions. Traditionally, land-use identification was inferred by human trajectory patterns as reflected by individual travel surveys recorded by respondents [19–21]. However, self-reported diaries suffer from major disadvantages, including a relatively small number of respondents, difficulty in obtaining a representative sample of the city population, and an experimental period that is usually limited to a few days because of high costs. Moreover, the diaries are self-reported; therefore, they are not considered to be fully reliable.

Sensing technologies, ubiquitous connectivity, and computing power have brought a variety of opportunities for smart cities, and specifically to land-use mapping [22]. Data sources, such as remote-sensing imagery, social media data, taxi trajectories, and mobile phone signals, have been utilized for cheaper and enhanced social land-use mapping research.

Some works have used spectral and textural characteristics. For example, Lu and Weng [23] integrated population density data and remote-sensing systems measuring land surface temperature and spectral reflectance to classify urban lands. Image processing and classification techniques of remote-sensing images were used in numerous research studies to capture physical aspects, such as land surface reflectivity and texture of urban space [24–26] or to accomplish urban land-use mapping [9]. However, inferring land use by analyzing remote-sensing images tells only part of the story because they cannot recognize functional interactions between city segments and social behavior [27–29].

Social media can be seen as complementary to remote-sensing image methodology, as it is valuable for identifying movement patterns and social dynamics [27, 29, 30]. A varied collection of social media data, such as social media check-ins, GPS trajectories, and points of interest (POI), has been used for monitoring urban residents' land-use dynamics [31]. Liu et al. [32] offered an unsupervised method that extracts patterns of temporal activity variations and spatial interactions between places based on taxi trajectories and discovers the common characteristics of lands of similar social function. Long and Thill [33] combined one-week period bus smart card data and household travel survey to analyze jobs–housing relationships in Beijing. Commuting trips from three typical residential communities to six main business zones were mapped and compared to analyze commuting patterns in Beijing, and then validated with those extracted from the survey. Also, Zhou et al. [34] used smart card data. They investigated how a rider allocates time in the vicinity of metro stations spatially and temporally to classify space–time activity patterns that may explain inter-personal and intra-personal behavioral variability. Shen and Karimi [35] used check-in-based data and analyzed the interaction between places in the city to infer their urban structure and related socioeconomic patterns. POIs associated with coordinates and a label such as "restaurant," "shopping center," and "theater" have been extensively leveraged for land-use identification [36]. Their biggest virtue is that they carry semantic information. Some methodologies offer to leverage POI datasets to discover regions of similar social function by classifying together lands of similar POI types' distribution and patterns [27, 37]. However, social media data's main demerit is its sparsity in space and time [29]. Social information hidden in GPS records allowed Khoroshevsky and Lerner [38] to discover mobility patterns and predict users' geographic and semantic locations alike, with no privacy violation by using only the user's own data and no semantic data voluntarily shared by him or by others. By properly selecting an evaluation metric of trajectory clustering and accounting for cluster density, they traded between prediction accuracy and information, providing more clusters that are smaller and denser, showing more meaningful locations, but less predictable, and vice versa. Using semantic mobility patterns determined from POIs in people's daily trajectories, Ben Zion and Lerner [39] could identify and predict person's lifestyle both for a novel trajectory and a novel user.

As all data sources are limited and capture specific aspects of urban dynamics, a recent movement in the research of land-use identification is to rely on several data sources of different types. Both the works of Liu et al. [31] and Hu et al. [8] combined remote-sensing images and social media data. The work of Yuan et al. [3] integrated POI datasets and datasets of 3 months of GPS trajectories generated by 12,000 taxicabs in Beijing to identify lands of different social functions using an unsupervised clustering algorithm. The work of Tu et al. [29] integrates a mobile phone signals dataset with social media data to infer the social function of land use. They estimated individuals' "home" and "work," and then aggregated the individuals together with social knowledge learned from social media check-in data into a collective social land-use map.

Numerous works leverage call detail records (CDR) for capturing spatiotemporal movement patterns and city dynamics [17, 30, 40]. CDR holds data of mobile phone signals collected and stored by telecom operators mainly for billing reasons [41]. They contain communication properties, such as start time and call duration, type of communication (call, SMS, internet), as well as the cell tower from which the communication originated. CDR also includes the location at which the communication occurred, calculated by triangulating the signal strengths from surrounding cell towers [4, 41, 42]. Its greatest virtue, as a location tool for human behavior evaluation, is that it is routinely produced by the telecom equipment when users make a phone call, send or receive a message, or browse web pages; hence, it is a low-cost and efficient location estimation source [43]. The respondents in an experiment are unaware of it, and are, thus, not interrupted by it, but still, their personal information is not violated, as the actual user identification is ciphered. CDR contains an enormous amount of data and covers the major part of civilized areas in the world, depicting a variety of users. However, CDRs have two prominent limitations as a source for tracking human activity: First, they are sparse in time because they are generated only when a user engages in cellular communication. Second, they are coarse in space because they record location only at the granularity of a cell tower [30, 44]; CDR-rendered coordinates have a varied inaccuracy of 50–350 m, depending on the density and arrangement of the towers. Another shortcoming is their lack of semantic information [30, 45].

Although incorporating several data resources is beneficial for achieving a high accuracy rate [9], in this work, we focused on achieving solid land-use identification with a simple and efficient methodology that requires only one data resource and little prior knowledge that can be obtained by domain experts. We wish to extract the most out of the information embodied in CDRs, and it can also be integrated with additional resources in future works. Several other works have already used CDRs as their main data resource for land-use identification. Toole et al. [40] utilized them for a supervised land-use classification method with a dataset consisting of CDRs for a period of three weeks in the greater Boston area. They classified urban space into five categories—residential, commercial, industrial, parks, and other, and relayed possession of ground truth land use as obtained by a zoning map. For the classification, they used Breiman's [46] random forest classification algorithm and post-processed the classification results with a neighbor smoothing algorithm. However, even with smoothing performed, in classifying the five land-use classes, the accuracy was relatively low, 54%. Pei et al. [18] also relied on CDRs and offered a semi-supervised algorithm for classifying the land of Singapore into the same five classes as Toole et al. [42]. They relied on the classification of a small number of labeled places, choosing 200 places to be labeled based on a few criteria aimed to ensure reliable labeling, and labeled them based on Singapore locals and Google Earth. They used the fuzzy c-means algorithm [47] and assumed possession of the "real" land-use labels of a small number of area segments. Their results also showed a relatively low detection rate of 58%. Zinman and Lerner [17] divided the space and time into spatiotemporal units, derived a varied collection of features to illuminate the social behavior of the units, and classified, with accuracies ranging from 84% to 91%, units in 62 days of cellular data recorded in nine cities in the Tel Aviv district according to their land use using a leveled hierarchy of semantic categories that include different levels of detail resolution.

3. SSK methodology

Our dataset consists of CDRs recorded by an Israeli telecommunications company during a 62-day period, each day between 4 a.m. and 10 p.m., in a region covering a major part of Israel's center district, including the city of Tel Aviv and its neighboring cities. The data include a diverse collection of human activity—a variety of settlements (cities and villages), open areas, highways, and industrial areas.

Our workflow (**Figure 1**) can be divided into five steps: (3.1) Area selection, (3.2) Division of smaller units of land with grid-like partitioning, (3.3) Land-use labeling, (3.4) Feature extraction, and (3.5) Usage of the SSK algorithm for land-use classification.

3.1 Area selection

We selected 61 areas with varied and known social functions, such as neighborhoods, industrial areas, office areas, highways, commercial streets, and shopping malls spread over nine cities, all located in the Tel Aviv metropolitan and its surrounding area (**Figure 2**): Tel Aviv, Holon, Ramat Gan, Petah Tikva, Rosh Haayin, Ra'anana, Ramat Hasharon, Givatayim, and Kfar Saba.

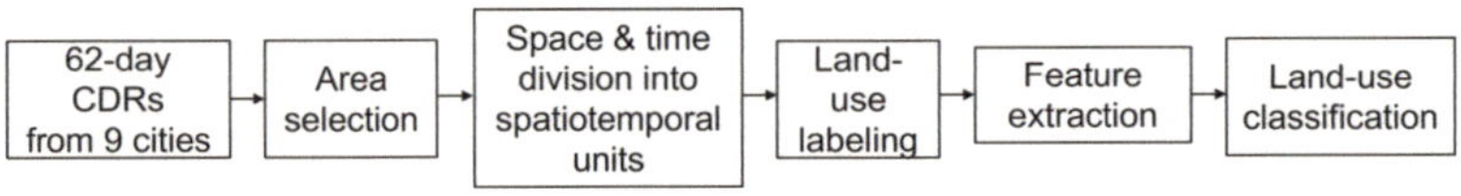

Figure 1.
Workflow of land-use classification using the SSK algorithm.

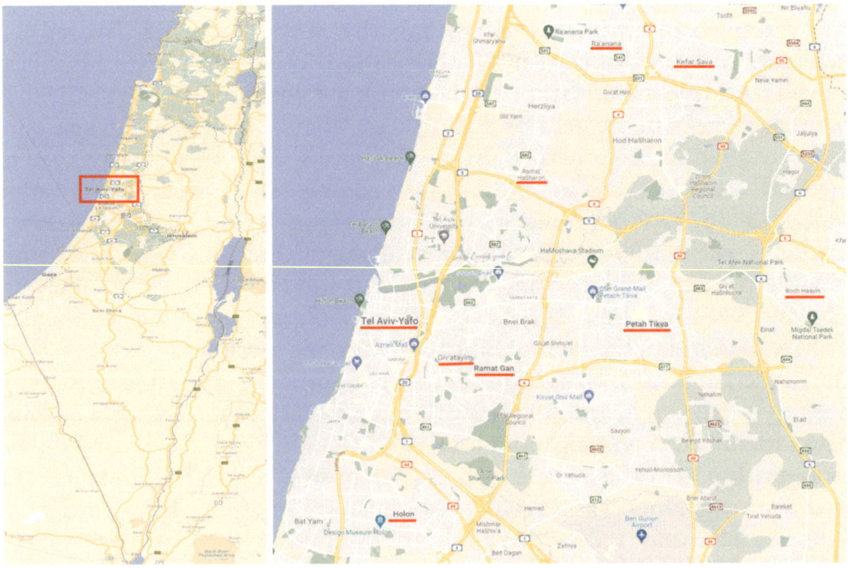

Figure 2.
(Left) A map of Israel with the area covered in the study marked by a red rectangular. (Right) A zoom-in map of this area including the Tel-Aviv metropolitan and its surrounding area with nine cities participating in the study (underlined in red): Tel Aviv, Holon, Ramat Gan, Petah Tikva, Rosh Haayin, Ra'anana, Ramat Hasharon, Givatayim, and Kfar Saba. Approximately 1 million people are living in this area.

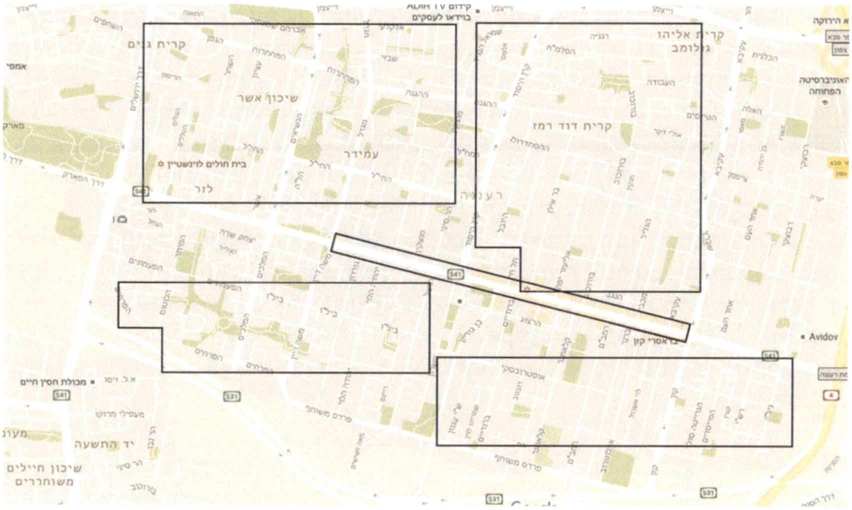

Figure 3.
Areas selected in the city of Ra'anana.

For example, see the five selected areas in the city of Ra'anana shown in **Figure 3**. Each area is represented as a polygon on the map. Four of the areas are wide; these cover residential neighborhoods. There is one narrow rectangle representing Ahuza Street, the main commercial street. It is narrow to include only the street without the surrounding area.

There is a need to discuss the choice to analyze segments of several cities that were deliberately chosen. Previous works, such as the works of Yuan et al. [3], Toole et al. [42], and Sun et al. [9], performed land-use mapping of whole cities, Beijing, Boston, and Shenzhen, respectively. However, in intentionally chosen areas, the social functions are less mixed. Classifying land of "pure" social function is easier; hence, we expect implementing this method on a whole city to yield a lower accuracy than achieved on this dataset. However, the deliberate choice of areas also has some notable advantages. Analyzing social land uses in their "pure" condition enables us to recognize the core behavior and patterns of the social functions. The areas chosen from different cities enable the examination of the inter-cities' resemblance of social function, as reflected by the use of cellular communication. Deliberately choosing areas causes the labeling process to be less expensive and time-consuming. More importantly, the granted labels are more accurate, and it enables more reliable tests and conclusions. Thus, this dataset enables a careful analysis, which is valuable for the assessment of the feasibility of the method.

3.2 Division of time and space into basic spatiotemporal units

We divided space and time into spatiotemporal units. The chosen areas were divided into smaller geographical units in a grid-like manner; we refer to each unit as a cell. Dividing the land into smaller parts reduces the variety of the social functions that take place in each; therefore, there is more homogenous land use, which is more suitable for land-use categorizing. However, using small fixed-size land parts may lose accuracy when the use of space is dynamic due to a mix of buildings of different uses in close proximity, or even different uses in the same building on different floors. We further note that others [48] found hexagonal cells advantageous over square cells, although the former are less intuitive for the urban environment, or used census blocks, where each partitioning system has its advantages and disadvantages [49]. We preliminary found the square grid suitable for our needs and selected the default size of the cell as 40,000 m^2, shaped as a 200 $\times$ 200 m^2. This is the same cell size and shape specified by Toole et al. [42] and Pei et al. [18]. However, because 30 of the 61 areas contained an edge smaller than 100 m, in these areas, we used narrower rectangles.

Land use is dynamic and varies during the day. For example, activity habits in a residential neighborhood at 7 p.m. (say, eating dinner and watching TV) are greatly different than the activity habits in the same neighborhood at 3 a.m. (say, sleeping). Therefore, in addition to dividing space, we also divided the day hourly, that is, 00:00 a.m. to 01:00 a.m. is one time unit, 01:00 a.m. to 02:00 a.m. is another time unit, and so on.

3.3 Land-use labeling

We labeled each cell per hour with a semantic social function of land use. As mentioned above, we chose to focus on areas that were relatively easy to label and, hence, we could label them with the help of a few locals. The labeled areas were then used as ground truth for training the land use classifier and evaluating its accuracy.

The semantic land-use labels include Residential, Commercial, Industrial, Highway (arterial roads), Office, Street, and No activity (no human activity is expected in this cell at this specific time, e.g., in industrial areas before work hours begin).

3.4 Feature extraction

In this work, we used 158 features that include varied aspects of the circadian nature of the activity in the cell [17]. We divided the features into five types: (1) Communication volume features measure the degree of communication activity. These features are designated to capture the difference between the activity volume typical to a specific social function (e.g., in commercial zones, there is more cellular communication compared to residential areas). (2) Daily pattern features are calculated by the calling volume in a specific hour relative to the communication volume at different hours of the day in the same zone. These features are designated to identify the circadian pattern of the communication activity typical to that area (e.g., in a residential area, the communication peak hours are in the mornings and evenings, while in industrial areas, the peak is during working hours). (3) Weekly pattern features capture the difference in cellular usage on weekdays compared to the weekend. Thus, it differentiates between land uses, such as residential, where their inhabitants return daily, and those like office zones, where workers do not go on weekends. (4) Contact features measure the number of different days on which people engage in at least one cellular communication in cell s in hour h, thus, differentiating between land uses with frequent visitors and those with occasional ones. (5) Communication habits features are a collection of features that aim to illustrate the land from the perspective of typical cellular communication usage habits, for example, call duration and usage distribution of different types of cellular communications (phone calls and internet usage). These 158 features were found very successful in land-use classification [17]. They predicted residential, industrial, and no activity land uses with F1 (see Eq. (5) below) values higher than 0.9 and provided average accuracy over seven land uses between 81% and 90% at any time of the day.

3.5 Semi-supervised self-labeled k-nearest neighbor

We developed a variation of the k-nearest neighbor algorithm combined with a self-labeled iterative technique that enlarges a labeled dataset when only a few labeled samples exist. We call this method the Semi-supervised Self-labeled K-nearest neighbor (SSK).

Gathering land-use labels of a few segments of an urban area is relatively attainable. This information can be gathered by inquiring locals. However, getting additional land-use labels is often out of reach or too expensive. In a condition of only a small number of labeled samples, the effectiveness of conservative supervised classification algorithms deteriorates. Therefore, we used the self-labeled technique designated to generate more labeled samples as an input for the classifier to tackle the lack of labeled data [50]. The self-labeled technique follows an iterative procedure—in each iteration, unlabeled data is labeled and added to the training set for the next iterations. In the first iteration, a classifier is trained based only on the labeled samples and classifies the unlabeled samples. In every iteration, the samples that the algorithm is most confident of classifying correctly are added to the labeled sample pool.

In our implementation, we used the Distance weighted variation of K-Nearest Neighbor (DKNN) as the classifier. We assumed possessing the "real" land use label of 5% of the samples. In every iteration, 5% of the samples, which the DKNN classifier is most confident of, are added to the training set. The samples used in the classification are the basic spatiotemporal unit described in Section 3.2, which we refer to as cell. We use x_i to refer to the cell i's sample.

We used DKNN, as introduced by Dudani [51]. In the classic version of KNN, assigning a class to each query sample (unlabeled sample) is determined by its k nearest neighbors in the training set, and each of the k neighbors has the same impact. In the distance-weighted version, again the k-nearest neighbors contribute to the classification of the query sample, but here, the closer the sample is to the query sample, the more impact on the classification it has. Each of the k neighbors of the query sample x_q's gets a weight $w_q^{(i)}$ that depends on how close it is to the query sample:

$$w_q^{(i)} = \frac{1}{d\left(x_q, x_i\right)^2} \quad \forall i \in 1, \dots, k, \tag{1}$$

where $d\left(x_q, x_i\right)$ is the feature-space Euclidean distance between the query sample x_q and its labeled neighbor x_i, and other distance-weighted versions may be considered as well, for example, the harmonic mean distance [52]. k determines the number of neighbors considered in the calculation. Since training the DKNN does not exist (all computation is done during prediction), the classifier training time and space complexities are $O(1)$, and the prediction time complexity is $O(knd)$ for n d-dimensional samples (and the prediction space complexity is also $O(1)$). Setting the number of neighbors k and a discussion about the considerations leading to its choice will follow below.

For example, let us assume that $k = 2$ and that x_q's two closest neighbors (labeled samples closest in the feature space to x_q) are x_a and x_b, and that their feature-space distance from x_q are 2 and 3, respectively. Then, according to Eq. (1), the weight of X_a is $\frac{1}{4}$ and that of X_b is $\frac{1}{9}$, as $x_a$is closer to x_q.

The SSK algorithm demonstrated in this section comprises the self-labeled technique and the DKNN classification algorithm. However, we have made some adjustments to make a version of DKNN that is more suitable for our problem. In regular classification, the labels used for training are assumed to be correct. However, this assumption cannot be taken when using the self-labeled technique because only the labels in the first iteration are ground truth labels, and the labels in the next iterations are samples that were not labeled but have been classified through the process. To address this issue, we would like neighbors whose label we are more confident is correct to have more impact on the classification.

Let O be the set of all cells (samples) and L be the original set of predefined ground truth labeled cells. The set of cells that are currently labeled in a certain iteration is G, and its complement set of cells that are not yet labeled Q $(Q = O \backslash G)$. In the first iteration of the algorithm, $G = L$. When describing the process, we will refer to the cell that its class is being considered as the query cell.

We would like to introduce the term land-use array, which is an object that we use to discuss the method. The number of entries in a land-use array is equal to the number of land uses. We denote the land-use array of x_i as A_i. Each array entry in A_i represents a land use, for example, entry 1 would be Residential, entry 2 Commercial, etc. The value of entry j represents the certainty that cell x_i is attributed to class j. Consider $A_i = (v_1, v_2, \dots, v_c)$. v_i is a value that represents the confidence we have that the land use of cell x_i is i. The sum of all entries in A_i is always 1. c is the number of land-use categories.

In the first iteration of the algorithm, the classification of the unlabeled cells is determined using the predefined labeled cells L, of which we assume 100% confidence. Before the first iteration, we initialize the land-use arrays of all the cells in L. Let us denote the land-use classes of the cells in L as C, meaning that the label of $x_i \in L$ is C_i. The initialization of the land-use array of cell $x_i \in L$ follows—entry number C_i (the class of x_i) in A_i is set to 1, and all the other entries are set to 0. For example, if cell x_i is labeled as Commercial, and we assume that Commercial is represented in the second entry, then its land-use array $A_i = (0, 1, 0, \dots, 0)$.

Setting the land-use arrays of the yet unlabeled cells is computed by the land-use arrays that were already calculated. Thus, the computation of the land-use array A_q for a query cell x_q is given by

$$A_q = \frac{\sum_{i=1}^{k} w_q^{(i)} A_i}{\sum_{i=1}^{k} w_q^{(i)}} \quad q \in Q, \tag{2}$$

where k is the number of neighbors configured for x_q, and $w_q^{(i)}$ is set by Eq. (1).

In the first iteration, the calculation of the land-use arrays is based only on the land-use arrays of the cells in L. At the end of the first iteration, the land-use arrays of the cells that were selected to be added to training set G of the next iteration will be set according to (2), and they will be used for the calculation of land-use arrays in the next iterations, and the process repeats itself in the next iterations.

For example, we will examine an hour with four land-use classes. For simplicity, let us assume that $k = 2$, meaning that for computing the land-use array A_q, we will consider only the two neighbors closest in the feature space. The two nearest neighbors of the query cell x_q are x_i and x_j. x_i is labeled as class 2 and x_j is labeled as class 4; therefore, their land-use arrays are $A_i = (0, 1, 0, 0)$ and $A_j = (0, 0, 0, 1)$. Their weights are $w_i = 6$ and $w_j = 2$. Notice, the weights indicate that x_i is closer to x_q than x_j. Calculating A_q:

$$A_q = \frac{w_q^{(i)} A_i + w_q^{(j)} A_j}{w_q^{(i)} + w_q^{(j)}} = \frac{6(0,1,0,0) + 2(0,0,0,1)}{6+2} = \left(0, \frac{3}{4}, 0, \frac{1}{4}\right). \quad (3)$$

A_q is calculated by the weighted average of the land-use arrays of its feature-space neighbors. For example, the value of the fourth entry in A_q ($\frac{1}{4}$), which represents the fourth land use, is the result of a weighted average of the fourth entry in A_i (equals 0) and A_j (equals 1), and it is calculated by $\frac{6\cdot 0+2\cdot 1}{6+2} = \frac{1}{4}$. The weighted average value $\frac{1}{4}$ is closer to A_i (equals 0) than to A_j (equals 1) because x_q is closer to x_i. Notice that (2) guarantees the land-use array entries always sum up to 1. In the example, the highest entry value is $\frac{3}{4}$, and its corresponding land-use class is 2; therefore, it is most reasonable to assign q to class 2. If x_q will be added to G at the end of the iteration, then A_q will be used to calculate land-use arrays in the next iterations.

However, we will classify x_q to class 2 only if it has high enough classification confidence, meaning only if we have relatively high confidence that its attribution is correct, we classify it and add it to the training set of the next iteration. The classification confidence of x_q is estimated by the entry with the maximal value in the land-use array:

$$confidence_q = max\left(A_q\right). \quad (4)$$

In the example, the classification confidence level of x_q is $\frac{3}{4}$ of it being attributed to class 2. In the example, x_q is a candidate for being classified as class 2, and it will be classified as class 2 if the confidence level $\frac{3}{4}$ is high enough.

In each iteration, we add 5% of all the cells to the training set for the next iteration. To consider a proper balance between the labels in the training set over the iterations, we do not blindly add to the training set the top 5% of the samples with the highest classification confidence. The number of cells added to the training set is proportional to the number of candidates for each land use in this iteration. For example, consider a simple case with only two land-use classes. Let us assume that the number of cells $|O| = 1000$, and therefore the number of cells added to the training set G in each iteration is 50 (5% of 1000). If in a specific iteration, 60% of the cells (600 cells) are candidates for class 1 (i.e., in 60% of the cells, the highest entry in the land-use array is 1), and the other 40% (400 cells) are candidates for class 2, then accordingly, 60% (30) of the cells added to the training set will be from class 1 and 40% (20) of the cells from class 2. The cells with the highest confidence are added to each class separately. In this example, the 30 cells with the highest values in entry 1 (represent class 1) will be labeled accordingly and added to the training set of the next iteration.

We would like to demonstrate in **Figure 4** the process of land-use classification using SSK with an example. We demonstrate classifying a query cell x_q to land use in the first iteration (**Figure 4(top)**), and then we demonstrate classifying another query cell x_s in the second iteration (**Figure 4(bottom)**). The bars in **Figure 4** represent the values of each entry in the land-use arrays. In the example, for simplicity, the neighborhood parameter $k = 2$, that is, the classification is based on the two samples that are closest to the query cell in the feature space. In this example, there are

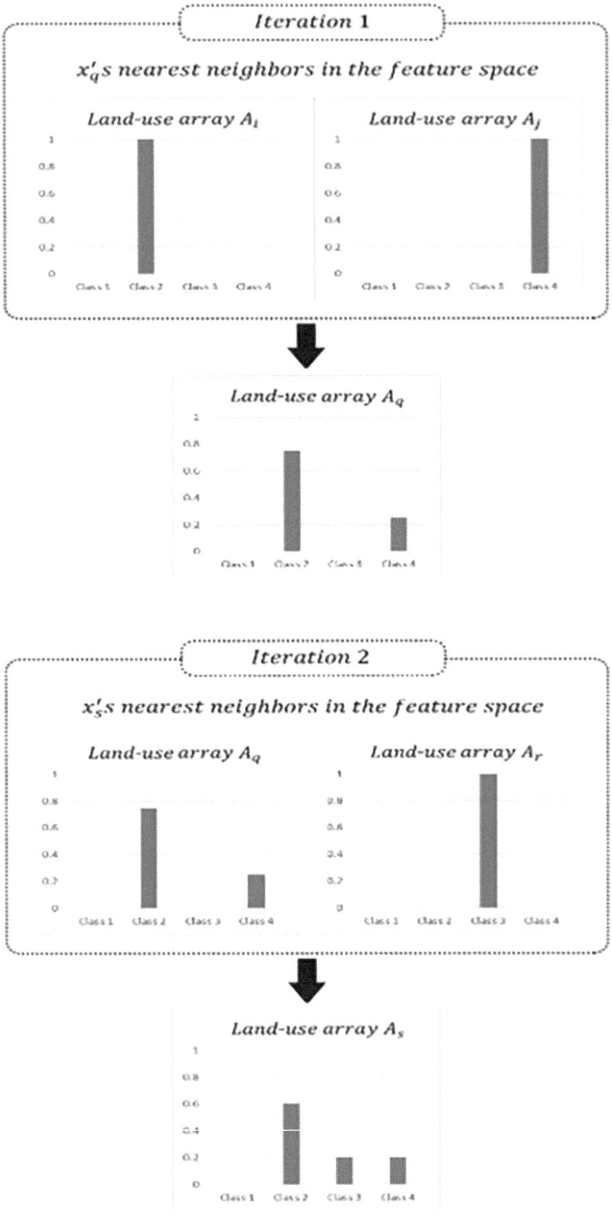

Figure 4.
Computing land-use arrays for (top) first and (bottom) second iterations of an example.

four land use classes. The computation of the land-use array of A_q in the first iteration (**Figure 4(top)**) was already demonstrated in the previous examples. We saw that after considering x_q's two nearest neighbors x_i and x_j, and based on their land-use arrays A_i and A_j, then $A_q = \left(0, \frac{3}{4}, 0, \frac{1}{4}\right)$ and $confidence_q = \frac{3}{4}$. Let us further assume that this confidence level of x_q was high enough, and thus x_q was labeled by class 2 and added to the training set for the second iteration.

In the second iteration (**Figure 4(bottom)**), there is another query cell x_s. In the example, x_s's two nearest neighbors are x_q (the cell that was added to the training set in iteration 1) and another cell x_r, and their land-use arrays are $A_q = \left(0, \frac{3}{4}, 0, \frac{1}{4}\right)$ (as already computed) and $A_r = (0, 0, 1, 0)$ and weights are $w_q = 4$ and $w_r = 1$, respectively. The land-use array of query cell A_s (Eq. (2)) is:

$$A_s = \frac{w_s^{(q)} A_q + w_s^{(r)} A_r}{w_s^{(q)} + w_s^{(r)}} = \frac{4\left(0, \frac{3}{4}, 0, \frac{1}{4}\right) + 1(0, 0, 1, 0)}{4 + 1} \left(0, \frac{3}{5}, \frac{1}{5}, \frac{1}{5}\right). \quad (5)$$

Figure 4(bottom) demonstrates that the land-use array A_s of cell x_s is mainly affected by cell x_q (belonging to class 2), which was labeled and introduced into the training set only in the previous iteration.

There is a need to specify the neighborhood parameter k that specifies the number of cells considered in the classification of each query cell. k controls the volume of the neighborhood and, consequently, the smoothness of the density estimates; thus, it plays an important role in the performance of the nearest neighbor classifier [53]. Increasing k decreases variance and increases bias; conversely, decreasing k increases variance and decreases bias [54]. Since the number of labeled cells gradually increases during the process of the self-labeled technique, we offer a dynamic k that changes through the iterations; its value depends on the size of $|G|$—the number of cells currently in the training set G. Through the iterations, k grows with the set of cells (samples) available for training. We used a rule-of-thumb offered by Duda et al. [55], setting the k value by:

$$k \approx \sqrt{|G|}. \quad (6)$$

For example, if the number of labeled cells $|G|$ in the first iteration is 50, then in the first iteration, $k = \sqrt{50} = 7.07 \approx 7$, and therefore the closest seven neighbors of each query cell will be considered in the classification. By the next iteration, 50 cells are added to G, then $|G| = 100$ and $k = \sqrt{100} = 10$, thus 10 neighbors will be considered next.

4. Empirical evaluation of SSK

In this section, we evaluate the performance of SSK classification. We compare it to the results of a classifier that possesses significantly more prior knowledge, demonstrate its performance with a few examples from different cities in Israel, analyze the process of the self-labeled technique, and discuss its overall accuracy and the accuracy in each land use separately.

We used the ground truth land-use labels for two purposes—for training the SSK classifier and for evaluating its performance. Five percent of the cells were randomly chosen at the beginning of the process, and the labels of these cells were treated as ground truth and were used for training the classifier. The performance of the classifier was estimated by the labels of the other 95% of the cells. We performed the classification in each hour separately, and in each hour, repeated the process five times, each with another randomly chosen 5% of the cells. Thus, using these permutations, we diminished the variance caused by the random aspect.

The accuracy rate of SSK averaged over all permutations and hours using labels for only 5% of the cells is 74.4%. Compared to the works of Toole et al. [42] and Pei et al. [18] who also attempted to identify land use based on CDR, our accuracy rate is exceptionally high; Toole et al. [42] and Pei et al. [18] achieved 54% and 58% accuracy rates, respectively. However, it is not possible to make conclusions based on comparing the accuracy rates of these works. The main reason is that these studies performed land-use mapping of a whole city, Boston in the work of Toole et al. [42], and Singapore in the work of Pei et al. [18], whereas we deliberately chose areas with a relatively "pure" and clear land-use function from different cities in Israel. Identification of the land use in lands of "pure" social function is an easier process.

Tables 1 and **2** illustrate the classification results in greater detail and the quality of the classification of each land-use category separately. **Table 1** demonstrates the confusion matrices of the results–predicted (columns) vs. true values (rows)–in different day parts: (a) between 4 a.m. and 7 a.m., (b) between 8 a.m. and 5 p.m., (c) between 5 p.m. and 7 p.m., and (d) between 8 p.m. and 10 p.m. Notice the set of social

	Residential	Street	Highway	No activity	
(a) 4 a.m.–7 a.m					
Residential	46.27	1.43	2.27	0.50	
Street	8.40	4.00	1.03	0.60	
Highway	3.13	0.67	1.03	0.63	
No activity	10.57	3.40	3.10	12.90	
	Residential	**Commercial**	**Industrial**	**Office**	
(b) 8 a.m.–5 p.m.					
Residential	44.71	1.33	0.29	0.12	
Commercial	9.99	10.30	1.13	0.12	
Industrial	4.99	2.27	22.42	0.28	
Office	0.66	0.14	0.62	0.62	
	Residential	**Commercial**	**Office**	**No activity**	
(c) 5 p.m.–7 p.m					
Residential	38.50	8.15	0.10	0.10	
Commercial	6.55	14.85	0.10	0.35	
Office	0.65	0.55	0.50	0.45	
No activity	4.55	6.15	1.55	17.00	
	Residential	**Street**	**Highway**	**Commercial**	**No activity**
(d) 8 p.m.–10 p.m					
Residential	41.80	2.40	2.15	0.05	0.85
Street	2.95	0.70	0.45	0.15	0.25
Highway	2.80	0.20	1.00	0.10	1.00
Commercial	2.05	0.30	1.35	7.20	1.90
No activity	5.65	0.55	2.85	0.80	20.70

Rows—true values; columns—predicted values. All values in %.

Table 1.
Confusion matrices of the classification results in four day parts: (a) 4 a.m.–7 a.m., (b) 8 a.m.–5 p.m., (c) 5 p.m.–7 p.m., and (d) 8 p.m.–10 p.m.

Land uses	Precision	Recall	F1
Residential	0.73	0.92	0.82
Commercial	0.70	0.52	0.59
Industrial	0.91	0.74	0.82
Office	0.46	0.28	0.35
Highway	0.25	0.19	0.21
Street	0.30	0.20	0.24
No activity	0.82	0.52	0.64

Table 2.
Precision, recall, and F1 of each land use.

land uses changes throughout the day. Some of the social functions, such as Commercial, occur only in specific hours (**Table 1b–d**), while other social functions, such as Highway and No activity, occur all day long, but not necessarily in the areas we chose. For example, in our dataset, there is no cell labeled as No activity between 8 a.m. and 5 p.m. While **Table 1** provides detailed accuracies for the different land uses in different time parts of the day, **Table 2** averages performance over the land uses and time parts and illustrates the precision, recall, and F1 score for the classification of each land use over all cells in the nine cities. Precision is the percentage of cells correctly classified to specific land use c, recall is the percentage of cells of the specific land use that are classified correctly, and the F1 score considers both recall and precision by calculating their harmonic average

$$F1 = 2\frac{Precision \bullet Recall}{Precision + Recall} \tag{7}$$

Thus, we use the F1 score as the best indicator for the quality of classification of certain land use.

Residential and Industrial are well identified (both have an F1 score of 0.82). Residential is the most common land use in urban areas; therefore, correct identification of it is important. In our work, 47% of the cells are Residential. All the land-use categories except Residential have higher precision than recall. It indicates that the classifier tends to classify as Residential, and all the other land uses are under-classified. Residential has a high Recall (0.92) and lower precision, while Industrial has high Precision (0.91) and lower recall. Commercial is relatively well-identified (F1 is 0.59). The commerce identification rate is damaged by the inaccuracy of location estimation more than other land uses. As mentioned in Section 2, CDR-rendered coordinate location estimation is inaccurate and can reach 350 m. Commercial streets, because of their long and narrow shape, are vulnerable to location estimation mistakes. Because they are often surrounded by a "sea" of residential neighborhoods, transmissions originating from the neighborhoods are mixed with transmissions originating from the commerce street. The result is a mixed cellular communication behavior that makes correct identification harder. Indeed, Commercial is often confused with Residential, as is shown in **Table 1b** and **c**. Later in the paper, we demonstrate an example of a Commercial street in the city of Ra'anana that is confused with its neighboring residential buildings. The same problem occurs in other narrow-shaped land uses, such as streets and highways; both have a low identification rate.

Street is also frequently confused with Residential (see **Table 1a** and **d**), rather not surprisingly because they are located in the heart of neighborhoods. No activity is relatively well-identified (F1 is 0.64).

We compared SSK performance that assumes possession of the social function of only 5% of the cells to a supervised random forest (RF) [46] classifier that assumes significantly more labeled cells. The RF classifier was trained on the same dataset and the same areas, except that it was trained with 8-fold cross-validation, thus in each fold, RF classified 1/8 of the cells based on the other 7/8 cells. Meaning, that compared to SKK, which assumed possession of 5% of the cells, RF assumed possession of 87.5% (7/8) of the cell. As expected, RF did achieve a higher accuracy rate of 84%; however, the accuracy rate of SSK (74.4%) is considerably high, considering the lack of labeled samples.

In **Figure 5**, we visualize the results on a map we refer to as a geographical confusion map. It resembles a confusion matrix, but it displays the results on a geographical map with each cell (sample) placed where it is located. **Figure 5** compares the geographical confusion maps of RF (**Figure 5a–c**) and SSK (**Figure 5d–f**) classification on the work hours between 8 a.m. and 5 p.m. in three cities: Ra'anana (RF **Figure 5a** and SSK **Figure 5d**), Ramat-Gan (RF **Figure 5b** and SSK **Figure 5e**), and Tel Aviv (RF **Figure 5c** and SSK **Figure 5f**). The legend displays the colors representing the four land-use classes in these hours. The colored circles beside each batch of cells indicate the "real" land-use label of the cell batch that lies to its side. The color of each of the cells indicates the land use it is classified to. Notice, some of the cells have more than one color. This is because the results in these maps accumulate 45 classification results, 9 hours from 8 a.m. to 5 p.m. X 5 random training–testing permutations.

Figure 6(left) focuses on part of Ramat-Gan's RF classification results (**Figure 5b**). See the cell marked "1"; it has three colors: blue, yellow, and a thin line of red. Fifty-three percent of the cell is blue, indicating it was classified as Residential in 53% of the runs (24 of the 45 runs). Also, almost half of the cell is yellow, indicating that it was frequently classified as Industrial, and it includes a thin red line that indicates it was also classified as Commercial (in 2 of the 45 runs). In contrast, the cell marked "2" is completely yellow, indicating that it was classified as Industrial in all runs.

Comparing the visualized results, one can see that SSK, which relies on a small number of labeled cells, suffers from higher classification variance than RF. In SSK, more cells are not unanimously classified to the same cell in all 45 runs, as indicated by more cells containing more than one color. For example, in **Figure 5c**, most of the cells of the commercial streets Ibn Gabirol and Dizengoff in Tel-Aviv classified by RF are uniformly red. This indicates that they were classified as Commercial in all runs.

However, the same streets classified by SSK (**Figure 5f**) are mostly red, indicating that in most runs, they are correctly classified as Commercial, but blue is also prominent, indicating that in a non-negligible number of the runs, they were classified as Residential (note, however, that in both streets, the ground floor of the buildings is stores and restaurants, that is, should be labeled Commercial, but the remaining, usually three, floors are residential, and thus should be labeled as Residential). SSK heavily relies on a random selection of the 5% cells used in the initial training set, in contrast to RF that relies on a large and consistent training set. Raanana's commerce street, Ahuza St. (**Figure 5a** and **d**), is confused with Residential. This is mostly because of the location estimation inaccuracy described earlier in this section, as the street is surrounded by neighborhoods and, hence, receives cellular transmissions of the neighboring Residential land use and is thereby confused with Residential.

DOI: http://dx.doi.org/10.5772/intechopen.104901

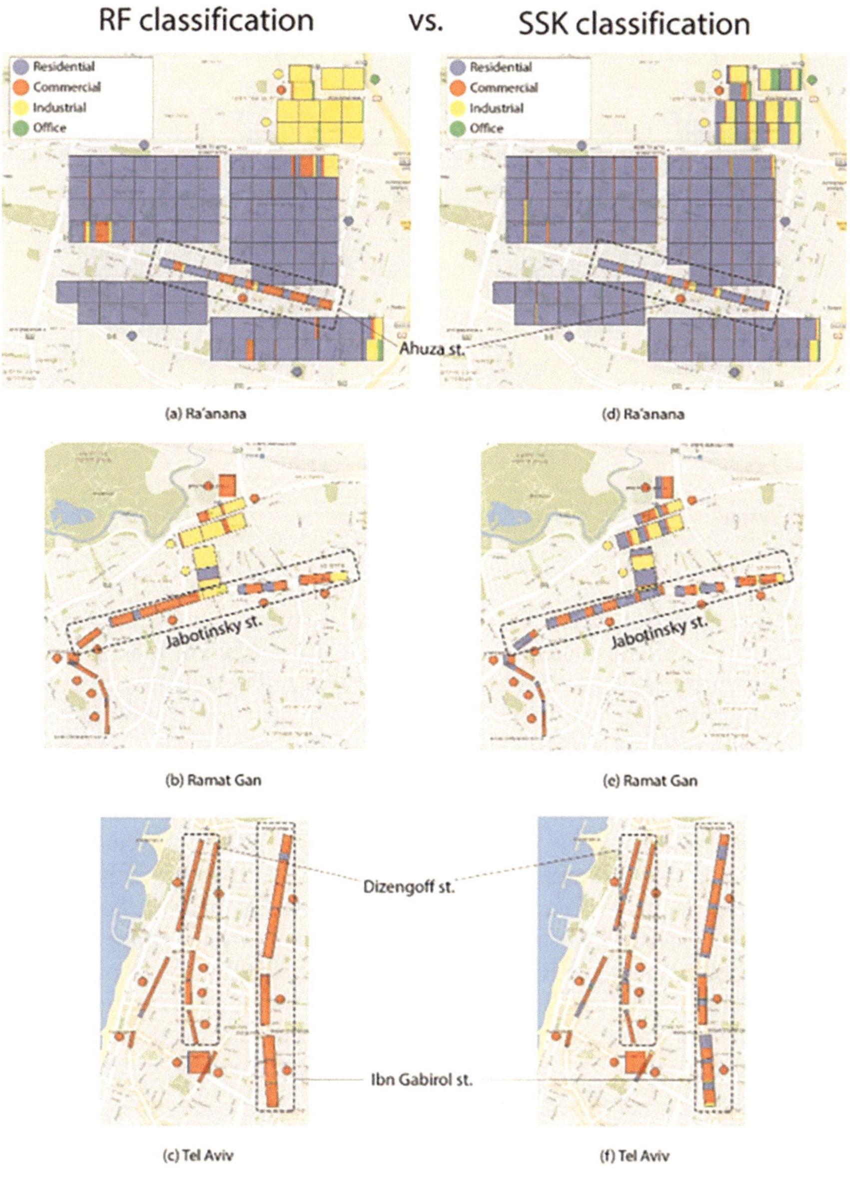

Figure 5.
Geographical confusion map comparison of RF (a)–(c) and SSK (d)–(f) for three cities shown in ***Figure** 2* *(bottom): (a) and (d) Ra'anana, (b) and (e) Ramat Gan, and (c) and (f) Tel Aviv.*

Moreover, this geographical confusion may be caused by residential buildings on the street itself that mix the social use of the land (as in the two streets in Tel Aviv).

SSK classification is more biased. As an example, we will examine the results of the commercial streets marked with a red circle beside them in Ramat-Gan (**Figure 5b** and **e**). Both algorithms classified the commercial streets inconsistently, sporadically classifying them as Commercial (correct) or as Residential (incorrect), but RF correctly classified the cells in most runs as Commercial (most cells are mostly red), whereas SSK classified some of the Commercial cells more as Residential (cells that are mostly blue).

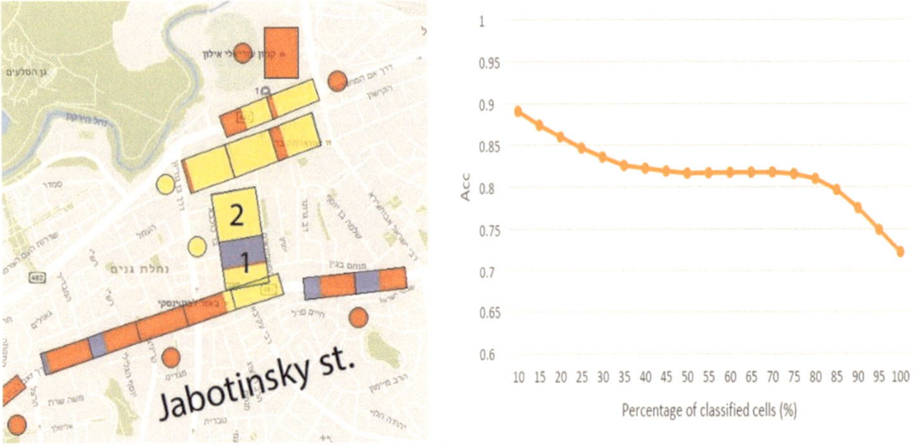

Figure 6.
*(left) "Zoom in" on part of Ramat Gan's geographical confusion map of the RF classification results (**Figure 5b**). (right) Accuracy rate (Acc) vs. the percentage of classified cells added in the self-labeled process.*

The accuracy of SSK is different across the different streets. Dizengoff St. (**Figure 5f**) for example, is correctly classified as Commercial in most runs. Another Commercial street in Tel Aviv, Ibn Gabirol St. (**Figure 5f**), is correctly classified at a lower rate than Dizengoff, while Jabotinsky St. in Ramat-Gan (**Figure 5e**) is mostly classified as Residential instead of Commercial. Analyzing the three streets indicates that they have different characteristics. Dizengoff and Ibn Gabirol have higher commercial densities than Jabotinsky, with many more shops, cafes, and bars. The automobile traffic on those streets is also different. All three have noticeable car traffic, but Ibn Gabirol is a wider road than Dizengoff, and Jabotinsky is much wider than Ibn Gabirol and serves as the main artery that connects several cities to Tel-Aviv. It may be that Jabotinsky is confused with Residential because there are more residents living there. On Jabotinsky, there are four-story residential buildings (and some 10–20-story ones as well), mainly inhabited by families. In comparison, on Dizengoff and Ibn Gabirol Streets, there are three-story buildings inhabited mostly by young single people. For all these reasons, it is not surprising that these streets are classified differently, as their social function differ.

In **Figure 6(right)**, we illustrate the accuracy rate through the self-labeled iterations. The figure demonstrates the accuracy rate (Acc) in accordance with the percentage of cells that were labeled. After the first iteration, 10% of the cells are classified (5% labeled by ground truth knowledge +5% classified in the first iteration), and the accuracy rate is high (89%). However, notice that, in this stage of the process, 90% of the cells are yet to be classified. Through the process, as more cells are classified, the accuracy rate gradually declines—from 89% after the first iteration to 72% at the end of the process when all cells are classified. There are two reasons for this. First, in each iteration, incorrect labels (due to erroneous labeling of previous iterations) are added to the training set, causing the quality of the training set to decline. Second, as the iterations go on, the samples added to the training set are those that the algorithm was the least confident of in previous iterations. Notice we could have stopped the iterations before all the cells were classified. The accuracy rate drops more rapidly in the classification of the last 20% of the cells. If we would have stopped the process when 80% of the cells were classified, then the accuracy rate would have been 81%. However, in that case, 20% of the cells would have been left unclassified, so this is left as a trade-off for the user.

5. Neighbor smoothing integrated into SSK

The lack of labeled data in our SSK semi-supervised methodology diminishes the classifier's ability. To achieve a more accurate classification, we used a smoothing process, which utilizes geographic neighbor similarity. Cells located close by in the geographic space have a greater chance of sharing the same land use because lands of unified social function are arbitrarily divided into cells and, thereby, neighboring cells tend to share similar social functions. To prevent confusion, we would like to emphasize that there are two different types of neighbors in the context of SSK—feature-space neighbors and geographic neighbors. Until this point in the paper, we have discussed feature-space neighbors. Two cells are considered feature-space neighbors if the Euclidian distance between their feature representations is relatively small. In the SSK without smoothing, only feature-space neighbors were considered. Geographic-space neighbors are cells closely located on the geographical map, and therefore, we use them for geographical smoothing.

Smoothing makes the results more homogenous in the geographical space. It causes the algorithm to be more accurate overall, but less sensitive to island land uses, relatively small lands that include a social function that is different from its surrounding areas. Because geographical space smoothing diminishes the chance of identifying these lands, we evaluated different degrees of smoothing, thus, controlling the trade-off between accuracy and sensitivity to island land uses.

The smoothing is integrated into the SSK process; in each iteration, before assigning a class, the geographic neighbors are also considered. The land-use array A_q, computed by the feature-space neighbors of x_q, is weighted with the geographical neighbors' land-use arrays (computed by their feature-space neighbors) to create an integrated array that is used for classification and confidence estimation. The rest remains the same—in every iteration, 5% of the samples are added to the training set G, with a proportion of the number of samples assigned to each class, and the process ends when all samples are labeled (or before, depending on the user/application).

To weigh between the query cell land-use array and its geographic neighbors' land-use arrays, we first need to define a neighbor. x_i is considered as x_q's geographic neighbor if the geographical distance between them is smaller than a distance denoted as $radius_q$. The distance between two cells is defined as the distance between their geographical centers. The neighbors' radius of query cell x_q is given by:

$$radius_q = 3\sqrt{(width_q/2)^2 + \left(height_q/2\right)^2}, \tag{8}$$

where $width_q$ and $height_q$ are x_q's width and height (meters).

The square root expression in Eq. (6) is the length of half of the cell's diagonal. That way, the radius is fitted to the size and shape of the cell. Half the diagonal is multiplied by 3 because, in a preliminary study, it was found to fit the problem. **Figure 7(left)** demonstrates the query cell's neighbor radius. Cell x_q is the default squared cell–$200 \times 200\ m^2$; therefore, $radius_q = 3\sqrt{(200/2)^2 + (200/2)^2} = 424.3m$. In the example

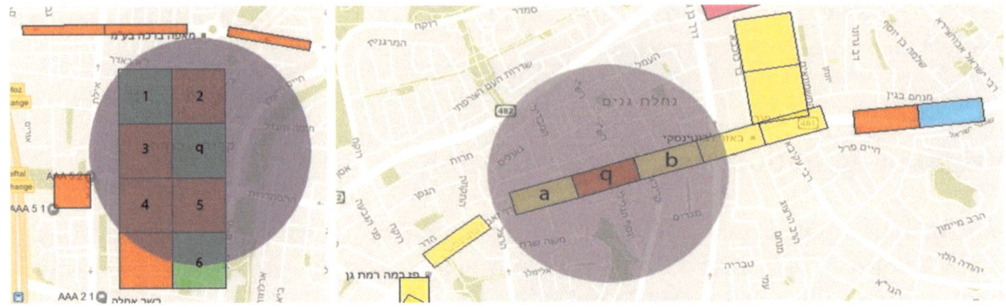

Figure 7.
(left) The neighbors' radius for the query cell q. (right) An example in which query cell x_q has two equally closed neighbors x_a and x_b.

in **Figure 7**, six cells' centers fall inside the circle formed by the neighbors' radius and, thus, those six cells, numbered 1 to 6, are considered as x_q's neighbors.

In **Figure 7(left)**, the cells within the neighbors' radius of x_q lay on different geographical distances from the center of x_q. For example, the centers of cells x_3, x_1, and x_6 are 200, 283, and 400 meters away, respectively. We want to weigh the contribution of a neighbor according to its distance from the query cell because the closer the neighbor is, the greater the chance that it shares the same land use as the query cell. The weights are given by:

$$W_q^{(i)} = \frac{1}{D(x_q, x_i)^2} \quad \forall i \in nbrs_q, \tag{9}$$

where $nbrs_q$ is the set of x_q's neighbors, and $D(x_q, x_i)$ is the geographical-based distance between query cell x_q and its neighbor x_i.

In the example demonstrated in **Figure 7(left)**, the weights of cells x_3, x_1, and x_6 are $W_q^{(3)} = 1/200^2$, $W_q^{(1)} = 1/283^2$, and $W_q^{(6)} = 1/400^2$. Notice that between these three cells, cell x_3 is the closest to cell x_q, thus its weight is the highest accordingly.

Notice, we denote distances differently in the feature space and the geographical space. Lower case d is a distance in the feature space (Eq. (1)), and upper case D is a distance in the geographical space (Eq. (7)).

We then compute an array NA_q that combines land-use array for x_q's neighbors by weighting every neighbor's distance from x_q:

$$NA_q = \frac{\sum_{i \in nbrs_q} W_q^{(i)} A_i}{\sum_{i \in nbrs_q} W_q^{(i)}}. \tag{10}$$

For demonstrating the mathematical equations used for integrating neighbor smoothing in SSK, we will use the example illustrated in **Figure 7(right)**. x_q has only two neighbors, x_a and x_b. Since x_a and x_b are located at the same distance from x_q, their weights are equal, $W_q^{(a)} = W_q^{(b)} = 1/268^2$.

Let us assume the land-use arrays are $A_a = (0, 0, 1, 0)$ and $A_b = (0, 0.8, 0, 0.2)$. Then NA_q is calculated by the weighted average of A_a and A_b:$NA_q = \frac{W_q^{(a)} A_a + W_q^{(b)} A_b}{W_q^{(a)} + W_q^{(b)}} = \frac{(1/268^2)A_a + (1/268^2)A_b}{(1/268^2) + (1/268^2)} = \frac{A_a + A_b}{2} = \frac{(0, 0, 1, 0) + (0, 0.8, 0, 0.2)}{2} = \frac{(0, 0.8, 1, 0.2)}{2} = (0, 0.4, 0.5, 0.1)$. As can be seen, the value in entry 3 (0.5) is the highest in the array, indicating that x_q's neighbors tend to be attributed to class 3, that is because x_a and its corresponding land-use array A_a are 100% attributed to class 3. However, x_q's neighbors also tend to be attributed to class 2, which is because x_b is most likely attributed to class 2.

A_q and NA_q, the query cell land-use array and its neighbor's land-use array, are integrated to IA_q by calculating their weighted average:

$$IA_q = P \bullet NA_q + (1-P) \bullet A_q, \tag{11}$$

where P is the weight of NA_q and, therefore, it is given to all of x_q's neighbors together. We denote P as the neighbor weight. For example, consider again the example in **Figure 7(right)** and assume $P = 0.3$ and $A_q = (0.1, 0.8, 0.1, 0)$. Then,

$$IA_q = 0.3 \cdot (0, 0.4, 0.5, 0.1) + 0.7 \cdot (0.1, 0.8, 0.1, 0) = (0.07, 0.68, 0.22, 0.03). \tag{12}$$

Examining A_q extracted by x_q's feature-space neighbors, it seems like x_q has the highest chance to be attributed to class 2, but examining NA_q, extracted by x_q's geographic-space neighbors, it seems most likely that it belongs to class 3. However, after incorporating both spaces, x_q is most likely attributed to class 2

The neighbor weight P depends on the number of geographic neighbors x_q has. The more neighbors it has, the more reliable their weighted array is, and we want it to have a more significant role in determining x_q's class. The formula for computing P

$$P\left(\left|nbrs_q\right|, \sigma\right) = \begin{cases} \sigma + \sigma \dfrac{\left(\left|nbrs_q\right| - 1\right)}{11} & \left|nbrs_q\right| > 0 \\ 0 & \left|nbrs_q\right| = 0 \end{cases}, \tag{13}$$

where $\left|nbrs_q\right|$ is the number of neighbors that x_q has, and σ is the smoothing parameter that determines the degree of influence that the neighbors have in the classification of the query cell. Setting a low σ, for example, will cause the neighbors of the query cells to be less significant in the classification.

In the example above, $P = 0.3$, because the number of neighbors $\left|nbrs_q\right| = 2$ (as can be seen in **Figure 7(right)**), and $\sigma = 0.275$. Therefore, $P\left(\left|nbrs_q\right|, \sigma\right) = 0.275 + 0.275\frac{(2-1)}{11} = 0.3$.

Eq. (9) is designed in a way that when x_q has only one neighbor, its neighbor weight is $P\left(\left|nbrs_q\right| = 1, \sigma\right) = \sigma$, whereas if x_q has 12 neighbors (the maximal number of neighbors because more neighbors cannot fit inside the neighbor's radius considering the shape and size of the cells), then $P\left(\left|nbrs_q\right| = 12, \sigma\right) = 2\sigma$. The value of P grows linearly between the case of only one neighbor and the case of 12 neighbors. If the query cell does not have any neighbors, then $P\left(\left|nbrs_q\right| = 0, \sigma\right) = 0$, and $IA_q = 0 \bullet NA_q + (1-0) \bullet A_q = A_q$. Because there are no neighbors to consider, NA_q will have no influence on setting IA_q, and $IA_q = A_q$.

The classification confidence is calculated as in Eq. (3), but here it is calculated over IA_q instead of A_q

$$confidence_q = max\left(IA_q\right), \tag{14}$$

where in the example, $confidence_q = max\,(0.07, 0.68, 0.22, 0.03) = 0.68$.

Again, in each iteration, the number of samples added to G from each class is proportional to the number of cells assigned to that class in this iteration. If $confidence_q$ is high enough, then x_q is classified as the class with the highest value in IA_q. The algorithm ends when all samples are added to G (or before based on the user/application).

The procedure of the SSK algorithm with neighbor smoothing:

1. Set σ (the smoothing parameter; can be set using a validation set)

2. $G \leftarrow L$ (set the training set G to be the predefined labeled samples L)

3. $Q \leftarrow O \backslash G$ (Q and O are the sets of unlabeled samples and all samples, respectively)

4. For each $x_q \in Q$ (for each yet unlabeled sample)

   a. $A_q = \frac{\sum_{i=1}^{k} w_q^{(i)} A_i}{\sum_{i=1}^{k} w_q^{(i)}}$ (land-use array) (Eq. (2))

   b. $radius_q = 3 * \sqrt{\left(\frac{width_q}{2}\right)^2 + \left(\frac{height_q}{2}\right)^2}$ (neighbor radius) (Eq. (5))

   c. $nbrs_q \leftarrow \varnothing$

   d. For each $x_i \in G$

      If $D(x_q, x_i) < radius_q$ then $nbrs_q \leftarrow (nbrs_q \cup x_i)$ (add to $nbrs_q$ the x_i neighbor)

   e. $w_q^{(i)} = \frac{1}{D(x_q, x_i)^2} \forall i \in nbrs_q$ (Eq. (7))

   f. $NA_q = \frac{\sum_{i \in nbrs_q} w_q^{(i)} A_i}{\sum_{i \in nbrs_q} w_q^{(i)}}$ (neighbors' land-use array) (Eq. (8))

   g. If $|nbrs_q| > 0$ $then P(|nbrs_q|, \sigma) = \sigma + \sigma \frac{(|nbrs_q| - 1)}{11}$

      Else $P(|nbrs_q|, \sigma) = 0$ (Eq. (10))

   h. $IA_q = P \bullet NA_q + (1 - P) \bullet A_q$ (integrated land-use array) (Eq. (9))

   i. $confidence_q = max(IA_q)$ (Eq. (11))

5. For each land-use class c

   a. $Z \leftarrow$ *sub areas with the highest confidence assigned to c*

   b. $G \leftarrow G \cup Z$; $Q \leftarrow Q \backslash Z$ (the cells assigned to class c with the highest confidence are added to G and subtracted from Q)

6. If $|Q| > 0$, then go to step 4, else output G

5.1 Example

Figure 8 illustrates an example of the classification of a query cell x_s after considering both spaces: x_s's neighbors in the feature space, under the title "Feature space" (**Figure 8(left)**), and x_s's neighbors in the geographical space, under the title "Geographical space" (**Figure 8(right)**).

In this example, the class assignment is based on the two samples that are closest in the feature space, and there are four land-use classes. x_s's two nearest neighbors in the feature space are x_r and x_q, and their land-use arrays are $A_r = (0, 0, 1, 0)$ and $A_q = \left(0, \frac{3}{4}, 0, \frac{1}{4}\right)$ with computed weights $w_s^{(r)} = 1$ and $w_s^{(q)} = 4$, respectively. Notice that $w_s^{(r)}$ and $w_s^{(q)}$ are set, respectively, according to the x_r and $x_q$feature space distances from the query cell x_s. In **Figure 8(left)**, under the title "Feature space," the two bar graphs represent the land-use arrays of x_r and x_q, which are A_r and A_q, respectively. For example, because A_r has 100% confidence of being attributed to class 3, the value

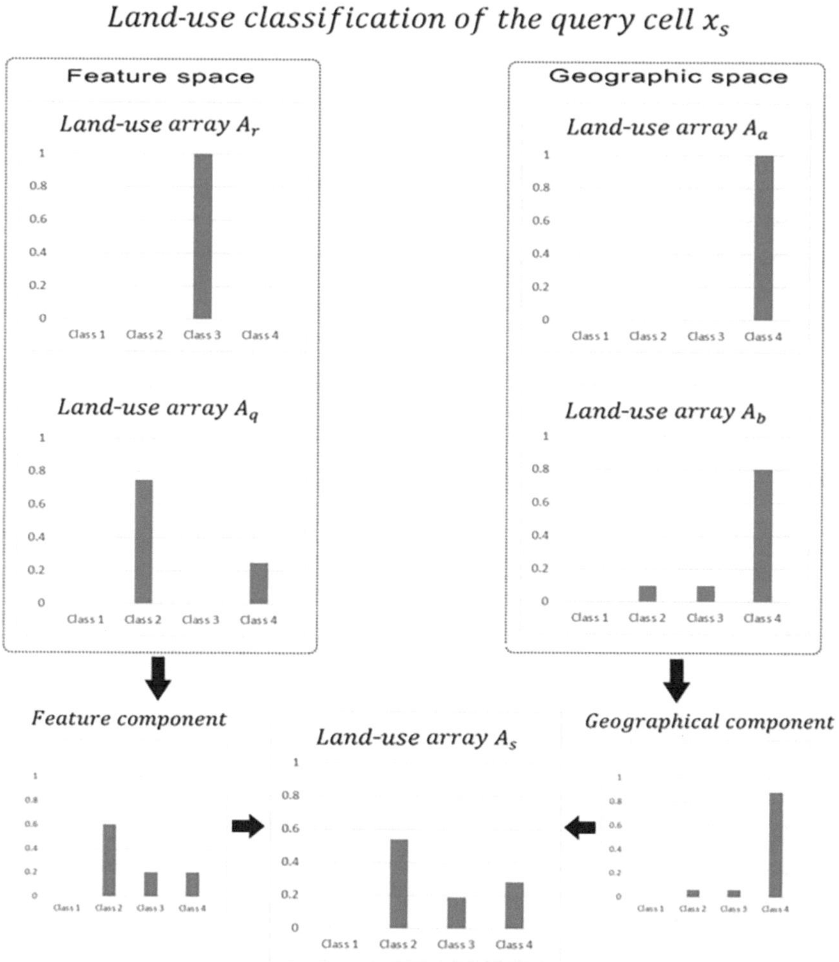

Figure 8.
Land-use classification of a query cell based on (left) only the feature space, (right) only the geographical space, and (bottom) both using neighbor smoothing.

of the bar of class 3 is 1, and the values of the other bars are 0. $x_s's$ land-use array is computed as a weighted average of A_r and A_q (Eq. (2)): $A_s = \frac{w_s^{(r)} A_r + w_s^{(q)} A_q}{w_s^{(r)} + w_s^{(q)}} =$ $(0, 0.6, 0.2, 0.2)$, as is demonstrated in **Figure 8(left)**, and it is the result of the weighted average of A_r and A_q. Without neighbor smoothing, assigning a class to x_s would have been decided at this point, and x_s would have been assigned to the class which is the highest in A_s, that is, class 2.

But here, we integrate the neighbors' land use in the classification decision. Let us assume x_s has two geographical neighbors x_a and x_b, and their land-use arrays are $A_a = (0, 0, 0, 1)$ and $A_b = (0, 0.1, 0.1, 0.8)$, and their weights are $W_s^{(a)} = 2$ and $W_s^{(b)} = 3$, respectively. Notice that $W_s^{(a)}$ and $W_s^{(b)}$ are set according to the Euclidean geographic distance of x_a and x_b from the query cell x_s. In **Figure 8(right)**, under the title "Geographic space," the two bar graphs represent the land-use arrays of x_a and x_b. x_s's neighbors' land-use array is computed by a weighted average of A_a and A_b (Eq. (7)): $NA_s = \frac{W_s^{(a)} A_a + W_s^{(b)} A_b}{W_s^{(a)} + W_s^{(b)}} = (0, 0.06, 0.06, 0.88)$. NA_s is demonstrated in **Figure 8 (right)** under the title "Geographical component." The maximal value of 0.88, based on the influential geographic neighbors of $x_s's$, challenge the cell's previous assignment of class 2 to that of class 4.

The final decision about assigning a class to x_s is after combining the feature component A_s and the geographic component NA_s. Let us set the smoothing parameter σ at 0.1, and thus the weight of the neighbors' component is (Eq. (9)): $(|nbrs_q| = 2, \sigma = 0.1) = 0.11.x_s$'s integrated land-use array (Eq. (8)) is $IA_s = 0.11 \bullet NA_s + (1 - 0.11) \bullet A_s = (0, 0.54, 0.18, 0.28)$, as is demonstrated in **Figure 8(bottom)** under the title "Land-use array x_s." If we consider IA_s's 0.54 confidence high enough, then x_s would be classified as class 2 and added to the training set G for the next iteration.

6. Empirical evaluation of neighbor smoothing integrated into SSK

In this section, we evaluate the effect of the neighbor smoothing integrated into SSK. **Figure 9** compares the SSK accuracy with different neighbor smoothing values σ, varying from 0 (no smoothing performed) to 0.25. As σ is higher, the accuracy rate is higher, varying from 74% when no smoothing is performed to 80% when σ is 0.25.

Recall that the accuracy rate of RF is 84%. Although not reaching RF's accuracy rate, the smoothing enables SSK accuracy to be significantly close to that of RF even though the latter is a supervised paradigm that uses a much bigger training set (87.5% of the cells are labeled and used as ground truth for training the RF in each of the eight cross-validation folds, comparing to only 5% of the cells that are used by the SSK). However, the effectivity of the smoothing process is overestimated because the neighbor similarity property that the neighbor smoothing relies on is exaggerated in our dataset. In the process of selecting the areas, we chose ones that are homogenous in land use, and their "real" land-use label is relatively easy for locals to determine. This means that most areas include only one land use in a specific hour. Homogenous areas have some advantages—they are practical for labeling, and they can serve to assess the process feasibility, but they are less representative of normal urban behavior. Thus, the areas we selected are overly homogenous. Therefore, the chance of neighboring cells sharing the same land use is higher than in normal urban behavior.

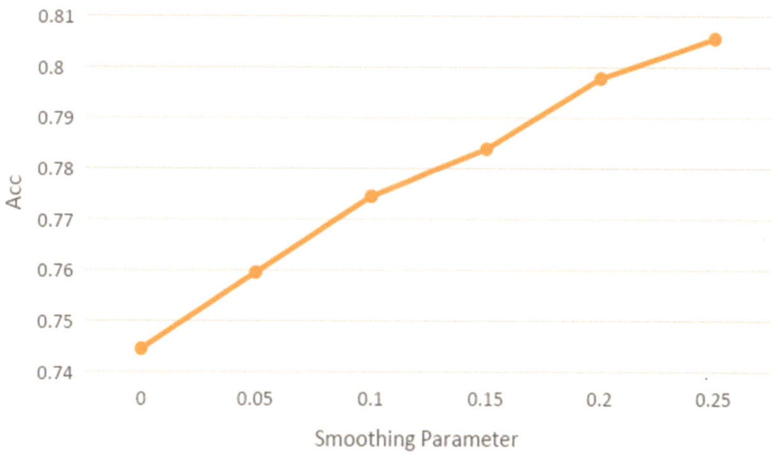

Figure 9.
Effect of smoothing parameter σ on the accuracy rate (Acc).

Island land uses located in the heart of other land uses, to which the neighbor smoothed SSK is less sensitive, occur less frequently in our data. We do expect this process to also perform well in a less homogenous dataset, however, in a more limited manner. We expect the algorithm to perform better when setting a higher smoothing parameter value, up to a point where the results become too homogenous, causing too many errors in identifying island land uses.

Figure 10 compares the geographical confusion maps of SSK classification without (**Figure 10a** and **b**) and with (**Figure 10c** and **d**) neighbor smoothing with $\sigma = 0.25$ on the work hours 8 a.m. to 5 p.m. in Ra'anana (**Figure 10a** and **c**) and Kiryat Arye, an industrial area of Petch Tikva (**Figure 10b** and **d**). Recall that the colors in each cell demonstrate accumulation of the classification results of the different hours and various random cells chosen to be used for the initial set of labeled cells.

The smoothing causes the classification assignment to be more consistent and less influenced by the randomness effect caused by randomly chosen cells with predefined land use. Considering more factors in the cell class assignment, that is, considering the cell's neighbors, diminishes the effect of randomness and lowers the classification variance. For example, see the classification of the industrial cells in Kiryat Arye. This is an area of homogenous social function, and the smoothing makes classification there more consistent. The cells are more uniformly colored in the same color (yellow) indicating that they were classified to the same class in more of the iterations. The smoothing also lowers SSK's bias. Because of the smoothing, all cells in Kiryat Arye are correctly classified as Industrial in most of the algorithm iterations. Without smoothing, 35 out of the 42 cells are well classified in most of the runs, while with smoothing, all 42 cells are well classified in most of them. For example, the bottom-right cell in Kiryat-Arye without smoothing (**Figure 10b**) is incorrectly classified in most runs (note the small yellow area indicating "Industrial" compared to the other colors), whereas with smoothing (**Figure 10d**), this cell is mostly correctly classified as "Industrial."

On the downside, neighbor smoothing diminishes the ability to identify "island" land uses. For example, see the commercial island street in Ra'anana located in the heart of several neighborhoods. Notice that even before smoothing (**Figure 10a**), SSK mostly classified it as Residential, as it is affected by nearby residential cells (as described above). Because the triangulating signal strength location estimation

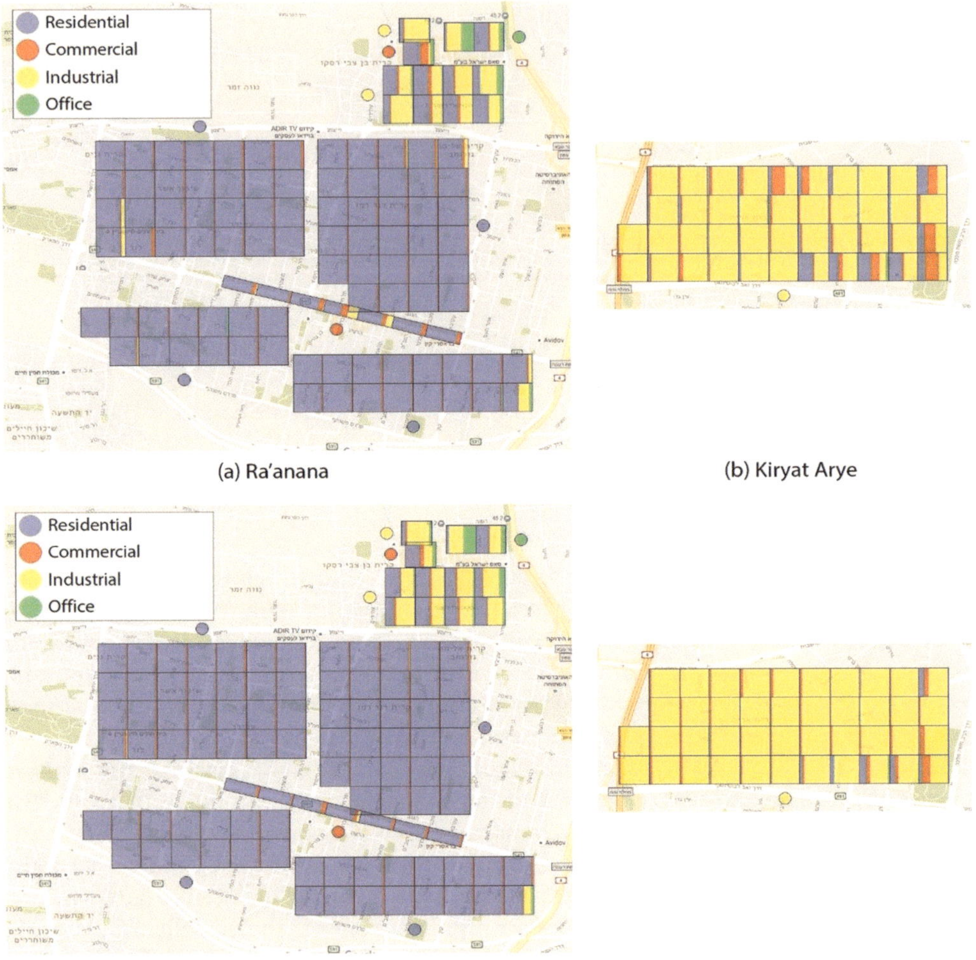

(a) Ra'anana (b) Kiryat Arye

(c) Ra'anana (d) Kiryat Arye

Figure 10.
Geographical confusion maps of SSK without (a, b) and with (c, d) smoothing ($\sigma = 0.25$).

technology used for the location estimation in this work suffers from inaccuracy, the extent of the problem is not negligible. Especially, small and narrow ("island") streets that are surrounded by a "sea" of residential neighborhoods are affected by this inaccuracy. Smoothing complicates the task of identifying island land use, as it makes the results more homogenous, and thus, the classifier is more decisive and mistakenly classifies more to Residential (in the case of Ra'anana; **Figure 10c**).

Smoothing influence depends on the geographical structure of the land use. We will distinguish between geographically wide-stretching land uses, such as Residential, and island land uses, which are usually located in the heart of a wide-stretching land use, such as commercial streets or shopping malls, or located at the borders between them, such as highways.

Neighbor smoothing causes the wide-stretching land uses to expand over island land uses and, consequently, more lands are classified as wide-stretching. Therefore, wide-stretching land uses recall increases—more cells are classified as wide-stretching with more cells identified correctly, but precision declines because some of the "new"

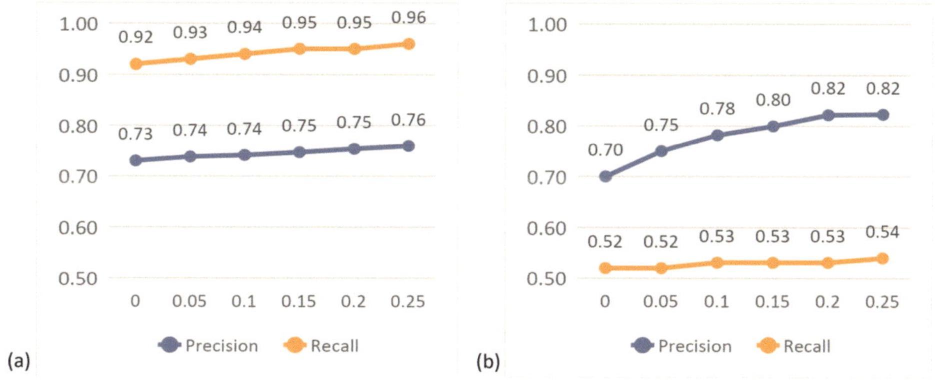

Figure 11.
Smoothing effect (σ) on the precision and recall performance measures in classifying (a) wide-stretching residential land uses and (b) narrow commercial island land uses.

wide-stretching cells belong to the neighboring island land use; thus, the percentage of correctly classified cells declines. The recall of island land uses decreases because fewer islands are identified, whereas precision increases because.

the cells classified as islands are those that are the most unambiguously correctly classified.

However, because our dataset is homogenous, both precision and recall improve in all land uses. **Figure 11** demonstrates the effect of the smoothing parameter on recall and precision of wide-stretching Residential (**Figure 11a**) and Commercial island land (**Figure 11b**) uses.

In the wide-stretching Residential example, recall ascends from 0.92 to 0.96; thus, 50% of the unidentified Residential cells are identified due to the smoothing. Whereas in the Commercial island land use, recall ascent is less prominent, from 0.52 to 0.54; thus, a 4% rise of the unidentified Commercial cells is identified due to the smoothing. As we would expect, the recall improvement in the wide-stretching land uses is considerably more significant. In the wide-stretching Residential cell, precision ascends from 0.73 to 0.76; thus, the percentage of cells incorrectly assigned as Residential is slightly reduced from 27–24%. Whereas in the Commercial island land use, precision rises significantly from 0.70 to 0.82; thus, the percentage of cells incorrectly assigned as Commercial is reduced from 30–18%. As we would expect, the precision improvement in the island land uses is considerably more significant.

7. Discussion and conclusions

Previous works dedicated to social land-use mapping mostly used more than one data resource and complex methodologies that integrate them. Other works assumed substantial prior knowledge about the examined lands but when used relatively little knowledge about the examined city achieved not satisfactory accuracy rates [18]. The main contribution of this paper is that it offers a method for social land-use mapping when only sparse prior knowledge about the examined city exists, and by relying on the CDR, an inexpensive and available data resource is routinely gathered by telecom operators.

We introduced SSK, a semi-supervised algorithm that requires a relatively small number of labeled samples and, therefore, fits the condition of sparse prior knowledge. The heart of SSK is the combination of the KNN classifier and the self-labeled technique that enables the enlargement of the training set in an iterative manner. SSK achieves an accuracy rate of 74.4%, a significantly higher rate than that achieved in the works of Toole et al. [42] and Pei et al. [18] of 54% and 58%, respectively. These works also relied mainly on CDR as their main data resource. However, it is not possible to infer that SSK performs better than their methodologies because our validation was on a very different dataset. Whereas they performed land-use mapping of a whole city, Boston in the work of Toole et al. [42], and Singapore in the work of Pei et al. [18], we chose areas of relatively homogenous social function from different cities in Israel. The task of classification in deliberately chosen areas of more "pure" social function is easier. We also compared the SSK's performance to that of a random forest (RF) classifier trained using many more labeled places, with 87.5% of the surface labeled (7/8 of the data set is used for training) compared to 5% in SSK. As expected, RF lowered the bias and variance of the classification and achieved a higher accuracy rate than SSK, but relative to the prior knowledge used in SSK, the performance gaps are mild. In a condition of only a small number of labeled samples, the effectiveness of conservative supervised classification algorithms, such as RF, deteriorates. Therefore, if getting additional land-use labels is out of reach or too expensive, it is better to use SSK.

SSK heavily relies on few labeled cells. If the land use in these cells is relatively mixed, then it has the potential to heavily damage the classification. Therefore, if cells of relatively "pure" social function cannot be obtained, then it is better to consider using an unsupervised method. The good thing is that, in most cases, the ground truth labeled cells are easier to be categorized to one land use (that is the reason they are chosen to be labeled); thus, they are relatively not mixed. Through the iterative steps, coverage of classified lands grows, but accuracy declines. We offer the option to stop the process before all land use is classified. For example, stopping the process at 80% of classified areas raises the accuracy rate to 81%, instead of 74.4%, if all areas are classified.

We also introduced a version of SSK that includes neighbor smoothing. We rely on the neighbor social land-use similarity property and offer a unique interpretation of KNN—a KNN that considers both the feature-space neighbors as in the regular KNN and the geographic space neighbors. We discussed the merits of incorporating smoothing, along with its drawbacks. Smoothing improves the overall accuracy; however, it degrades the chances to discover narrow land of a social function that is different than its surroundings. Therefore, the algorithm enables a parameter that sets the level of smoothing performed and, thus, controls the trade-off between overall accuracy and sensitivity to an exceptional social function. High levels of neighbor smoothing should be most effective in cities that are more "planned"; these cities tend to be more divided into functional parts of homogenous social function. Validating neighbors' smoothing shows that it indeed improves SSK's accuracy rate to 80% with the most smoothed results. In our dataset, it also improves the discovery rate of island land uses. This is mainly due to the homogeneity of the social function of the areas we chose to include in this work.

SSK is assembled of several components, each aiming to tackle some of the difficulties in the problem of mapping social functions (e.g., lack of labeled samples). In addition, SSK leverages opportunities inherent in the problem:

1. Self-labeled technique – While it might be costly to attain sufficient labeled samples needed for a classic classifier, it is relatively easy to attain labels of few

locations in a city. Residents can participate in the process of self-labeling of their city and thereby contribute to the efforts to make their own city smarter.

2. Neighbor smoothing – Usage of only CDR as a data resource requires creative solutions for improving the accuracy of the identification. One property that can be utilized is the resemblance in terms of the social function of neighboring parts of the city. Neighbor smoothing incorporates the geographic neighbors in the classification, and, in our case, it proved to improve the average accuracy rate from 74% to 80%. By integrating a smoothing parameter, we limited the effect of neighbor smoothing to prevent overly homogenous classification that is not sensitive to an exceptional social function.

3. Usage of KNN classifier—KNN fits perfectly for integrating the two spaces—feature space and geographic space and thus incorporates neighbor smoothing.

4. Usage of the distance weighted version of KNN-DKNN, which gives in the classification higher weight to closer neighbors, is mainly implemented for integrating the geographic space. Obviously, adjacent lands tend to share a similar social function, while lands that are relatively close but not adjacent have a lower probability to share the same social function. Therefore, we chose to use DKNN, which would cause the classification to rely more on the closest lands. The same logic is applied to the feature space, mainly for uniformity purposes between the two spaces.

In future work, we would like to validate the offered methodology on a whole city. Because some of the social functions are not well identified, creative solutions will be needed to identify them more consistently. In addition, further research may lead to an enhanced smoothing logic that is more sensitive to island land uses. A limitation of our approach may be that cellular communication cannot always capture the differences between some land uses (e.g., when the communication is limited in less populated areas), and then more data resources will be needed. Therefore, it may also be interesting to examine combining this methodology with other data resources, such as POI and remote-sensing imagery.

Acknowledgements

This work was supported by the Israel Ministry of Science and Technology.

Author details

Oded Zinman and Boaz Lerner*
Industrial Engineering and Management, Ben-Gurion University of the Negev, Israel

*Address all correspondence to: boaz@bgu.ac.il

References

[1] Alberti M, Marzluff JM, Shulenberger E, Bradley G, Ryan C, Zumbrunnen C. Integrating humans into ecology: Opportunities and challenges for studying urban ecosystems. AIBS Bulletin. 2003;**53**(12):1169-1179

[2] Zhang X, Du S. A linear Dirichlet mixture model for decomposing scenes: Application to analyzing urban functional zonings. Remote Sensing of Environment. 2015;**169**:37-49

[3] Yuan J, Zheng Y, Xie X (2012) Discovering regions of different functions in a city using human mobility and POIs. Proceedings of the 18th ACM SIGKDD International Conference on Knowledge Discovery and Data Mining. ACM, Beijing, pp. 186-194.

[4] Zheng Y, Capra L, Wolfson O, Yang H. Urban computing: Concepts, methodologies, and applications. ACM Transactions on Intelligent Systems and Technology (TIST). 2014; **5**(3):38

[5] Li C, Wang J, Wang L, Hu L, Gong P. Comparison of classification algorithms and training sample sizes in urban land classification with Landsat thematic mapper imagery. Remote Sensing. 2014; **6**(2):964-983

[6] Okafor CC, Aigbavboa C, Thwala WD. A bibliometric evaluation and critical review of the smart city concept–making a case for social equity. Journal of Science and Technology Policy Management. 2022. Available from: https://doi-org.ezproxy.bgu.ac.il/10.1108/JSTPM-06-2020-0098

[7] Kim HM, Sabri S, Kent A. Smart cities as a platform for technological and social innovation in productivity, sustainability, and livability: A conceptual framework. Smart Cities for Technological and Social Innovation. 2021. pp. 9-28

[8] Hu T, Yang J, Li X, Gong P. Mapping urban land use by using Landsat images and open social data. Remote Sensing. 2016;**8**(2):151

[9] Sun B, Zhang Y, Zhou Q, Zhang X. Effectiveness of semi-supervised learning and multi-source data in detailed urban landuse mapping with a few labeled samples. Remote Sensing. 2022;**14**(3):648

[10] Pan S, Zhou W, Piramuthu S, Giannikas V, Chen C. Smart city for sustainable urban freight logistics. International Journal of Production Research. 2021;**59**(7):2079-2089

[11] Kaginalkar A, Kumar S, Gargava P, Niyogi D. Review of urban computing in air quality management as smart city service: An integrated IoT, AI, and cloud technology perspective. Urban Climate. 2021;**39**:100972

[12] Bibri SE. Eco-districts and data-driven smart eco-cities: Emerging approaches to strategic planning by design and spatial scaling and evaluation by technology. Land Use Policy. 2022;**113**:105830

[13] Bibri SE. Data-driven smart sustainable cities of the future: Urban computing and intelligence for strategic, short-term, and joined-up planning. Computational Urban Science. 2021;**1**(1): 1-29

[14] Wang A, Lin W, Liu B, Wang H, Xu H. Does smart city construction improve the green utilization efficiency of urban land? Land. 2021; **10**(6):657

[15] Laurini R. A primer of knowledge management for smart city governance. Land Use Policy. 2021:111

[16] Arribas-Bel D, Tranos E. Characterizing the spatial structure(s) of cities "on the fly": The space-time calendar. Geographical Analysis. 2018; **50**(2):162-181

[17] Zinman O, Lerner B. Utilizing digital traces of mobile phones for understanding social dynamics in urban areas. Personal and Ubiquitous Computing. 2020;**24**:535-549

[18] Pei T, Sobolevsky S, Ratti C, Shaw SL, Li T, Zhou C. A new insight into land use classification based on aggregated mobile phone data. International Journal of Geographical Information Science. 2014;**28**(9): 1988-2007

[19] Goodchild MF, Janelle DG. The city around the clock: Space-time patterns of urban ecological structure. Environment and Planning A. 1984;**16**(6):807-820

[20] Jiang S, Ferreira J, González MC. Clustering daily patterns of human activities in the city. Data Mining and Knowledge Discovery. 2012;**25**(3): 478-510

[21] Yue Y, Lan T, Yeh AG, Li QQ. Zooming into individuals to understand the collective: A review of trajectory-based travel behaviour studies. Travel Behaviour and Society. 2014;**1**(2):69-78

[22] Batty M. Big data, smart cities and city planning. Dialogues in Human Geography. 2013;**3**(3):274-279

[23] Lu D, Weng Q. Use of impervious surface in urban land-use classification. Remote Sensing of Environment. 2006; **102**(1):146-160

[24] Heiden U, Heldens W, Roessner S, Segl K, Esch T, Mueller A. Urban structure type characterization using hyperspectral remote sensing and height information. Landscape and Urban Planning. 2012;**105**(4):361-375

[25] Wen D, Huang X, Zhang L, Benediktsson JA. A novel automatic change detection method for urban high-resolution remotely sensed imagery based on multiindex scene representation. Geoscience and Remote Sensing. 2016;**54**(1):609-625

[26] Wu C, Zhang L, Zhang L. A scene change detection framework for multi-temporal very high resolution remote sensing images. Signal Processing. 2016; **124**:184-197

[27] Gao S, Janowicz K, Couclelis H. Extracting urban functional regions from points of interest and human activities on location-based social networks. Transactions in GIS. 2017; **21**(3):446-467

[28] Liu Y, Liu X, Gao S, Gong L, Kang C, Zhi Y, et al. Social sensing: A new approach to understanding our socioeconomic environments. Annals of the Association of American Geographers. 2015;**105**(3):512-530

[29] Tu W, Cao J, Yue Y, Shaw SL, Zhou M, Wang Z, et al. Coupling mobile phone and social media data: A new approach to understanding urban functions and diurnal patterns. International Journal of Geographical Information Science. 2017;**31**(12): 2331-2358

[30] Toch E, Lerner B, Ben-Zion E, Ben-Gal I. Analyzing large-scale human mobility data: A survey of machine learning methods and applications. Knowledge and Information System. 2019;**58**:501-523

[31] Liu X, He J, Yao Y, Zhang J, Liang H, Wang H, et al. Classifying urban land use by integrating remote sensing and social media data. International Journal of Geographical Information Science. 2017; **31**(8):1675-1696

[32] Liu X, Kang C, Gong L, Liu Y. Incorporating spatial interaction patterns in classifying and understanding urban land use. International Journal of Geographical Information Science. 2016;**30**(2): 334-350

[33] Long Y, Thill J-C. Combining smart card data and household travel survey to analyze jobs–housing relationships in Be ijing. Computers, Environment and Urban Systems. 2015;**53**:19-35

[34] Zhou Y, Thill J-C, Xu Y, Fang Z. Variability in individual home-work activity patterns. Journal of Transport Geography. 2021;**90**

[35] Shen Y, Karimi K. Urban function connectivity: Characterisation of functional urban streets with social media check-in data. Cities. 2016; **55**:9-21

[36] Ye M, Yin P, Lee WC, Lee DL. Exploiting geographical influence for collaborative point-of-interest recommendation. In: Proceedings of the 34th International ACM SIGIR Conference on Research and Development in Information Retrieval. Beijing. 2011. pp. 325-334.

[37] Sheng C, Zheng Y, Hsu W, Lee ML, Xie X. Answering top-k similar region queries. In: International Conference on Database Systems for Advanced Applications. Berlin, Heidelberg: Springer; 2010. pp. 186-201

[38] Khoroshevsky F, Lerner B. Human mobility-pattern discovery and next-place prediction from GPS data. In: Schwenker F, Scherer S, editors. Multimodal Pattern Recognition of Social Signals in Human-Computer-Interaction (MPRSS). Berlin: Springer; 2017

[39] Ben Zion E, Lerner B. Identifying and predicting social lifestyles in people's trajectories by neural networks. EPJ Data Science. 2018;**7**(45):1-27

[40] Zhao Z, Shaw SL, Xu Y, Lu F, Chen J, Yin L. Understanding the bias of call detail records in human mobility research. International Journal of Geographical Information Science. 2016; **30**(9):1738-1762

[41] Trasarti R, Olteanu-Raimond AM, Nanni M, Couronné T, Furletti B, Giannotti F, et al. Discovering urban and country dynamics from mobile phone data with spatial correlation patterns. Telecommunications Policy. 2015;**39**(3): 347-362

[42] Toole JL, Ulm M, González MC, Bauer D. Inferring land use from mobile phone activity. In: Proceedings of the ACM SIGKDD International Workshop on Urban Computing. ACM, Beijing. 2012. pp. 1-8

[43] Wang H, Calabrese F, Di Lorenzo G, Ratti C. Transportation mode inference from anonymized and aggregated mobile phone call detail records. In: Intelligent Transportation Systems (ITSC), 2010 13th International IEEE Conference. Funchal, Portugal. 2010. pp. 318-323

[44] Isaacman S, Becker R, C'aceres R, Kobourov S. Identifying important places in people's lives from cellular network data. In: International Conference on Pervasive Computing. 2011. pp. 133-151

[45] Calabrese F, Ferrari L, Blondel VD. Urban sensing using mobile phone network data: A survey of research. ACM Computing Surveys. 2015;**47**(2):25

[46] Breiman L. Random forests. Machine Learning. 2001;**45**(1):5-32

[47] Bezdek JC, Ehrlich R, Full W. FCM: The fuzzy c-means clustering algorithm. Computers & Geosciences. 1984;**10**(2-3, 203):191

[48] Nugraha AT, Waterson B, Blainey S, Nash F. On the consistency of urban cellular automata models based on hexagonal and square cells. Environment and Planning B: Urban Analytics and City Science. 2021;**48**:845-860

[49] Leyk S, Balk D, Jones B, et al. The heterogeneity and change in the urban structure of metropolitan areas in the United States, 1990–2010. Sci Data. 2019;**6**:321

[50] Triguero I, García S, Herrera F. Self-labeled techniques for semi-supervised learning: Taxonomy, software and empirical study. Knowledge and Information Systems. 2015;**42**(2): 245-284

[51] Dudani SA. The distance-weighted k-nearest-neighbor rule. IEEE Transactions on Systems, Man, and Cybernetics. 1976;**4**:325-327

[52] Mehta S, Shen X, Gou J, Niu D. A new nearest centroid neighbor classifier based on K local means using harmonic mean distance. Information. 2018;**9**(9):234

[53] Ghosh AK. On optimum choice of k in nearest neighbor classification. Computational Statistics & Data Analysis. 2006;**50**(11):3113-3123

[54] Fortmann-Roe S. Understanding the bias-variance tradeoff. 2012. Available online at http://scott.fortmann-roe.com/docs/BiasVariance.html. [Accessed 9 November, 2018]

[55] Duda RO, Hart PE, Stork DG. Pattern Classification. John Wiley & Sons; 2012